# THE
# GOOD MENU
# GUIDE

Edited by

**Chris Barrett**
and
**Jeremy Longley**

© **GMG Publishing**

*The Good Menu Guide* is published by:

GMG Publishing
PO BOX 78
Evesham
Worcestershire
WR11 5ZB

© 1997 GMG Publishing

ISBN: 1-901681-01-7

Front Cover photographs reproduced by kind permission of:
*(clockwise from top left)*
Brockencote Hall, Chaddesley Corbett; Oaks, Ludlow;
Merchant House, Ludlow; Raven Arms, Much Wenlock.

Back Cover photograph reproduced by kind permission of:
Moat House, Acton Trussell

Contents Page photographs reproduced by kind permission of:
Julian's, Eccleshall; Bull's Head, Wootton Wawen.

Page 5 photograph reproduced by kind permission of:
Crown Inn, Hopton Wafers

All the other photographs in this book are reproduced
by the kind permission of the participating restaurants.

Printed and bound in Great Britain.

Although every effort has been made to ensure that the information
contained in this book is correct, the publishers, GMG Publishing,
accept no responsibility whatsoever for any errors or omissions.
The restaurants featured in this book reserve the right to change
their menus and prices without prior notice.

Also published in this series:
**The Good Menu Guide - *The Cotswolds***

# Contents

# Welcome to the first Midlands edition of *The Good Menu Guide.*

The aim of this book is to introduce you to our selection of the very best places to eat in The Midlands. Entries range from the top hotel restaurants to period country pubs and intimate bistros, with the criteria for selection being placed very firmly on the high quality food which they all serve.

It must be stressed that **no-one pays, directly or otherwise, to be in this guide** and we personally recommend them all.

Because our taste in style of food and type of restaurant may well differ from your own, we have tried not to let on which are our own particular favourites. We simply want to encourage you to go out for a meal and discover some of the many wonderful establishments that are featured in the following pages.

So we let the menus that accompany every entry tell their own story.

Please bear in mind that restaurant menus change frequently, some seasonally, some daily. All the menus and prices were correct at the time of going to press and, when ultimately they change, should still be indicative of the style and value for money of that particular restaurant.

We would also like to say that we welcome your comments and criticisms. So if you have had a great meal (or a bad meal) or you think we have missed somewhere worthy of inclusion, then please let us know!

In the meantime, let our recommendations whet your appetite, then indulge yourself. You will not be disappointed.

# How to use *The Good Menu Guide* and other useful information

The main entries featured on pages 6 to 251 are all displayed in the same easy-to-use format - menus appear on the left and colour photographs, a brief description of the establishment and the style of food, directions and useful information are shown opposite. They are in alphabetical order by the name of their nearest town or village. These names appear at the top of each page, together with the page number.

At the back of the book you will find two indexes to help you locate a particular restaurant:
  i) Alphabetical index of main entries
  ii) Index of main entries by county, including nearest major town.

Abbreviations for charge cards used in this book:
V=Visa, MC=Mastercard, S=Switch, D=Delta, AE=American Express, DC=Diners Club

The majority of establishments featured in this edition welcome disabled customers. However, due to the age of many of the buildings, the facilities are not always ideal for those in wheelchairs and may occasionally involve being helped down a stair or to the toilets. We strongly advise you to check when making your reservation, in order to avoid any potential inconvenience or discomfort that may later affect your enjoyment.

**Please mention *The Good Menu Guide* when making a reservation.**

We hope you enjoy our selections
featured on the following pages ...

*Bon appetit!*

# THE ALDERLEY EDGE HOTEL

### Tel: (01625) 583033

Macclesfield Road, Alderley Edge, Cheshire, SK9 7BJ

## *Signatures*

'Marjolaine' of Horseradish and Cucumber Mousse
with a Tartare of Scallop and Salmon
on a Lobster Salad
£9.95

Seared King Scallops with a Salad of Plum Tomatoes
and Crispy Italian Ham and Vermouth Dressing
£9.75 / £19.50

Terrine of Goose and Chicken Livers
with Sun-dried Tomatoes, Leeks
and Fig Jam
£9.75

'Charlotte' of Cheshire Ham
with a Purée of Tomato Pickles
£8.75

\* \* \*

Market Fish
Grilled with a Fennel Butter
on Asparagus and Citrus Potatoes
£19.50

Trio of Game with Vegetables
and a Sauté of Potatoes
£18.50

Beef Fillet Mignons Roasted
with Braised Leeks infused with Tarragon
on a Celeriac Purée
£21.50

Rack of Lamb Marinated and Roasted
with a Gratin of Potatoes and Spinach
on a Parsley Juice Sauce
£19.75

The Alderley Edge Hotel, now recognised as one of the finest country house hotels in the country, was originally built in 1850 as the private home of one of Manchester's wealthy cotton barons.

The food served here is quite superb. The seasonal à la carte menu is beautifully presented as a collection of the award-winning Head Chef Steve Kitchen's 'signature' dishes (a few of these are shown opposite). A Market Menu, featuring three special dishes such as Monkfish Collops with a Vegetable Cous Cous and Basil Butter Sauce (£16.55), changes twice a week, and at luncheon a weekly table d'hôte is offered (2 or 3 courses £13.50/15.50). An evening table d'hôte (3 courses £22.95) is also available.

The delicious sweets, like Open Apple Flan with Calvados Ice Cream (£4.55) and French Crêpe and Orange Gateau (£4.50) are all home-made, as are the breads, cakes and pastries fresh from the hotel's own bakery.

Directions: Alderley Edge is about 14 miles south of Manchester on the A34. Take the B5087 towards Macclesfield and the hotel is a few hundred yards further along on the right.

## USEFUL INFORMATION

**SERVING TIMES:**
Lunch 12pm-2pm (every day)
Dinner 7pm-10pm (every day)
**SEATING CAPACITY:** 80
**C/C:** V, MC, S, D, AE, DC
**OUTDOOR EATING:** no
**OFF-STREET PARKING:** yes

**NUMBER OF WINES:** 700
**HOUSE WINE:** £12.95
**RESERVATIONS:** advisable
**DRESS CODE:** jacket and tie
**ACCOMMODATION:** 32 rooms
(single £89.50, double £99.50)

# THE GROSVENOR ARMS

### Tel: (01244) 620228

Chester Road, Aldford, near Chester, Cheshire, CH3 6HJ

Farfale pasta with a fresh chilli, roasted pepper and tomato sauce
garnished with Italian meats and parmesan £3.75
Mushrooms cooked with tomato and fresh basil,
topped with farmhouse cheddar £3.95
A tart filled with Caerphilly, Cheddar, Double Gloucester and cream,
topped with bacon and served with a country garden chutney £4.25
A plate of Scottish smoked salmon with cracked pepper
on a bed of iceberg lettuce £5.45
A small salad of thinly sliced smoked chicken breast
with a fresh coriander dressing £3.95
Fresh mussels cooked with white wine, cream, shallots and garlic £4.95

Roast half shoulder of lamb with rosemary sauce £9.95
Steak and mushroom pie with a puff pastry lid £8.95
Pan-fried duck breast served with a rich raspberry and pear sauce £10.95
Fillets of tuna, halibut and cod served with a lime butter £9.95
8oz Fillet steak £15.45 or 10oz Rump steak £11.45
served with garlic butter and French fries
(The above dishes are served with potatoes and vegetables)

Spirals of pasta served with a Provençale sauce £5.95
Stir-fried vegetables on a large floured tortilla served with guacamole £5.95
Sautéed chicken on the bone with chunky potatoes and vegetables
covered in a tarragon sauce £7.95
Puff pastry pillow filled with leeks in a rich cheese sauce £4.75
Salmon and haddock fishcakes served with a tomato and onion salad
and lemon mayonnaise £5.95
Chicken livers pan-fried with tarragon mustard, cream and red wine
served on a bed of leaves £4.95
Barbequed rack of pork ribs
served with a barbequed sauce, coleslaw and French fries £7.95
A casserole of marinated pheasant with bacon, red wine and mushrooms
served with creamed potatoes £8.95
Cumberland sausage with creamed potatoes and a rich onion gravy £5.25

Bread and butter pudding £3.25          Chocolate truffle cake £3.25
Vanilla crème brûlée £3.25          Banoffee pie £3.25
Citrus tart with cinnamon berries £3.25
Apple and mincemeat lattice tart £3.25

The village of Aldford dates from the time of the 1st Duke of Westminster (the last non-royal duke to be created in England) and is built in a style typical of the area, with barley sugar twist chimneys, patterned brickwork and diamond-patterned windows.

The Grosvenor Arms, a country pub with period charm, is one of the largest buildings in the village. It has been recently restored using traditional furnishings to create a comfortable homely atmosphere, complemented by excellent food and fine ales and wines.

Directions: The Grosvenor Arms is situated approximately 4 miles to the south of Chester on the B5130.

## USEFUL INFORMATION

**SERVING TIMES:**
Lunch 12pm-2pm (Mon-Fri)
Dinner 6pm-10pm (Mon-Fri)
Food served all day Sat 12pm-10pm
          all day Sun 12pm-9pm
**SEATING CAPACITY:** 130
**C/C:** V, MC, S, D, AE

**NUMBER OF WINES:** 20
**HOUSE WINE:** £8.75
**RESERVATIONS:** advisable
**CHILDREN:** welcome at lunch
only and until 6pm on Sat & Sun
**OUTDOOR EATING:** yes
**OFF-STREET PARKING:** yes

# JUNIPER

### Tel: (0161) 929 4008

21 The Downs, Altrincham, Greater Manchester, WA14 2QD

**Starters**
All at £6.00

Char-Grilled Scallops with Tomato Consommé and Noodles

Avocado, Tomato and Crème Fraîche Terrine with Saffron Vinaigrette

Roast Codling with Leek and Ginger Sauce

Roast Saddle of Hare with Mushroom Feuilleté

Confit of Chicken Terrine with Aubergine

**Main Courses**
All at £16.00

Roast Fillet of Beef with Port Wine and Winter Vegetables

Local Corn-Fed Chicken with Black-Pudding and Juniper

Grilled Brill Bonne Femme with Truffle Sauce

Grilled Salmon Fillet with Scallops, Cucumber and Red Wine

Roast Duckling with Creamy Mushroom Duxelle and Garlic

**Desserts**
All at £5.50

Poached Fig Tarte Tatin

Glazed Lemon Tart

White Chocolate Mille Feuille

Rice Pudding Soufflé

Baked Egg Custard Tart

Poached Pears and Green Apple Sorbet

Although open for only eighteen months, Juniper has already won many accolades on the way to becoming one of the top restaurants in the area. Split over two floors, the interior is stylishly modern, and yet the atmosphere is delightfully welcoming. One immediately expects something rather special.

Chef Paul Kitching heads a team of five 'serious' chefs, and using only the best ingredients prepares modern French food with innovative personal touches. Everything is individually cooked and the results are superb. The bread and chocolates are made in-house.

The evening à la carte (an example is shown opposite) changes daily, but always offers a choice of five dishes with each course. This is supplemented by a selection of daily gourmet specials - perhaps a Chicken Bouillon with White Truffle, Cauliflower, Leeks and Barley (£6) to start, with an Assiette of Fish with Mediterranean Vegetables, White Beans and Chive Oil (£16) to follow. At lunch a slightly less extensive à la carte is offered.

Directions: Altrincham is found about 6 miles south of Manchester city centre on the A56. Follow the signs to the town centre and continue up the high street with the bus station on your left. After a few hundred yards take the right-hand fork and the restaurant is found on the left.

## USEFUL INFORMATION

**SERVING TIMES:**
Lunch 12pm-2pm (Tues-Fri)
Dinner 7pm-9.30pm (Mon-Sat)
**CLOSED:** Monday lunch, Saturday lunch, and all day Sunday
**SEATING CAPACITY:** 50
**C/C:** V, MC, S, D, AE

**NUMBER OF WINES:** 40
**HOUSE WINE:** £12.50
**OFF-STREET PARKING:** no
**RESERVATIONS:** advisable
**DRESS CODE:** smart
**OUTDOOR EATING:** no

# THE OLD PACKET HOUSE

### Tel: (0161) 929 1331

Navigation Road, Broadheath, Altrincham, Greater Manchester, WA14 1LW

## *A selection from the Blackboard*

### *Starters and Snacks*

*Home-made Chicken, Leek & Asparagus Soup £2.50*
*Chef's Pâté Salad with Toast £3.95*
*Baked Haddock topped with a Prawn Sauce £4.95*
*Chilled Tropical Platter £4.95*
*Lamb Samosas & Onion Bhajis with a Mango Chilli Dip £4.95*
*Venison Sausage with Creamed Potatoes & Mushrooms £4.95*

### *Main Dishes*

*Deep-fried King Cod in Batter £7.95*
*Traditional Roast Beef & Yorkshire Pudding £7.95*
*Braised Lamb's Liver & Bacon Pie £5.45*
*Home-made Lamb & Apricot Pie £7.45*
*Poached Fillet of Trout on a bed of Vegetables £7.45*
*Roast Cheshire Turkey & Cranberry Sauce £7.95*
*Spaghetti Carbonara £6.45*
*Ribeye Steak with a Pepper Sauce £9.50*
*Cod & Prawn Mornay £7.45*
*Individual Lamb Roast & Mint Sauce £7.95*
*Chicken Supreme with a Pepper or Chasseur Sauce £7.45*
*Poached Salmon in a Prawn Sauce £7.45*
*Vegetarian Ravioli with a Neetrine & Courgette Salsa £6.95*
*Pan-fried Chicken Kiev £7.45*

*All served with fresh vegetables and potatoes*

### *Puddings all £2.95*

*Hot Banana Crêpe*
*Chocolate Sponge and Custard*
*Summer Pudding*
*Bread and Butter Pudding*
*Apple and Blueberry Pie*
*Chocolate Box Cake*

Despite a rather inauspicious roadside location, walking into this pub really is a very pleasant surprise. The Old Packet House, with original open fires, dark panelling, tiled floors and exposed brickwork is a delightful olde worlde inn dating back to the late 18th Century.

As we have come to expect of a pub owned by Frances and Jim Cunningham (their other pubs, The Swettenham Arms and The Dog Inn, are featured elsewhere in this guide), the atmosphere here is warm and friendly, and the food superb. A blackboard menu (shown opposite), featuring an extensive selection of starters and main courses, changes daily. There is also a Sandwich Menu with all the old favourites (from £2.40) and more imaginative creations such as Mexican Chicken on Ciabatta Bread (£3.75), as well as a good range of salads and ploughmans.

Directions: Easily found a mile north of Altrincham on the A56 at Broadheath.

## USEFUL INFORMATION

**SERVING TIMES:**
Lunch 12pm-2.30pm (every day)
Dinner 6.30pm-9.30pm (Mon-Sat)
**CLOSED:** Sunday evening for food
**SEATING CAPACITY:** 50
**C/C:** V, MC, S, D
**OFF-STREET PARKING:** yes
**CHILDREN:** welcome

**NUMBER OF WINES:** 37
**HOUSE WINE:** £7.20
**RESERVATIONS:** advisable
**OUTDOOR EATING:** yes
**NO SMOKING** area available
**ACCOMMODATION:** 4 rooms
(single £45, double £62.50)

# THE MILL AT ALVECHURCH
### Tel: (0121) 447 7005
Radford Road, Alvechurch, Birmingham, West Midlands, B48 7LD

## STARTERS

* Freshly Prepared Soup of the Day £2.95
* Mixed Salad Leaves with Avocado, Croutons
& a Wholegrain Mustard Dressing £3.75
* Salmon Fishcake on a Bed of Creamed Leeks £4.25
Mediterranean Fish Soup with Rouille Croutons £4.50
Parfait of Chicken Livers
served on Warm Brioche Toast with Cumberland Sauce £3.75
Lasagne of Wild Mushrooms & Asparagus with a Chervil Butter Sauce £6.25
Escalope of Salmon with a lightly poached Egg
glazed with a White Wine Sauce £5.50
Galia Melon with an Exotic Fruit Compôte £4.95

## MAIN COURSES

* Braised Pork Meatballs with Tagliatelle in a Spicy Tomato Sauce £10.75
* Roast Fillet of Cod with a Parsley Butter Sauce £11.50
* Onion & Mushroom Tart with a Tomato Salad £9.50
Fillet of Beef with Shallots, Mushrooms & Red Wine Sauce £14.75
Breast of Duck with Caramelised Kumquats & Oranges £13.25
Roast Rack of Lamb with Rosemary & Redcurrant Sauce £14.50
Medallions of Pork Fillet
set on a Bed of Onion Purée with Roasted Vegetables £13.75
Supreme of Chicken filled with Mozzarella Cheese
and wrapped in Parma Ham £13.50
Fillet of Monkfish served on a Bed of Leeks
with a Saffron Sauce and Braised Rice £14.75
A Selection of Fresh Seasonal Vegetables is included with all main courses

## DESSERTS

* Lime Mousse with Marinated Kiwi Fruit £3.50
* Nougatine Ice Cream with Caramel Sauce £3.50
Bread & Butter Pudding with Lemon & Honey Glaze £4.25
Aniseed Parfait with Blackberry Sauce £4.25
Passion Fruit Tart with Pineapple & Lime Sorbet £4.25
White Chocolate Tear Mousse with a Rich Dark Chocolate Ice Cream £5.00
* A Selection of Fine English and French Cheeses £4.25

The Mill at Alvechurch is a popular restaurant housed in a converted red brick mill in a quiet village not far from the M42. The cosy dining room is divided into two sections by the original wooden beams and the whole atmosphere is reminiscent of an English country house.

The menu, a sample of which is featured on the facing page, changes every two months to reflect the seasons' produce. Although at first glance it appears to be à la carte, the dishes preceded by an asterisk form part of the set price menu available. You can choose any two courses for £14, or any three courses for £16, with coffee included. This menu is only available from Tuesday to Thursday.

The modern British cooking is complemented by an extensive wine list, with 200 bins from all the world's main growing regions, supplemented by a Fine Wine List, which is not normally offered unless specifically requested.

Directions: The Mill is set back from the A441 which runs through the village of Alvechurch.

## USEFUL INFORMATION

**SERVING TIMES:**
Lunch 12.30pm-2pm (Sunday only)
Dinner 7pm-9pm (Tues-Fri)
        7pm-9.30pm (Sat)
**CLOSED:** lunch (Mon-Sat), Sunday evening and all day Monday
**SEATING CAPACITY:** 34
**C/C:** V, MC, AE

**NUMBER OF WINES:** 200
**HOUSE WINE:** £8.25
**RESERVATIONS:** advisable
**OUTDOOR EATING:** no
**NO SMOKING** in the restaurant
**NO WHEELCHAIR ACCESS**
**OFF-STREET PARKING:** yes

# BEECHES
### Tel: (01889) 590288
Waldley, Doveridge, nr Ashbourne, Derbyshire, DE6 5LR

*A selection from the A La Carte*

## to start

| | | |
|---|---|---|
| SOUP | *home-made soup of the day* | £2.25 |
| MERMEASTER | *prawns in a cream an mustard sauce with a crisp topping* | £3.25 |
| DUCK | *galantine of duck with chicken, lime and Savoy cabbage served hot on a lemon cream sauce* | £5.25 |
| MELON | *fan of melon with a sorbet of Victoria Plum and Sloe gin* | £3.75 |
| CHEESE | *goats cheese coated with herbs and hazelnuts served with home-made marrow chutney* | £3.95 |
| WOODPIGEON | *confit of pigeon breast on a rich savoury stuffing with an ale and oyster mushroom sauce* | £4.25 |

## main courses

| | | |
|---|---|---|
| DUCK | *breast of English duck on a bed of lentils with smoked bacon and red wine* | £11.95 |
| PLAICE | *roast fillet of plaice with a herb crust on an orange butter sauce* | £13.25 |
| BEEF | *local boneless rib of beef, glazed onions and home-pickled walnuts and Guinness sauce* | £11.95 |
| CHICKEN | *breast of chicken filled with Conference pears on a bed of celeriac with blue cheese sauce* | £8.50 |
| PHEASANT | *breast of pheasant with a caramelised apple and cider sauce on sautéed apples and celery* | £11.25 |
| STEAK AND KIDNEY | *a rich pudding with layers of delicate suet pastry* | £8.95 |

## desserts

| | |
|---|---|
| *A selection of home-made desserts from our trolley* | £3.50 |
| *A selection of farmhouse English cheeses served with exotic fruits* | £3.50 |
| *Freshly ground coffee or a speciality tea with mints* | £1.75 |

Lovingly restored by Barbara and Paul Tunnicliffe, Beeches is a beautiful 18th Century farmhouse hotel and restaurant found deep in the heart of Derbyshire countryside. Forming part of a fully working farm (which guests are warmly invited to look around and enjoy), the restaurant has earned an enviable reputation for presenting food of the highest quality without ever losing touch with the best traditions of farmhouse cooking - the best product available, served simply and at a very good price!

The evening à la carte (shown opposite) changes seasonally, but is supplemented by chef's specials such as Fresh English Mussels in a Garlic Cream Sauce (£3.95) and Braised Lamb on a Parsnip Crumble with a Rich Sage Gravy (£13.50). From Monday to Thursday there is also a very good value Stable Menu, when a three course dinner will come to about £14. At lunch a daily table d'hôte is offered (2 or 3 courses for £8.95 and £10.95 respectively), and their Sunday lunch (4 courses £12.50) is extremely popular.

Directions: About 2 miles east of Uttoxeter on the A50, take the left turn at Doveridge signposted to Waldley. A mile and a half down this country lane fork right, and Beeches is about 50 yards along on the left.

## USEFUL INFORMATION

**SERVING TIMES:**
Lunch 12pm-2pm (every day)
Dinner 7pm-9pm (Mon-Sat)
**CLOSED:** Sunday evening
**SEATING CAPACITY:** 70
**C/C:** V, MC, S, D, AE, DC
**NO SMOKING** requested in the
restaurant before coffee

**NUMBER OF WINES:** 38
**HOUSE WINE:** £7.75
**CHILDREN:** welcome
**OFF-STREET PARKING:** yes
**RESERVATIONS:** advisable
**OUTDOOR EATING:** yes
**ACCOMMODATION:** 10 rooms
(B&B single £39.50, double fr £50)

# CALLOW HALL

## Tel: (01335) 343403

Mappleton Road, Ashbourne, Derbyshire, DE6 2AA

### *EVENING DINNER MENU £33.00*

*Fresh Asparagus with Tomato Coulis & Oregano*

*Cream of Celeriac Soup with Toasted Almonds*

*Mixed Leaf Salad with Sautéed Guinea Fowl Livers & Bacon Lardons*

\* \* \* \* \*

*Roulade of Lemon Sole, Stuffed with Crab, Dill Butter Sauce*

*Fresh Fruit Sorbet*

\* \* \* \* \*

*Roast Loin of Lamb with Braised Red Cabbage, Rosemary & Red Wine Sauce*

*Monkfish Tail Baked in Parma Ham with White Wine Sauce & Fennel Seeds*

*Breast of Barbary Duck with Bramley Apple & Blueberries, Honey Glaze*

\* \* \* \* \*

*Selection of Fresh Vegetables*

\* \* \* \* \*

*Home-made Desserts & Pastries*

*Selection of Cheeses, English & Continental*

\* \* \* \* \*

*Coffee or Tea with Petits Fours*

\* \* \* \* \*

Nestling in 44 acres of picturesque countryside, Callow Hall is an elegant hotel and restaurant with a deserving reputation for its friendly service, comprehensive wine list and highest quality cuisine.

Dining here is described as the "complete experience", and David Spencer and his team draw from the very best of local produce to present a wonderful array of English and continental dishes, complemented by delicious home-made breads, puddings and pastries.

In addition to the dinner menu featured opposite, which changes daily, there is a seasonal à la carte with an exceptional choice of fresh fish dishes such as Grilled Fillet of Sea Bass with Red Peppers, Leek & Sauce Noilly Prat (£9.85 or £18.65) which may be taken as starters or main courses. Every Sunday there is a set menu at lunch (3 courses £15.50).

Directions:  Take the A515 from Ashbourne in the direction of Buxton. After about a quarter of a mile turn left on the brow of the hill by the Bowling Green pub. Then take the first right into Mappleton Road, and Callow Hall is on the right just after a humpback bridge.

## USEFUL INFORMATION

**SERVING TIMES:**
Lunch 12.30pm-2pm (Sunday)
and by reservation only (Mon-Sat)
Dinner 7.30pm-9pm (Mon-Sat)
**CLOSED:** Sunday evening
**SEATING CAPACITY:** 80 divided
between 3 dining rooms
**C/C:** V, MC, S, D, AE, DC
**NO SMOKING** in the dining rooms

**NUMBER OF WINES:** 120
**HOUSE WINE:** £9.75
**OFF-STREET PARKING:** yes
**RESERVATIONS:** advisable, and
compulsory for lunch
**OUTDOOR EATING:** yes
**CHILDREN:** welcome
**ACCOMMODATION:** 16 rooms
(single fr £70, double fr £105)

# RIVERSIDE HOTEL
## Tel: (01629) 814275
Ashford-in-the-Water, nr Bakewell, Derbyshire, DE4 1QF

### *A selection from the Menu Gourmande*

**TO START**

Boudin Blanc with sautéed
spinach and haricot beans in a tomato sauce

Wild Mushroom and Potato Pavé
served on a saffron water dressing and herb salad

Pan Fried Fillets of Red Mullet,
ricotta cheese tortellini and tapenade dressing

Terrine of Goats Cheese and Foie Gras
with a red pepper and courgette salad

**HEART OF YOUR MEAL**

Pan Fried Beef Fillet with braised oxtail on parsley creamed
potatoes and glazed baby vegetables in a red wine sauce

Seared Rosette of Salmon with a ragoût of mussels,
leeks and artichokes in a red wine fumet

Roasted Lamb Cutlets and pan-fried lambs liver with a polenta,
aubergine and pipperade torte on a plum tomato, olive and coriander jus

Loin of Venison on a risotto of savoy cabbage and smoked
bacon in a juniper, port and celery sauce

**DESSERT**

Pecan Nut and Maple Syrup Sponge Pudding
served with traditional custard sauce

Rhubarb and Ginger Soufflé
with a fresh strawberry sauce

Passion Fruit Crème Brûlée and Lime Sorbet
layered with tuille biscuits and a mango coulis

White Chocolate and Griottine Cherry Bavarois
with dark chocolate ice cream

*Five Course Dinner Menu £33*

The Riverside Hotel is a beautiful Georgian country house enjoying an idyllic setting on the banks of the River Wye in the Peak District National Park.

Whether you choose to dine in the elegant restaurant, which is made up of two dining-rooms, or the more relaxed atmosphere of the Buttery, the food is all freshly prepared and quite delicious, with game in season from nearby Chatsworth, and locally caught fish being house specialities.

At luncheon a table d'hôte menu is offered (2 or 3 courses for £14.50 and £18.95 respectively), and this changes weekly. There is also a table d'hôte in the evening and a selection from it is featured opposite. From Sunday to Thursday you may opt for only two or three courses from the same menu (£22.50 or £27). There are additional daily specials.

Meanwhile the Terrace Buttery Menu has dishes to cater for all sizes of appetite, with a good selection of sandwiches, salads and 'lite bites' such as Baked Ciabatta topped with Mozzarella Cheese, Plum Tomatoes, Olives with Pesto Dressing (£6.50), as well as more substantial meals like Braised Shoulder of Lamb with Creamed Potatoes in a Garlic Fumet (£9.50).

Directions: About a mile west of Bakewell on the A6, the Riverside is easily found in the centre of the village.

## USEFUL INFORMATION

**SERVING TIMES:**
Lunch 12pm-1.30pm (every day)
Dinner 7pm-9.30pm (every day)
The Buttery 9.30am-9.30pm (every day)
**SEATING CAPACITY:** 50 in the restaurant, 25 in the Buttery
**C/C:** V, MC, S, D, AE
**OUTDOOR EATING:** yes
**NO SMOKING** in the restaurant

**NUMBER OF WINES:** 89
**HOUSE WINE:** £12.65
**RESERVATIONS:** advisable
**OFF-STREET PARKING:** yes
**CHILDREN:** welcome
**DRESS CODE:** smart in the restaurant
**ACCOMMODATION:** 15 rooms (single from £75, double from £85)

# SLATER'S

### Tel: (01782) 680052

Stone Road, Baldwins Gate, Newcastle, Staffordshire, ST5 5ED

---

*A selection from the A La Carte*

**FRESH SEASONAL MELON £2.10**
**FILLET OF SMOKED MACKEREL £2.85**
**TUNA AND PASTA SALAD £2.55**
**GARLIC MUSHROOMS £2.95**

**FISH DISHES**

**SALMON STEAK MEUNIERE £8.95**
pan fried and finished with lemon juice
**FRESH SALMON STEAK £9.35**
served with a light champagne sauce
**GRILLED LEMON SOLE MEUNIERE £9.25**
**FILLET OF PLAICE JOSEPHINE £9.25**
served with a mellow cream & tomato sauce & garnished with prawns

**POULTRY DISHES**

**GARLIC CHICKEN SUPREME £8.75**
sautéed with onions, mushrooms and parsley butter
**ROAST DUCKLING BIRRIAGADE £8.75**
fresh half duckling served with an orange & red wine birriagade sauce
**SUPREME OF CHICKEN PRINCESS £8.75**

**GRILLS AND MEAT DISHES**

**PORK LOIN STROGANOFF £10.25**
pork loin slices sautéed with a mushroom, brandy & French mustard sauce
**ENTRECOTE STEAK £11.25**
served with a pepper, cream and brandy sauce
**PAN FRIED FILLET DIANE £12.75**
served with mushroom, cream, tarragon, brandy & French mustard sauce
**GRILLED GAMON STEAK GARNI £8.95**
prime gammon steak topped with a fried egg and pineapple

**VEGETARIAN SPECIALITIES**

**MUSHROOM STROGANOFF £7.95**
**BROCCOLI AND PASTA BAKE £7.85**
**AUBERGINE, MUSHROOM & TOMATO PANCAKE £7.95**

Converted from old farm buildings dating back to the 18th Century, Slater's enjoys a lovely setting in rural Staffordshire. Despite extensive refurbishment, the olde worlde charm has been retained and there is a very relaxing and friendly atmosphere.

Food is available in both the bar and restaurant. The bar menu changes regularly to accommodate seasonal dishes and is complemented by a daily specials board. Everything is bought locally and prepared fresh to order, right down to the delicious home-made chips.

In the restaurant an extensive à la carte menu is offered along with daily house specialities like Scampi Newburg (£11.75) and Lamb Cutlets with Stilton and Port (£10.45).

Directions:  Baldwins Gate is about 5 miles west of junction 15 of the M6. Slater's is signposted from the A53 and is found on the side of the A51.

### USEFUL INFORMATION

**SERVING TIMES:**
Lunch 12pm-3pm (daily in the bar)
Dinner 7pm-10pm (Wed-Sat restaurant)
        6pm-9.30pm (daily in the bar)
All day Sunday (until 3pm in restaurant)
**CLOSED:** in the restaurant on
Monday and Tuesday
**SEATING CAPACITY:** 76 in the
restaurant, 55 in the bar
**C/C:** V, MC, S, D

**NUMBER OF WINES:** 32
**HOUSE WINE:** £7.90
**OFF-STREET PARKING:** yes
**RESERVATIONS:** are compulsory
at weekends in the restaurant
**OUTDOOR EATING:** yes
**CHILDREN** welcome
**NO SMOKING** in the restaurant
**ACCOMMODATION:** 6 rooms
(from £35 per night)

# RENAISSANCE RESTAURANT
### Tel: (01629) 812687
Bath Street, Bakewell, Derbyshire, DE45 1BX

### *A Selection from the 3 Course Menu £17.95*

#### *To Start*

***Crème d'oignons au Porto***
Creamed onion soup with port

***Moules Marinières accompagnée d'un pain à l'ail***
Mussels cooked in white wine and cream served with garlic bread

***Fagot d'asperges glacée d'une sauce choron***
A bundle of asparagus glazed with a tomato hollondaise £1.99 extra

***Oeuf pochée cuit en filo servit sur une sauce de poireaux***
Poached egg baked in filo pastry served on a leek sauce

#### *Main Courses*

***Boeuf Bourguignon Façon Renaissance***
Beef stew cooked in a rich merlot wine sauce

***250g Sirloin Steacks au Poivre finis d'une sauce au Cognac***
8oz peppered sirloin steak finished with a brandy sauce £3.50 extra

***Poisson Frais du jour***
Today's fresh fish from the market

***Suprème de Faisan cuit au cidre et finit avec des pommes glacée à brun***
Breast of pheasant cooked in cider and garnished with caramelised apples

***Beignets de tomate accompagnée d'une sauce piquante***
Croquettes of tomato in a piquante sauce

#### *Gourmet Dishes*

***Demi Homard et coquille St Jacque Thermidor et sa Julienne de legumes***
Half lobster and scallops Thermidor with a vegetable julienne £5.50 extra

### *A Choice from our Sweet Menu*

Renaissance, an elegant French restaurant in a listed building, has established itself in a mere two years as one of the premier places to eat in Derbyshire. Whether you choose to eat in the elegant and refined restaurant, or the more relaxed atmosphere of the eaterie, the food is always beautifully prepared and quite delicious.

The table d'hôte menu includes a free sorbet as an intermediate and is available at lunch and dinner. The sweet menu offers six enticing choices and may include the very popular Crêpes Suzette or Eric Renaissance Gateaux au Chocolat. Both these menus change every eight weeks.

For those after a lighter meal then the blackboard menu in the eaterie may well provide the answer, with dishes like home-made soup (£1.90). The Sunday lunch (3 courses for £12.95) offers a choice of traditional and continental cuisine.

Directions: Renaissance Restaurant is easily found in Bath Street just off the town centre of Bakewell, which is on the A619 about 10 miles west of Chesterfield.

### USEFUL INFORMATION

**SERVING TIMES:**
Lunch 12pm-2pm (Tues-Sun)
Dinner 7pm-10pm (Tues-Sat)
**CLOSED:** All day Monday and Sunday evening
**SEATING CAPACITY:** 45 in the restaurant, 25 in the eaterie
**C/C:** V, MC, S, D

**NUMBER OF WINES:** 52
**HOUSE WINE:** £9.80
**OFF-STREET PARKING:** no
**OUTDOOR EATING:** yes
**CHILDREN** welcome
**RESERVATIONS:** are compulsory in the restaurant
**NO SMOKING** in the restaurant

# CAVENDISH HOTEL
### Tel: (01246) 582311
Baslow, Derbyshire, DE45 1SP

## The First Course

**Oxtail soup**
*this clear soup served with oxtail, carrots and parsley dumplings*
**Buckwheat pancake**
*filled with avocado, poached pear and fromage frais spiced with
cracked black pepper, glazed with a minted hollandaise*
**Ham knuckle and parsley terrine**
*pressed and set with its own jelly and offered with honey and lentil dressing*
**Parma ham and feta cheese**
*cheese, basil and tomato wrapped in parma ham, lightly pan fried
and served with a black raisin sauce*
**Seared tuna**
*the medallion cooked pink on a niçoise salad with shaved parmesan in olive oil*

## The Main Course

**Medallions of beef**
*chargrilled to your liking with red onion marmalade and Béarnaise sauce*
**Breast of Deben duck**
*stuffed with apple noodles, served with a nutmeg and beetroot sauce,
vegetables and gaufrette potatoes*
**Norwegian cod fillet**
*cooked in stock, this healthy dish of vegetable diamonds and
aromatic seaweed served with mixed leaf salad*
**One pot chicken**
*the breast braised with smoked bacon, burgundy and garlic,
offered with baby vegetables and potatoes*
**Fillet of salmon**
*pan fried in a basil cream crust, served on a bed of chargrilled vegetables
offered with a warm tomato dressing*
**Spinach and goats cheese**
*double baked soufflé with a lemon and cardamom sauce
accompanied by a citrus salad*

## The Dessert

**Iced honey and lavender parfait, Vanilla and apple strudel
Steamed cherry pudding, Camembert fritter
Hot dessert of the day, Cold dessert of the day**

Enjoying a prime location in the heart of the Peak District on the Chatsworth Estate, the Cavendish with its open fires, oak beams and antique furniture effuses a charm and elegance of a bygone era.

Lunch and dinner may be taken either formally in The Restaurant or casually in The Garden Room, and the food prepared by chef director Nicholas Buckingham is superb. The table d'hôte restaurant menu featured opposite (2,3 or 4 courses at £26.75, £32.25 and £37.75 respectively) includes an intermediate course and house favourites at a supplementary charge. This changes monthly, as does the less expensive Garden Room menu with dishes such as Ham and Eggs (£9.75) and Sweet Chilli Chicken (£9.75). There is also a daily blackboard menu.

For the gourmet gurus amongst you, then the novel Kitchen Table is well worth considering. This excellent idea allows you to sit in the kitchen and watch the chef prepare a special menu for two (£40 per person).

Directions:  About 10 miles west of Chesterfield, Cavendish Hotel is easily found in the centre of Baslow on the A623.

## USEFUL INFORMATION

**SERVING TIMES:**
Lunch 12.30pm-2pm (every day)
Dinner 7pm-10pm (every day)
Garden Room 11am-11pm (every day)
**SEATING CAPACITY:** 50 in the restaurant, 30 in the Garden Room
**C/C:** V, MC, S, D, AE, DC
**DRESS CODE:** jacket and tie in the restaurant, casual in the Garden Room
**OUTDOOR EATING:** no
**CHILDREN** welcome

**NUMBER OF WINES:** 120
**HOUSE WINE:** £13.50
**OFF-STREET PARKING:** yes
**RESERVATIONS:** advisable in the restaurant but not offered in the Garden Room
**NO SMOKING** in the restaurant but permitted in the Garden Room
**ACCOMMODATION:** 24 rooms (single £79, double £99)

# FISCHER'S BASLOW HALL
### Tel: (01246) 583259
Calver Road, Baslow, Derbyshire, DE45 1RR

*Gourmet Menu £42.00*

## To Start

Terrine of Foie Gras with Duck Confit

Calves' Liver with Ginger and Lime

Sea Scallops, Szechuan Vegetables, Spicy Sauce Vierge

Gourmet Assiette
salmon & poached oyster, smoked salmon mousse, langoustine salad,
cod brandade, quail's egg & caviar

Langoustine Ravioli with a Parsley Cream Sauce

## Main Dishes

Turbot, steamed with Mussel Minestrone

Fish of the Day

Naturally reared Beef Fillet with Béarnaise Sauce

Saddle of Venison, Roast Winter Vegetables, Game Pepper Sauce

Breast of Duckling, Sesame Cabbage, Oriental Sauce

Pigs Trotter, Pommes Purées and Morel Mushroom

Roast Saddle of Lamb with Flageolet Beans

Veal Steak with home-preserved Cep Mushrooms

## Dessert or Cheese from our List

## Coffee and Petits Fours

Baslow Hall is a beautiful Derbyshire manor house which enjoys an enviable location on the edge of the magnificent Chatsworth Estate. Established by Max and Susan Fischer in 1988 as a 'Restaurant with Rooms', it has an outstanding reputation among connoisseurs for its impeccable cuisine.

As you would expect, Max cooks with the seasons using the very best local produce alongside imported luxuries such as Foie Gras and Truffles. The fixed price Gourmet Menu (featured opposite) changes monthly and includes delicious canapés and a chef's surprise savoury at the table. Desserts may feature delights such as Millefeuille of Pineapple or Glazed French Lemon Tart. At luncheon a weekly table d'hôte is offered (2 or 3 courses for £18 and £22 respectively). Sunday lunch is also a table d'hôte (3 courses £21.50).

For those after something a little less formal, the Café-Max menu offers a brasserie style cuisine of the highest quality. Perhaps Salmon Fishcakes (£4.50) to start, and Confit of Rabbit legs (£12.50) to follow.

Directions: Approaching Baslow on the A619 from Bakewell, take the A623 turning at the roundabout on the outskirts of the village. Baslow Hall is found on the right after about half a mile.

## USEFUL INFORMATION

**SERVING TIMES:**
Lunch 12pm-2pm (every day)
Dinner 7pm-9.30pm (Mon-Sat)
**CLOSED:** Sunday for dinner
**SEATING CAPACITY:** 40 in the restaurant, 24 in the café
**C/C:** V, MC, S, D, AE, DC
**NO SMOKING** in the restaurants
**CHILDREN:** over 12 welcome

**NUMBER OF WINES:** 119
**HOUSE WINE:** £9.50
**OFF-STREET PARKING:** yes
**RESERVATIONS:** advisable
**DRESS CODE:** jacket and tie is preferred
**OUTDOOR EATING:** yes
**ACCOMMODATION:** 6 rooms (B&B single fr £75, double fr £95)

# THE BUCKLEMAKER

**Tel: (0121) 200 2515**

30 Mary Ann Street, St. Paul's Square, Birmingham, B3 1RL

## STARTERS

King Prawns with Garlic Butter
£2.50 each

Fresh Native Irish Oysters served on a
bed of Crushed Ice
£1.25 each

Caesar's Salad £3.50

Plate of Smoked Salmon with Lemon &
Fresh Creamed Horseradish £5.25

Coarse Game Terrine
with an Orange & Mango Chutney £3.50

Sautéed Wild Mushrooms, Smoked
Bacon & Black Pudding, served en
croûte with a Red Wine Glaze £4.95

Plate of Parma Ham served with Baby
Gherkins & Silver Skin Onions £5.95

Spinach, Onion, Garlic & Potato Rosti
with a light cream Tarragon Sauce £3.50

Fish Cakes with a Red Pepper
& Coriander Confit £4.95

Deep Fried Spicy Fish
with a hot Salsa Dip £3.75

Watercress, Orange & Pine Kernel
Salad with a hot dressing of Lime &
Lemon Juice with White Wine & Mint
£3.25

Warm Breast of Chicken, marinated with
Lemon, Garlic, White Wine & Fresh
Basil, served on Mixed Leaves £3.75

## VEGETABLES

Braised Red Cabbage £1.25
Buttered Spinach, Onion & Garlic £1.25
Purée Carrots with Dill £1.25
Green Beans with Garlic £1.25
Mange-tout £1.25
Home-made Chips £2.00
Dish of Potatoes £2.00
Green Salad £1.25
Watercress & Orange Salad £1.25

## MAIN COURSES

Bangers & Mash
with Onion Gravy £6.25

Braised Faggots with Mushy Peas £6.50

Beef Fillet, Kidney, Mushroom & Ale Pie
£8.50

Pan Fried Breast of Chicken with
Mushrooms, Cream & Peppers served
on Pilaf Rice £8.50

Filo Pastry filled with Wild Mushrooms &
Leeks in a Sauce of Brandy Paprika &
Cream £7.95

Deep Fried Cheese, Spinach & Potato
Roulade wrapped in a Herb Crust with a
Spicy Tomato Sauce £7.95

Calves' Liver & Bacon
with a Piquant Onion Sauce £11.25

Pan Fried Venison Steak with Red
Cabbage, braised with Apples &
Sultanas, with Natural Jus £10.50

Flash Roasted Rack of English Lamb
with a Redcurrant Sauce £10.50

Honey Glazed Breast of Duck with
Fresh Kumquats & Natural Jus £11.25

Pan Fried Veal Escalope coated with
Garlic Breadcrumbs, served with Lime &
a Nut Brown Butter Sauce £12.75

Prime Fillet Steak with Tomato,
Mushrooms & Gaufrettes £14.50

## FRESH PUDDINGS (£3.50)

Bread & Butter Pudding with Custard

Fresh Fruit Crumble

Rich Dark Chocolate Mousse

Fresh Strawberries & Vanilla Ice Cream

Lemon or Cassis Sorbet

Bananas & Hot Custard

The Bucklemaker is a city-centre wine house and restaurant offering subterranean dining in the converted cellars of a 17th Century (yes, you've guessed it!) buckle maker's shop. In addition to the walk-in wine shop, there are two separate dining areas: the bar, where filled baguettes and excellent tapas (£3.25 each) are served, and the restaurant, with the menu featured opposite.

The Bucklemaker has probably the most extensive range of fresh fish in the city, with scallops and oysters generally available. The fish specials are written up on the blackboards daily and might include Sautéed Monkfish with Sun Dried Tomatoes (£11.50), Fresh Tuna Steak with a Hot Lime & Tarragon Dressing (£9.95), Whole Grilled Sardines with a Spicy Tomato Sauce (£3.75 as a starter), Whole Baked Sea Bass filled with Basil & Onions (£17.95) or a Fillet of John Dory served with a Mixed Fruit Salsa (£12.50).

You could do worse than ordering a glass of wine and a plain bowl of home-made chips - after all, they're famous for them!

Directions: The Bucklemaker is situated just off St. Paul's Square near Birmingham's Jewellery Quarter.

## USEFUL INFORMATION

**SERVING TIMES:**
Lunch 12pm-2.30pm (Mon-Fri)
Dinner 5.30pm-10.30pm (Mon-Fri)
        7pm-10.30pm (Sat)
**CLOSED:** Sat lunch & all day Sun
**SEATING CAPACITY:** 60 in the
restaurant, 50 in the bar area
**C/C:** V, MC, S, D, AE

**NUMBER OF WINES:** 80
**HOUSE WINE:** £8.95
**RESERVATIONS:** advisable
**CHILDREN:** welcome
**NO WHEELCHAIR ACCESS**
**ON-STREET PARKING:** yes
**FULLY AIR-CONDITIONED**

# LEFTBANK
### Tel: (0121) 643 4464
Broad Street, Birmingham, B15 1QA

Two courses £12     ## LUNCH MENU     Three Courses £14.50

### First Dishes

Broccoli Soup finished with a Goats' Cheese Ravioli

Terrine of Pressed Duck with Red Cabbage confit & a Fruit Jam

Warm Escalope of Salmon with a Pine Nut & Mango Salad

Tomato & Basil Tart with Mozzarella,
surrounded by a Tapenade dressing

Pan Fried Chicken Livers,
with Mushy Peas & Red Wine Sauce

### Principal Dishes

Roasted Fish with Herb Risotto

Seared Salmon with Stir Fried Vegetables & Squid Ink Pasta

Braised Rump of Lamb on Chargrilled Vegetables

Cassoulet of Chicken with Chorizo Sausage

Artichoke Heart with Poached Egg,
Tomato Confit & Roasted Onions

### Desserts

Chocolate Truffle Torte on a Lime Coulis

Nougat Parfait with Fruit Sauces

Ginger & Caramel Brûlée

Pear & Cinnamon Turnover

English Cheeses with Bramble Chutney

The Leftbank is a city centre restaurant with a frivolously chic interior of rattan, gilt and oils on canvas in a stylishly converted banking hall in the centre of Broad Street near the ICC and the Symphony Hall.

Head chef Bill Marmion, previously of Charingworth Manor, offers excellent modern British cooking through a set price luncheon menu (featured opposite) and the à la carte dinner menu that changes seasonally.

Starters on the *carte* might include a Salad of Wild Mushrooms and Lardons dressed with Balsamic & Tomato Vinaigrette (£4.90), or Tortellini of Lobster with Lentils and Smoked Bacon (£6.75). Main courses could feature Steamed Supreme of Salmon with Mussels and Thai Herb Sauce (£12.50) or Tournedos of Beef with Chicken and Wild Mushroom Soufflé (£15.50).

Directions: Leftbank is easily found in the centre of Birmingham on Broad Street, midway between The Swallow Hotel and The Hyatt Regency.

### USEFUL INFORMATION

**SERVING TIMES:**
Lunch 12pm-2pm (Mon-Fri)
Dinner 7pm-10pm (Mon-Sat)
**CLOSED:** Sat lunch & all day Sun
**SEATING CAPACITY:** 70
**C/C:** V, MC, S, D, AE, DC

**NUMBER OF WINES:** 40
**HOUSE WINE:** £9.90
**RESERVATIONS:** advisable
**OFF-STREET PARKING:** no
**OUTDOOR EATING:** no

# MAHARAJA
### Tel: (0121) 622 2641
23-25 Hurst Street, Birmingham, B5 4SA

### STARTERS
Maharaja Tikkian £2.35
Panir Pakora £2.35
Aloo Tikkian £2.25
Tandoori Mix £3.35
Tandoori Chicken £1.95
Seekh Kebab £2.65
Lamb Tikka £2.75
Chicken Tikka £2.75
Tandoori King Prawn £3.75

### TANDOORI SPECIALITIES
Tandoori Chicken
Half £3.70     Full £7.30
Seekh Kebab £5.30
Lamb Tikka £5.50
Chicken Tikka £5.50
Tandoori King Prawn £7.50

### CHICKEN DISHES
Chicken Curry £5.80
Chicken Do-Piaza £5.90
Chicken Madras £5.90
Chicken Sagwala £5.90
Chicken Dhansak £5.90
Chicken Patiala £5.95
Chicken Korma £5.95
Chicken Bhuna Masala £5.95
Chicken Mughlai £5.95
Murg Mussalam £5.95
Butter Chicken £6.05
Chicken Tikka Masala £6.05

### LAMB DISHES
Lamb Curry £5.70
Bhuna Gost £5.85
Lamb Do-Piaza £5.85
Gobi Meat £5.85
Sag Meat £5.85
Rogan Josh £5.90
Lamb Pasanda £5.90

Lamb Mughlai £5.90
Shahi Korma £5.90
Lamb Madras £5.90
Lamb Dhansak £5.90
Bhuna Keema £5.90
Keema Mattar £5.90

### PRAWN DISHES
Prawn Curry £5.70
Prawn and Mushroom £5.70
Bhuna Prawn £5.70
Prawn Madras £5.70
King Prawn Curry £7.45
Bhuna King Prawn Masala £7.55
King Prawn Masala £7.55
King Prawn Madras £7.55

### VEGETABLES
Baingan £3.75
Chana Masaladar £3.75
Dal of the Day £3.75
Mixed Vegetable Curry £3.75
Vegetable Kofta £3.75
Aloo Gobi £3.75
Mushroom and Peas £3.75
Sag Panir £3.75
Aloo Palak £3.75
Bhindi £3.75
Shahi Panir Korma £3.75
Kamal Kakri and Mattar £3.75
Aloo Mattar £3.75

### RICE AND BIRYANI
Boiled Rice £1.70
Pillau Rice £1.80
Peas Pillau £2.05
Vegetable Biryani £3.75
Maharaja Biryani £4.15
Prawn Biryani £4.15
Chicken Biryani £4.15
Lamb Biryani £4.15

Maharaja prides itself on recreating the flavours of the real India, with its team of talented cooks preparing the Punjabi and Mughlai dishes exactly as they would in their own homes.

They have been importing their exotic spices from the same supplier in Delhi for over twenty years, drying them, grinding them and blending them on site for a more authentic taste. Indeed the restaurant's head chef refuses to enter a certain well-known Indian wholesaler's annual cooking competition for fear that his customers will think that he uses their products!

The traditional charcoal-fired tandoori ovens are specially made in India and shipped across every three or four years when they need replacing. The à la carte menu featured on the facing page is supplemented by daily specials and two fixed price meals costing £11.65.

Directions: Maharaja is on the corner of Thorpe Street and Hurst Street in the Chinatown district of the city.

## USEFUL INFORMATION

**SERVING TIMES:**
Lunch 12pm-2pm (Mon-Sat)
Dinner 6pm-11pm (Mon-Sat)
**CLOSED:** all day Sunday
**SEATING CAPACITY:** 62
**C/C:** V, MC, S, D, AE, DC
**OUTDOOR EATING:** no

**NUMBER OF WINES:** 26
**HOUSE WINE:** £7.15
**RESERVATIONS:** advisable
**DRESS CODE:** smart
**CHILDREN:** welcome
**OFF-STREET PARKING:** no

# NUMBER 282
### Tel: (0121) 643 1234
The Hyatt Regency Birmingham, 2 Bridge Street, Birmingham B1 2JZ

## TWO-COURSE DINNER FROM £17.00

### APPETIZERS

**Traditional French Onion Soup**

**Assortment of Anti Pasta**

**Shrimp Bisque**

**Smoked Trout with Vegetable Carpaccio**
with Horseradish Sauce

**Caesar Salad with Parmesan Tuille**
Garlic Croutons and Duck Crackling

**Smoked Salmon Crêpes**
on Dill Mousse

**Chicken Mousseline Parcels**
with Red Pepper Sauce

**Shrimp Salad with Carrot Essence**
and Celery Heart

**Millefeuille of Crayfish and Tomato**
Vinaigrette of Tomatoes

**Grilled Vegetable Terrine**
with a Wild Mushroom Salad,
dressed with Balsamic Vinaigrette

**Potato, Leek and Stilton Brûlée**
served with Celery Salad

**********

**Side Orders (all £1.95 each)**

Chicory Pear and Potato Gratin
Sautéed Potatoes
Creamed Spinach
Seasonal Vegetables
Creamed Potatoes with Wild
Mushrooms

### MAIN COURSES

**Beef Tenderloin (supp £3.00)**
with Mushroom Ragoût and Steak Fries

**Casserole of Seafood**
with Saffron and Leek

**Escalope of Salmon**
on a Bed of Creamed Spinach with
Tomato and Sorrel Sauce

**Fillet of Swordfish (supp £2.00)**
with Spicy Harissa, Chickpeas and
Papaya Salsa

**Panfried Supreme of Chicken**
with Orange, Rosemary and Almonds

**Pan Roasted Duck Breast**
with Raspberry Vinaigrette Sauce,
Papaya and Green Eggplant

**Potato Gnocchi**
with a Walnut and Pumpkin Sauce

**Seared Scallops (supp £2.00)**
with Cous Cous, Chives
and Ginger Sauce

**Seasonal Roast Vegetable Casserole**
with Mushroom Potato
and Braised Cabbage

**Grilled Rack of Lamb (supp £2.00)**
with Artichoke Sauce
and Goat's Cheese Gratin

**Traditional Sirloin Steak (supp £2.00)**
with Celery Root Sauce, Onion Tatin
and Sautéed Mushrooms

**Veal Sweetbreads**
with Honey and Chilli Sauce

Located within the Hyatt Regency Birmingham, *Number 282* offers formal dining, providing guests with a blend of internationally renowned dishes and local seasonal favourites. The restaurant stands on what were originally the BBC Radio studios - the popular series "The Archers" was performed and broadcast from this very spot.

Inside the restaurant, the marble tables, natural light and modern design project a warm, comfortable feel and service is efficient without being overly obtrusive. A pleasant touch is that a personalised greeting or message can be added to the placemat-style menus to surprise a friend.

The menu featured on the facing page allows a choice of appetizer and main course for £17.00 (with various supplements for certain dishes), followed by dessert priced at £4.95. With visitors to Symphony Hall and theatre-goers in mind, a fixed price Symphony Menu (£18.50) is also available. This enables you to enjoy your first two courses before the performance and return afterwards to relax over dessert and coffee. Luncheon is a light, one-hour experience, with three courses and coffee good value at £16.00 per person.

Directions: The Hyatt Regency is directly opposite the International Convention Centre on the intersection of Bridge Street and Broad Street in the heart of the city.

### USEFUL INFORMATION

**SERVING TIMES:**
Lunch 12.30pm-2.30pm (Mon-Fri)
Dinner 6pm-10.30pm (Mon-Sat)
**CLOSED:** Sat lunch & all day Sun
**SEATING CAPACITY:** 80
**C/C:** V, MC, S, D, AE, DC
**NO SMOKING** area available
**OFF-STREET PARKING:** yes

**NUMBER OF WINES:** 60
**HOUSE WINE:** £13.75
**OUTDOOR EATING:** no
**DRESS CODE:** smart
**RESERVATIONS:** advisable
**CHILDREN:** welcome
**ACCOMMODATION:** 319 rooms
(weekend breaks fr £69, room only)

# RAJDOOT

## Tel: (0121) 643 8805

12-22 Albert Street, Birmingham, B4 7UD

### STARTERS

Tandoori Chicken £3.00
Chicken Tikka £3.30
Chilli Chicken Tikka £3.30
Chicken Shashlik £3.30
Rashmi Kebab £3.30
Tandoori Quail £3.60
Duck Tikka £4.40
Lamb Tikka £3.30
Shish Kebab £3.30
Tandoori Fish (Mackerel) £3.80
Fish Tikka (Cod) £3.80
Jumbo Prawn Kebab £6.00
Vegetable Shashlik £3.00
Mixed Pakoras £3.20
Rajdoot Platter (for 2 people) £12.00

### SPECIALITY OF THE HOUSE

Chicken Tikka Masala £7.20
Makhani Chicken Tikka £7.60
Chicken Tikka Badami £7.40
Chicken Chilli Garlic £7.20
Saag Chicken £6.80
Duck Chilli Garlic £9.20
Lamb Pasanda £7.20
Lamb Punjabi Massalla £7.20
Fish Kashmiri £6.90
King Prawn Chilli Garlic £8.80

### CHICKEN DISHES

Chicken Jaipur £6.40
Chicken Jalfrazi £6.40
Chicken Shajahan £6.40
Chicken Korma £6.40
Chicken Keema £6.40
Quail Jaipur £7.40
Duck Jaipur £8.80

### LAMB DISHES

Rogan Josh £6.60
Lamb Jaipur £6.60
Lamb Jalfrazi £6.60
Lamb Chilli Garlic £6.90
Lamb Korma £6.60
Saag Gosht £6.50
Keema Peas £6.50

### SEAFOOD

Fish Jaipur £6.60
Fish Korma £6.60
Fish Shajahan £6.60
King Prawn Jaipur £8.60
Jumbo Prawn Jaipur £12.00
Jumbo Prawn Chilli Garlic £12.60

### VEGETABLES

Mixed Vegetables £3.90
Bhindi Bhaji £4.20
Bengan Bhaji £4.20
Mushroom Bhuna £3.90
Matter Paneer £3.90
Saag Paneer £4.20
Kofta Korma £3.90
Shahi Paneer £4.20
Bombay Aloo Jeera £3.90
Aloo Gobi £3.90
Channa Bhuna £3.90
Dal of the Day £3.90

### SUNDRIES

Lamb Tikka Biryani £9.80
Chicken Tikka Biryani £9.80
King Prawn Biryani £11.20
Vegetable Biryani £7.80

Rajdoot was opened in Birmingham in 1972 following the success of its sister restaurant in Chelsea, the first Tandoori restaurant in Europe. Tandoori, barbecued in traditional charcoal fired clay ovens, is their speciality, together with the subtle North Indian style of Moghlai cooking.

The chefs are sought out from India or Nepal, then trained in five-star hotels in India before being brought over to this country to recreate their authentic Indian cuisine in the heart of the city.

In addition to the à la carte menu featured opposite, there are four set price meals ranging in price from £14.00 to £19.50 per head. An "Executive Lunch" is available every day except Sunday, with three courses costing £6.95 per person.

Directions: Rajdoot can be found alongside *Marks & Spencer* between the High Street and Queensway.

## USEFUL INFORMATION

**SERVING TIMES:**
Lunch 12pm-2.30pm (Mon-Sat)
Dinner 6.30pm-11.30pm (every day)
**CLOSED:** Sunday lunch
**SEATING CAPACITY:** 86
**C/C:** V, MC, S, D, AE, DC
**OUTDOOR EATING:** no

**NUMBER OF WINES:** 24
**HOUSE WINE:** £7.95
**RESERVATIONS:** advisable
**DRESS CODE:** smart
**CHILDREN:** welcome
**OFF-STREET PARKING:** yes,
(5 spaces available across the road)

# SAINT PAULS

## Tel: (0121) 605 1001

50-54 St. Paul's Square, Hockley, Birmingham, B3 1QS

## STARTERS

Spinach, Glazed Goats Cheese & Orange Salad  £3.80
with Herb and Hazelnut Oil
Confit of Duck  £4.50
with a Smoked Bacon and Mixed Leaf Salad
Oak Smoked Salmon  £4.00
on Rocket Leaves with a Pink Peppercorn and Paprika Vinaigrette
St. Pauls Antipasti  £5.50
Continental Meats and Fresh Fish on a bed of Dressed Salad Leaves
served with Salsa Verde and Parmesan shavings, accompanied by Ciabatta Bread
Grilled Field Mushrooms  £2.95
with a Garlic and Onion Marinade on toasted French Bread

## MAIN COURSES

Pan Fried Cod Fillet  £9.50
with a Basil and Garlic Potato Cake, dressed with a Rocket Salsa
Chestnut and Oyster Mushrooms  £7.50
sautéed with Leeks and Pinenuts, finished with Goats Cheese, in a Filo Pastry case
Pan Fried Medallions of Pork Fillet  £8.95
marinated in Olive Oil, Honey and Fennel with Caramelised Apples
Baked Chicken Fillet  £8.50
stuffed with Blanched Leaf Spinach and Gruyère, on a sharp Cranberry Coulis
Roast Rack of Lamb  £9.00
stuffed with Pistachio Nut and Mint served on a Redcurrant and Port Sauce
Roast Mediterranean Vegetables  £7.50
in a Pastry Case browned with Parmesan with a Basil and Cream Sauce
Fillet of Beef  £11.95
marinated in Garlic, Wine, Herbs and Mustard with Sweet Red Onions
Monkfish Fillets  £11.50
sautéed with Lemon and Basil on Crisp Fried Spinach with a Red Pimiento Sauce
Grilled Chicken Breast  £8.95
seasoned with Garlic and Thyme with Baby Mushrooms and Sundried Tomatoes

## PASTA
served with one of the following sauces ...

Spinach, Pesto and St. Pauls Ham  £5.50     Spicy Lamb Meatballs  £5.50
Chargrilled Vegetables £5.50     Tomato, Basil, Garlic and Chilli  £5.00

Saint Pauls Bar & Restaurant overlooks the church in the peace and quiet of St. Paul's Square in the heart of Birmingham's Jewellery Quarter. The upstairs bar is modern and bright, with paintings by local artists on the walls, and a spiral staircase leads down to the basement restaurant (although the menu is the same wherever you decide to sit).

The dishes reflect the fashion of the moment with daily specials always available. The bar area can get very crowded on certain evenings and it is good to see people of all ages and haircuts mixing and enjoying themselves. Everything is cooked from fresh and offers good value for money. Sunday lunch ("with a bit of flair") is very popular, with their three-course meal priced at £12.95 per person.

Directions: Saint Pauls is easily found in St. Paul's Square in Birmingham.

### USEFUL INFORMATION

**SERVING TIMES:**
12pm-9.30pm (all day Mon-Thur)
12pm-10.30pm (all day Fri & Sat)
12.30pm-4pm and 6pm-9.30pm (Sun)
**SEATING CAPACITY:** 50 in the
restaurant, 30 in the bar upstairs
**C/C:** V, MC, S, D, AE

**NUMBER OF WINES:** 29
**HOUSE WINE:** £8.95
**RESERVATIONS:** advisable, but
essential at weekends
**OFF-STREET PARKING:** no
**OUTDOOR EATING:** yes

# THE WATERFRONT
### Tel: (0121) 333 5255
Waterlinks, Aston Cross, Rocky Lane, Birmingham, B6 5QR

**Open Fish Ravioli with Roasted Garlic £4.25**
*served with Fresh Tomato & Dill Sauce*
**Smoked Halibut & Mackerel Mousse wrapped in Smoked Salmon £5.25**
*with Fresh Lime & Horseradish Dressing*
**Chicken Livers Flamed in Calvados £3.95**
*with Apple, Cayenne Pepper & Croutons served on Mixed Leaves*
**Oyster Mushrooms Sautéed in Garlic £3.95**
*served with Hot Toast*
**Oven Baked Bruschetta £3.75**
*with Tomato, Olive Oil, Garlic & Mozzarella*
**Pigeon & Venison Terrine £4.95**
*served with an Apricot Chutney*
**Parma Ham with Pickled Shallots £5.25**
*with Fresh Parmesan Shavings*
**Avocado, Mozzarella & Sundried Tomato Tart £3.25**
*served with a Fresh Basil Dressing*
**Warm Lamb Fillet £4.95**
*on a Bed of Mixed Leaves with a Fresh Mint Dressing*

**Pasta with Broccoli, Fennel & Mushrooms £6.50**
*in a White Wine & Crème Fraîche Sauce*
**Cabbage Leaves Filled with Onion, Tomato, Rice, Nuts & Fresh Mint £7.25**
*served with a Tomato, Coriander & Garlic Sauce*
**Pan Fried Medallions of Pork £6.95**
*served with Garlic Mash & Braised Red Cabbage*
**Pan Fried Breast of Duck £11.25**
*with a Peach Liqueur & Honey Sauce*
**Breast of Chicken Filled with a Mushroom & Tarragon Mousse £9.75**
*served with a Brandy & Cream Sauce*
**Flash Roasted Rack of Lamb £10.75**
*with a Fresh Redcurrant & Rosemary Sauce*
**Pan Fried Calves Liver & Smoked Bacon £11.95**
*with a Caramelised Onion Gravy*
**Veal Escalope Filled with a Garlic Ratatouille £12.95**
*served with a Shallot & Thyme Sauce*

**White & Dark Chocolate Mousse with Cointreau £3.95**
**Tiramisu on a Coffee Cream Sauce £3.95**
**Crème Brûlée served with Peppered Strawberries £3.95**
**Oven Baked Cheesecake with Fresh Fruit Coulis £3.95**

The Waterfront is a new bar/restaurant which is situated in the Aston Waterlinks development, just a short taxi ride away from Birmingham city centre. This modern restaurant caters primarily for the business market at lunchtimes and in the evenings for the international visitor and local clientele.

The upstairs restaurant, which overlooks Birmingham's famous canals, offers a seasonally-changing menu based around modern European cuisine. In addition to the *carte* featured on the facing page, there are daily fish specials, such as Filo Wrapped Salmon with Fresh Herbs served with a Basil Cream Sauce (£11.50), Pan-fried Monkfish with Sundried Tomato & Spring Onion Sauce (£11.95), Grouper Fillet baked *en papillote* with Tomato, White Wine & Coriander (£10.50) or Grilled Swordfish Steak on a bed of Mixed Leaves with a Roasted Pepper Coulis (£11.50).

Directions: The Waterfront is found off Rocky Lane (B4144) off the Lichfield Road (A5127) which is directly linked with Junction 6 of the M6.

## USEFUL INFORMATION

**SERVING TIMES:**
Lunch 12pm-2.30pm (Mon-Fri)
Dinner 6pm-10.30pm (Mon-Sat)
**CLOSED:** Sat lunch & all day Sun
**SEATING CAPACITY:** 90
**C/C:** V, MC, S, D, AE, DC
**NO SMOKING** area available

**NUMBER OF WINES:** 51
**HOUSE WINE:** £8.95
**RESERVATIONS:** advisable
**OFF-STREET PARKING:** yes
**CHILDREN:** welcome
**OUTDOOR EATING:** yes

# MALLORY COURT

### Tel: (01926) 330214

Bishops Tachbrook, Leamington Spa, Warwickshire, CV33 9QB

## Luncheon

### First Courses or light main courses
(all first courses - £8)

Smoked Scottish salmon with scrambled eggs
Caesar salad
Ham terrine with parsley and white wine jelly and pickles
Potted duck with spiced pears
Crab and saffron tart
Smoked haddock fishcakes with parsley sauce
Globe artichoke with wild mushrooms, poached egg and Hollandaise sauce
Creamed haricot bean soup with bacon and garlic butter

### Main Courses
(all main courses - £10.50)

Deep fried cod in a beer batter with chips and tartare sauce
Skate 'au poivre' with a red wine sauce
Rabbit in Dijon mustard sauce
Grilled entrecôte steak with Café de Paris butter and chipped potatoes
Steak, kidney and mushroom pie with creamed potato
Veal escalope with chicory, Mozzarella, spinach and Parmesan
Confit de canard with a port wine sauce, braised cabbage and Pomme Anna
Devilled lambs' kidneys served with saffron rice

### Desserts
(all desserts - £7.50)

Chocolate, pear and almond tart with cinnamon ice cream
Rhubarb compôte with iced tangerine mousse
Hot apple tart with caramel sauce and vanilla ice cream (£3 supplement)
Caramel cream with sultanas
Mascarpone Cheesecake with bananas and hot butterscotch sauce
Choice of the Cheese board

Cafetière coffee with chocolate truffles - £3.75

*There is no service charge and none is expected*

Mallory Court is an outstanding example of period architecture, built in mellow stone with leaded light windows and set in ten acres of landscaped grounds. In an area renowned for its stately homes, the hotel faithfully recreates the traditions of the English country house. Its interior combines elegance with comfort and tranquillity. Owners Allan Holland and Jeremy Mort strive to provide for their guests the three essentials of country house living - hospitality, comfort and superb cuisine.

The panelled restaurant forms a graceful frame for the award-winning cooking. The menu, which changes seasonally, is light and innovative, using only the finest ingredients. Fresh vegetables and herbs from the gardens are used extensively, and home-made canapés, breads and petits fours help make every meal here a celebration.

In addition to the luncheon menu opposite (priced by the number of courses taken), there is a superb à la carte dinner menu, supported by a table d'hôte costing £30 for three courses inclusive of coffee.

Directions: Mallory Court is located north of the village of Bishops Tachbrook approximately 3 miles south of Leamington Spa. The hotel is signposted from the B4087 Leamington Spa to Wellesbourne road.

### USEFUL INFORMATION

**SERVING TIMES:**
Lunch 12.30pm-1.45pm (every day)
Dinner 7pm-9.45pm (every day)
**SEATING CAPACITY:** 50
**C/C:** V, MC, S, D, AE, DC
**OFF-STREET PARKING:** yes
**OUTDOOR EATING:** yes

**NUMBER OF WINES:** 200
**HOUSE WINE:** £16.00
**RESERVATIONS:** advisable
**CHILDREN:** welcome (over 9 yrs)
**DRESS CODE:** smart
**ACCOMMODATION:** 10 rooms
(B&B sgl fr £120, dbl fr £170)

# MAURO'S RESTAURANT

### Tel: (01625) 573898

88 Palmerston Street, Bollington, Cheshire, SK10 5PW

### Antipasti (Starters)

**Prosciutto e Melone £6.10**
Parma Ham &Melon
**Bresaola di Cinghiale £6.75**
Wild Boar Ham with Mozzarella
Cheese & Artichokes
**Insalata Caprese £4.70**
Mozzarella Cheese & Tomato Salad
with Olive Oil, Basil & Oregano
**Funghi con Aglio £4.20**
Mushrooms in Garlic Butter
**Soup of the Day £2.90**
**Stracciatella alla Romana £2.90**
Consommé with beaten Egg, Parmesan
Cheese and Parsley

### Pasta (Starters)

**Spaghetti Napoli £4.65**
Spaghetti in Tomato Sauce with Garlic
**Fettucine alla Romana £4.95**
Green Noodles with Cream,
Mushrooms, Peas and Ham
**Linguine ai Gamberetti £6.10**
Linguine with Prawns, Parsley, Garlic
and a touch of Tomato and Brandy
**Maccheroni all Tiberio £5.50**
Macaroni in a creamy sauce with
Smoked Cheese and finely chopped
Red Peppers
**Tubetti al Salmone £5.60**
Tubetti with Smoked Salmon, Cream
& Dill Sauce with a touch of Tomato
**Gnocchi alla Contadina £4.85**
Home-made Potato Gnocchi with a
mixed vegetable sauce with Basil

**Main Course Portion of Pasta
£1.85 extra**

### Pollo (Chicken)

**Pollo agli Agrumi £9.80**
Breast of Chicken with a Mixed Citrus
Fruit and Dry Martini Sauce
**Pollo Sorpresa £9.65**
Crumbed Breast of Chicken, stuffed
with Home-made Pâté & Garlic Butter
**Pollo alla Vesuviano £8.70**
Crumbed Escalope of Chicken, topped
with Mozzarella Cheese, Asparagus
and Tomato Sauce
**Pollo alla Cacciatore £8.95**
Boned leg of Chicken with Sweet
Pepper, Tomato, Mushroom and Onion
Sauce, with a hint of Chilli

### Carne (Meat)

**Filetto Dolcelatte £13.50**
Fillet Steak with Dolcelatte Cheese
and Cream Sauce
**Medaglioni Pizzaiola £13.10**
Fillet Steak in Tomato Sauce with
Oregano and Garlic
**Vitello alla Milanese £11.20**
Veal in breadcrumbs, served with
Spaghetti in Tomato Sauce with Garlic
**Piccata al Limone £10.90**
Veal Escalopes in Butter, Lemon and
White Wine Sauce
**Saltimbocca alla Romana £11.40**
Veal Escalopes topped with Parma
Ham in Sage and White Wine Sauce
**Scaloppine Valdostana £11.30**
Veal Escalopes topped with Ham
and Cheese

**All main dishes (except Pasta) are
served with two vegetables & potatoes**

Dating back to the 19th Century, and at one time a greengrocer's shop, Mauro's has established itself over the last ten years as one of the premier Italian restaurants in the north of England. The atmosphere, like the decor, is sunny and Mediterranean, with pictures from Capri adorning the bright yellow walls, and the wonderful aroma of Italian food wafting out from a bustling kitchen.

Although the main menu (featured opposite) is in itself quite extensive, it is the weekly specials and daily fish dishes that have really made this place so popular. Regulars often ignore the menu completely and simply ask Vincenzo what he's going to make for them today! The starters are supplemented by a mouth-watering array of hors d'oeuvres presented each day on a trolley, and the sweets are all home-made and quite delicious.

Directions: Bollington is a few miles north of Macclesfield. From the A523 follow the signs to Bollington and Mauro's is found on the right at the far end of the town.

## USEFUL INFORMATION

**SERVING TIMES:**
Lunch 12.15pm-2pm (Mon-Sat)
Dinner 7pm-10pm (Mon Sat)
**CLOSED:** Sunday
**SEATING CAPACITY:** 45
**C/C:** V, MC, S, D, AE

**NUMBER OF WINES:** 54
**HOUSE WINE:** £9.00
**RESERVATIONS:** advisable
**OUTDOOR EATING:** no
**OFF-STREET PARKING:** no
**CHILDREN:** welcome

# THE FEATHERS
## Tel: (01746) 785202
Brockton, near Much Wenlock, Shropshire, TF13 6JR

**Home-made Soup of the Day £2.45**
A full-flavoured soup, always without meat
**Crostini £2.95**
Garlic bread topped with chopped bacon, peppers and melted cheddar
**Greek Salad £3.75**
Chopped onion, cucumber and tomato with Feta cheese and olives
**Garlic King Prawns £5.75**
Shell-on prawns, pan-fried in garlic
**Lamb Kofta £3.95**
Grilled kebabs of minced lamb and herbs with a minted yoghurt dip

**Teriyaki Duck £9.75**
Duckling breast marinaded in wine, herbs, soy sauce and garlic, finished crisp
**Steak au Poivre £11.95**
Pan-fried prime fillet steak, cooked to your liking in a peppercorn sauce
**Flash Fried Chicken £8.95**
Strips of chicken breast, flash fried with mushrooms, peppers and onions,
finished in an Oriental (hot spicy) sauce
**Roulade of Pork £9.75**
Pork fillet, rolled and filled with sausage meat and herbs,
finished in a creamy stilton and onion sauce
**Half Duckling £11.95**
Roasted crisp, finished in a light gravy
**Chilli Garlic Chicken £7.95**
Boneless chicken breast baked in a skillet, in a spicy chilli, garlic & tomato sauce
**Stuffed Lamb Fillet £9.75**
Lamb fillet filled with fresh herb stuffing, baked in a red wine & redcurrant sauce
**Fillet of Fresh Fish £8.95**
Fillet of white fish, grilled with a lemon and chive crust,
finished with a lemon butter sauce
**Bouchées of Toasted Vegetables £7.65**
Toasted vegetables in puff pastry nests, finished with cream and tarragon sauce
**Penne Pasta £6.95**
Baked with spinach, tomato and pumpkin seeds, finished with mozzarella

**Baked Rice Pudding** with a Caramel Sauce **£3.25**
**Chocolate Marquise** with a Whisky and White Chocolate Sauce **£3.25**
**Baked Rice Pudding** with a Caramel Sauce **£3.25**
**Fresh Strawberry Meringue £3.25**

The Feathers looks for all the world like a traditional country pub, but owners Andrea and Martin Hayward have created something entirely unique in the middle of the Shropshire countryside. The 17th Century building still retains its characteristic low beams and exposed brickwork, but the atmosphere now is one of a friendly bistro, with a menu to match.

There are several different dining areas, from a modern conservatory to small snugs with collections of bric-a-brac. The menus are all written on blackboards, with excellent daily specials such as Aubergine Gateau finished with Three Cheeses in a Wild Mushroom Sauce (£7.95), Smoked Haddock on a Bed of Leek and Potato with a Cream and Chive Sauce (£7.95), or Roasted Fillet of Scottish Salmon dressed with Sushi Salmon and Cucumber (£9.75).

Directions: Feathers is situated on the crossroads in the centre of the village of Brockton, approximately 4 miles south-west of Much Wenlock on the B4378.

## USEFUL INFORMATION

**SERVING TIMES:**
Lunch 12pm-2pm (Sat & Sun only)
Dinner 6.30pm-9.30pm (Tues-Sun)
**CLOSED:** lunch (Mon-Fri), Mon night
**SEATING CAPACITY:** 56
**C/C:** S, D
**NO SMOKING** area available

**NUMBER OF WINES:** 20
**HOUSE WINE:** £9.75
**RESERVATIONS:** only accepted for parties of 6 or more
**OUTDOOR EATING:** no
**OFF-STREET PARKING:** yes
**CHILDREN:** welcome

# GRAFTON MANOR

### Tel: (01527) 579007

Grafton Lane, Bromsgrove, Worcestershire, B61 7HA

### 4-Course Dinner
### £31.50

Turnip, Honey and Lemon Soup

\* \* \* \* \*

Gravadlax served with a Wild Mustard and Dill Sauce
Pheasant Liver Parfait accompanied by Creamed Leeks and Leek Crisps
Terrine of Sole served on a Purée of Butter Beans
accompanied by a Pink Prawn and Chive Sauce
Goats Cheese encased in Filo Pastry with a Sundried Tomato and Marjoram
Dressing served on a Mixed Pepper and Parmesan Gratin

\* \* \* \* \*

Confit of Duck roasted until crisp,
served on a bed of Sauerkraut with a Green Lentil Sauce
Fillet of Beef, cooked pink, served with a Red Wine and Morel Sauce
Fillet of Salmon, grilled lightly with Olive Oil and Black Pepper,
served with Moules Marinières and Rosti Potato
Boned Leg of Worcestershire Lamb, cooked on a skillet,
served on a bed of Roast Cumin Cous Cous, with a Mint Jus and Brinjal Relish

Selection of seasonal vegetables or fresh leaf salad

\* \* \* \* \*

Selection of Sweets

\* \* \* \* \*

Cheese Board £3.25

\* \* \* \* \*

Freshly ground coffee and petits fours £2.60

Grafton Manor is a stylish country house hotel surrounded by six acres of beautiful grounds and a tranquil water garden bordering the lake. The present manor was commissioned in 1567 by Sir Gilbert Talbot, then Earl of Shrewsbury, and retains its original grace and proportions despite being substantially rebuilt in the early 18th Century after the Great Fire in 1710.

The elegant dining room is the focal point of a visit to Grafton, together with the sumptuous Grand Parlour for post-prandial drinks. Simon Morris changes his imaginative menus on a daily basis and selects from only the freshest ingredients, many of which are produced on the estate.

In addition to the dinner menu featured opposite, a three-course table d'hôte menu is served for both lunch and dinner priced at £25.95, with Sunday luncheon costing £18.50.

Directions: Grafton Manor is located approximately 1fi miles south of Bromsgrove town centre and is signposted from the B4091 Worcester road.

## USEFUL INFORMATION

**SERVING TIMES:**
Lunch 12.30pm-1.30pm (Sun-Fri)
Dinner 7.30pm-9pm (Mon-Sat)
**CLOSED:** Sat lunch & Sun evening
**SEATING CAPACITY:** 50
**C/C:** V, MC, S, D, AE, DC
**OFF-STREET PARKING:** yes
**OUTDOOR EATING:** no

**NUMBER OF WINES:** 93
**HOUSE WINE:** £10.95
**NO SMOKING** in the restaurant
**DRESS CODE:** no jeans, trainers
**RESERVATIONS:** very advisable
**CHILDREN:** welcome
**ACCOMMODATION:** 9 rooms
(B&B sgl fr £85, dbl fr £105)

# BROXTON HALL

**Tel: (01829) 782321**

Whitchurch Road, Broxton, Cheshire, CH3 9JS

*A selection from the table d'hôte menu £24.90*

*Chef's Home-made Soup of the Day*
*Smoked Haddock, Prawn and Mushroom Gratin*
*Traditional Fish Soup with a Rouille Croûton*
*Lambs Kidneys sautéed in a Herb and Garlic Butter with a Red Wine Sauce*
*Giant Prawns & Smoked Salmon with a delicious Seafood Sauce (£3 extra)*
*Mussels cooked in White Wine, Garlic, Parsley and Shallots*
*garnished with toasted Croûtons*
*Avocado Salad with a Warm Crispy Bacon Vinaigrette Dressing*

~~~~~~~~~~
*Sorbet*
~~~~~~~~~~

*Pöelled Supreme of Chicken on a bed of Tagliatelle served with a Stilton Sauce*
*Grilled Prime Fillet Steak with Sauce Archiduc (£3 extra)*
*Fillet of Beef Stroganoff served with Basmati Rice*
*Salmon en Croûte, Supreme of Salmon with a Dill Butter, wrapped in light*
*Puff Pastry and served with a White Wine and Cream Sauce*
*Braised Lamb Shank cooked with Tomato and Mediterranean Vegetables,*
*flavoured with Thyme and Rosemary*
*Goujons of Plaice served with a Sauce Tartare*
*Grilled Lambs' Liver and Bacon served with an Onion Marmalade*
*Roast Cheshire Duckling with an Orange and Grand Marnier Sauce*
*Medallions of Pork with an Apple, Sage and Calvados Sauce*
*Chef's Vegetarian Dish of the Day*

*Selection of Fresh Seasonal Vegetables*

*Apricot and Almond Frangipane Tart with Crème Fraîche*
*Sauternes Syllabub with Sultanas steeped in Brandy*
*Crêpes with Ice Cream covered in a Hot Chocolate Sauce*
*Crêpes filled with Apple and Cinnamon served with a Vanilla Ice Cream*
*Chef's delicious Bread and Butter Pudding with a hint of Brandy*
*Chocolate Roulade filled with Pears and Kummel Cream*
*Hot Raspberries served with Vanilla Ice Cream*
*Hot Syrup Sponge served with Custard or Ice Cream*

*Coffee and Chocolate Mints*

Set in five acres of beautiful grounds and gardens, Broxton Hall is an elegant half-timbered hotel dating back to the 17th Century. Oak-panelled walls, large open fireplaces, and antique furniture help to create an atmosphere of olde worlde charm and luxury.

The restaurant, which overlooks the gardens, has an excellent reputation for its French and English cuisine. At lunch there is a good value table d'hôte (3 courses £15.50) or a more extensive à la carte. Lighter lunches such as Toasted Steak Sandwich with Caramelised Onions (£5.50), Lasagne with Salad and French Bread (£5.75) and sandwiches (from £3) are also available.

Featured opposite is an example of the evening table d'hôte (an à la carte was being introduced at the time of publication), and as with the luncheon menu it changes seasonally. A traditional roast with a good choice of dishes is offered on Sunday (3 courses £13.90).

Directions: About 9 miles south of Chester on the A41 Chester to Whitchurch Road. Broxton Hall is 200 yards along on the left after the roundabout junction with the A534.

## USEFUL INFORMATION

**SERVING TIMES:**
Lunch 12pm-2pm (every day)
Dinner 7pm-9.30pm (Mon-Sat)
7pm-9pm (Sunday)
**SEATING CAPACITY:** 60
**C/C:** V, MC, S, D, AE, DC
**OUTDOOR EATING:** yes

**NUMBER OF WINES:** 65
**HOUSE WINE:** £10.75
**RESERVATIONS:** advisable
**OFF-STREET PARKING:** yes
**CHILDREN:** welcome
**ACCOMMODATION:** 11 rooms
(B&B single £60, double from £70)

# FROGG MANOR
## Tel: (01829) 782629
Nantwich Road, Broxton, Cheshire, CH3 9JH

### *A selection from the A La Carte £25.95*

**FRESHLY MADE SOUP**
**GRILLED "CHEVRE BLANC"**
A full fat soft cheese made from goats milk served with spring onions, sweet peppers, celery, nuts and fruit, pan fried in a raspberry vinaigrette
**POONA PRAWN VOL AU VENT**
Poached Royal Greenland prawns served in a cream of oriental spices on a vol au vent
**MELON**
With Royal Greenland prawns in marie rose sauce
**POACHED PEAR AND ROQUEFORT**
A green salad, tossed in a vinaigrette "Frogg Manor style", served with Roquefort cheese and pear poached in red wine
**GREENLAND PARCEL**
A medium fat soft cheese made from goats milk, baked in filo pastry and served with natural yoghurt flavoured with lime juice, on salad

### MAIN COURSES

**FILLET OF SALMON**
Fillet of salmon, dipped in crushed black peppercorns, oven baked and served with a béchamel sauce suprème. With Basmati rice or vegetables of the day
**POACHED FILLET OF LEMON SOLE**
Poached fillet of lemon sole with spinach and king prawns, served with a cream of parsley butter sauce. With Basmati rice or vegetables of the day
**ROAST BREAST OF GRESSINGHAM DUCK**
Served with a rich black cherry sauce
**CHICKEN SPARTEN**
Supreme of chicken, sautéed in olive oil and butter, served on a bed of buttered spinach, with chives, new potatoes and carrots
**THE WHOLE FILLET OF LAMB**
Whole fillet of lamb served with port and red wine savoury gravy *£7.70 extra*
**INDIVIDUAL STEAK PIE**
Individual steak, onion, mushroom and celery pie made using only the finest and purest of local beef in a rich red wine gravy
**SEAFOOD CREME DE BELLE**
Prawns, scallops, salmon, and cream potato, poached and baked, served with a cream of white wine and parsley butter sauce

### DESSERTS

Welcome to The Twilight Zone. Frogg Manor is a grade II listed Georgian house which stands peacefully in its own nine acres of pretty gardens. But as one might expect of a hotel called Frogg (named after the proprietor's girlfriend "Froggy"), everything here is a bit surreal. Welcomed by a human-sized frog in a polka dot tie, the experience is a wonderful mix of luxury and eccentricity, with huge doses of the latter being supplied by proprietor and host, John Sykes. Don't expect him to be polite just because you are his guest.

Lunch and dinner are by reservation only (you may try turning up without one, but it all depends on the mood of the chef as to whether you get fed) and the food is all freshly prepared. The menu is constantly evolving to include seasonal specialities. Beef dishes carry a supplement (from £6 extra), as well as a house guarantee that 'you are more likely to win the lottery twice in succession than be harmed by the meat served in this establishment'.

Directions: About 12 miles west of Nantwich on the A534, Frogg Manor is on the left a mile before the A41.

### USEFUL INFORMATION

**SERVING TIMES:**
Lunch by reservation only
Dinner by reservation only
**CLOSED:** New Year's Day
**SEATING CAPACITY:** 55
**C/C:** V, MC, S, D, AE, DC
**OUTDOOR EATING:** yes
**NO SMOKING** area available

**NUMBER OF WINES:** 37
**HOUSE WINE:** £10
**RESERVATIONS:** compulsory
**OFF-STREET PARKING:** yes
**CHILDREN:** welcome
**ACCOMMODATION:** 6 rooms
(single £50-£87, double £66-£120)

# THE WILD BOAR HOTEL
## Tel: (01829) 260309
Whitchurch Road, Beeston, nr Bunbury, Cheshire, CW6 9NW

*A selection from the Winter A La Carte Menu*

**SMOKED SALMON MOUSSELINE**
*Served in a blanched seedless beef tomato, with horseradish crème fraîche and surrounded by an avocado and green salad £6.95*
**A TERRINE OF PHEASANT, QUAIL AND PIGEON**
*Bound in a chicken liver parfait and served with home-made brioche and a cranberry and juniper chutney £6.25*
**A DUO OF GALIA AND WATER MELONS**
*Served with a passion fruit mousse with plum sorbet and plum sauce £5.25*
**A WARM SALAD OF FRIED QUEEN SCALLOPS**
*Served with lardons of smoked bacon in a vermouth, shallot, chive, garlic and oyster sauce £7.95*
**A PRESSED VEGETABLE TERRINE**
*Consisting of aubergine, tomato, basil and mozzarella cheese served with a spiced herb olive oil, winter salad and pickled walnuts £5.25*

## MAIN COURSES

**OVEN BAKED BREAST OF CHESHIRE CHICKEN**
*Filled with blue cheese and accompanied by a parsley butter sauce and ribbons of tomato pasta tossed in shallot, garlic, diced tomato and herbs £16.25*
**ROAST RACK OF HILL LAMB**
*Served with a panaché of wilted greens, buttered potatoes, cherry tomatoes and a pommery mustard dressing £17.60*
**FRESH 16oz DOVER SOLE GRILLED OR MEUNIERE**
*Removed from the bone unless requested whole £22.00*
**CHAR-GRILLED PRIME LOCAL SIRLOIN STEAK**
*Cooked with a grilled tomato and glazed mushrooms £17.50*
**CHINESE CHICKEN**
*Strips of chicken cooked in honey, soy, garlic, chillis, balsamic vinegar, mango chutney and sesame seeds £19.00*
**PROVENCALE SCAMPI**
*Tails of scampi cooked with aubergine, courgette, peppers and garlic in a tomato and basil sauce £23.00*

## PUDDINGS

*A selection of hand-made sweets and pastries from the trolley £4.10*

The Wild Boar Hotel nestles in beautiful Cheshire countryside beneath the outcrop of Beeston Castle. Originally a 17th Century hunting lodge, this dramatic half-timbered black and white building is now a splendid hotel, renowned for its gourmet restaurant.

In addition to the seasonal à la carte shown opposite, the elegant Tower Restaurant offers a lunchtime table d'hôte (5 courses £14.50) and an evening table d'hôte (5 courses £22), both of which change daily. There is also a Sunday dinner table d'hôte (5 courses £15.95) which is very popular, and those after a less formal meal may well find the answer in the bar on the menu or specials board.

Directions:  Easily found on the A49 about ten miles north of Whitchurch.

### <u>USEFUL INFORMATION</u>

**SERVING TIMES:**
Lunch 12pm-2pm (every day)
Dinner 7pm-9.45pm (every day)
**SEATING CAPACITY:** 75 in the restaurant, 75 in the bar
**C/C:** V, MC, S, D, AE
**OUTDOOR EATING:** yes
**CHILDREN** welcome

**NUMBER OF WINES:** 70
**HOUSE WINE:** £9.90
**OFF-STREET PARKING:** yes
**RESERVATIONS:** advisable
**NO SMOKING** requested in the restaurant
**ACCOMMODATION:** 37 rooms (single £59, double £75)

# THE HORSESHOE INN

## Tel: (01283) 564913

Main Street, Tatenhill, nr Burton upon Trent, Staffordshire, DE13 9SD

**Smoked Black Forest Ham £2.30**
thinly sliced, served with tossed salad leaves, olive oil & black pepper

**Garlic Mushrooms & Cheese £2.55**
cooked in garlic butter & topped with melted stilton or cheddar cheese, served with garlic bread

**Prawn Waldorf £2.95**
prawns, apple, celery & walnuts, tossed in marie rose sauce &served on a bed of mixed leaves

**Filo Pastry Prawns £2.95**
served with your choice of dip, choose from korma, garlic or blue cheese

**Oven-baked Smoked Mackerel £2.20**
fillet of mackerel served with a gooseberry sauce

**Pedigree Pie £3.95**
steak, kidney & mushrooms braised in a rich pedigree gravy & topped with puff pastry

**Home-made Lasagne Verdi £4.95**
layers of pasta & minced beef with a cheesy sauce

**Lambs Liver & Bacon £4.35**
pan-fried liver served with a rich bacon & onion gravy

**Home-made Salmon Fishcakes £5.30**
salmon fillet flaked & mixed with wine, shallots, parsley & mashed potato, coated in fresh white breadcrumbs, deep fried & served with a lemon butter sauce

**Lamb Steak £6.95**
an 8oz lamb steak marinated in rosemary & mint & grilled to perfection

**Fisherman's Bake £5.75**
poached salmon, cod & scallops cooked in a white wine & cream sauce, topped with a light cheese & breadcrumb crust

**Bangers 'n' Mash £4.35**
delicious pork & herb sausages in a rich onion gravy, served with mashed potatoes & peas

**King Prawn Tagliatelle £4.45**
cooked in garlic butter & pesto sauce on a bed of tagliatelle, served with ciabatta bread

**Savoury Pancake £4.25**
herb pancakes filled with broccoli florets & a creamy stilton sauce

**Sesame Roasted Salmon Fillet £6.65**
scotch salmon seasoned with sea salt, pepper & sesame seeds, served with hollandaise sauce

**Sirloin Steak £8.75**
8oz sirloin steak, grilled, served with cherry tomatoes, mushrooms & crispy onion rings

**Rich Chocolate Fudge Cake £2.10**
served hot or cold

**Luxury Bread & Butter Pudding £2.15**
served with cream, custard or ice cream

The Horseshoe Inn, parts of which are believed to date back to the 15th Century, is a country inn that serves traditional pub fayre in welcoming surroundings. Exposed beams, tiled flooring and wooden panelling all help the building retain much of its original character.

There is a separate restaurant, although the menu (a selection is featured opposite) remains the same as the bar area. In addition to these dishes, which give excellent value for money, there are specials on the blackboard that change daily, such as Cajun Chicken (£5.40), Beef & Mushroom Pie (£3.25), Half a Roast Chicken with Stuffing (4.95), 14oz Rump Steak with all the trimmings (£12.95), or a Pork Chop in Cider Gravy (£5.50).

Directions: The Horseshoe Inn is in the village of Tatenhill, approximately 2 miles to the south-west of Burton upon Trent and signposted from the A38.

## USEFUL INFORMATION

**SERVING TIMES:**
Lunch 12pm-2pm (Mon-Fri)
        12pm-2.30pm (Sat & Sun)
Dinner 6pm-10pm (Mon-Fri)
        5.30pm-9.30pm (Sat & Sun)
**SEATING CAPACITY:** 120
**NO SMOKING** area available

**NUMBER OF WINES:** 25
**HOUSE WINE:** £7.40
**OUTDOOR EATING:** yes
**RESERVATIONS:** advisable
**CHILDREN:** welcome
**C/C:** V, MC, S, D, AE
**OFF-STREET PARKING:** yes

# THE CASTLE HOTEL
## Tel: (01433) 620578
Castle Street, Castleton, Hope Valley, Derbyshire, S30 2WG

## STARTERS

### Savoury Bacon and Cheddar Melt
Pan-fried bacon, mushrooms, onion and tomato mixed with English mustard and served on a toasted garlic bloomer bread with cheddar cheese melted over
**£2.50**

### Fresh Soup of the Day
Served with a wedge of fresh bloomer bread
**£1.95**

### Breaded Mushrooms
Breaded button mushrooms, deep fried and served on a mixed leaf salad with a garlic and sour cream dip
**£2.25**

### Prawn Cocktail
Served with buttered crusty granary bread
**£2.50**

## MAINS

### 8oz Gammon Steak
Grilled and served with pineapple, fried egg, seasoned chips & fresh seasonal vegetables
**£4.95**

### Breaded Scampi
Whole tail scampi, deep fried & served with lemon, tartare sauce, seasoned chips & peas
**£5.25**

### Beef and Ale Pie
Filled with beef & mushrooms in Bass ale gravy, with fresh vegetables, cheddar mash
**£5.25**

### Chicken, Ham & Mushroom Pie
With fresh vegetables & cheddar mash
**£5.25**

## MAINS

### Hunters Chicken
Grilled double breast of chicken & bacon covered with smoky barbecue sauce and melted cheddar cheese, served with cheddar mash & fresh seasonal vegetables
**£6.95**

### 8oz Rump Steak
Brushed with seasoned oil and grilled as you asked. Served with onion rings and pan-fried button mushrooms, seasoned chips and fresh seasonal vegetables
**£6.95**

### Lemon Chicken
Two breadcrumbed chicken breasts, deep fried and topped with melting lemon and parsley butter. Served with seasoned chips and fresh seasonal vegetables
**£5.25**

### Cod and Chips
A whale of a fish, battered and deep fried, served with lemon, tartare sauce, seasoned chips and peas
**£5.25**

### Hot Chicken Salad
Grilled Double breast of chicken sliced and served on a fresh mixed salad with croutons
**£5.45**

### Seafood Salad
Sliced smoked salmon, tuna in mayonnaise and peeled prawns served on a fresh mixed salad with lemon and croutons
**£5.95**

### Vegetarian
See the blackboard for today's vegetarian dish and other specials

The Castle Hotel is a 17th Century coaching inn set in the heart of the Peak District. It has recently undergone extensive renovation, and offers guests a warm welcome amidst low beams, ancient stone walls and a giant log fire. At the latest count there were four friendly ghosts, including that of a jilted bride and a middle-aged man in a pin-striped suit!

Only traditional British food is served here. The main menu changes seasonally and is complemented by excellent blackboard daily specials, including huge starters like Yorkshire Pudding filled with Three Lincolnshire Sausages and Onion Gravy, Cheddar Mash and Vegetables (£4.75), and mouthwatering main dishes such as Halibut Steak with Lobster Sauce (£8.25). The puddings are appropriately rich, with the School Pud (£1.95) being a particular favourite.

Directions: The Castle Hotel is easily found on the A625 in the middle of Castleton.

## USEFUL INFORMATION

**SERVING TIMES:**
Food served 11am-10pm (every day)
**SEATING CAPACITY:** 160
**C/C:** V, MC, S, D, AE
**CHILDREN** welcome
**OUTDOOR EATING:** yes
**OFF-STREET PARKING:** yes

**NUMBER OF WINES:** 40
**HOUSE WINE:** £7.45
**RESERVATIONS:** are not available for dining
**NO SMOKING** area available
**ACCOMMODATION:** 9 rooms
(B&B single £39.50, double £59)

# YE OLDE NAGS HEAD
### Tel: (01433) 620248
Castleton, Derbyshire, S30 2WH

### *TABLE D'HOTE DINNER MENU £22.50*

#### *To Start*

*Crab and asparagus gateau served in a chive cream*

*A savoury onion tart glazed with blue cheese and served with a hazelnut salad*

*Seasonal melon served with a pot pourri of exotic fruits and berries*

*Terrine of lamb fillet accompanied by a salad of oranges and truffle oil*

*A warm salad of black pudding and smoked bacon topped with poached egg
in a balsamic vinegar dressing*

#### *Main Course*

*Roast monkfish tail wrapped in smoked bacon surrounded by a tomato
and saffron butter sauce*

*Supreme of chicken braised in white wine, served with salmon dumplings
in a tarragon butter sauce*

*Fillet of beef (cooked pink) with garlic butter and spaghetti pizziola*

*Rack of lamb served with colcannon purée and spring onion mash
together in a madeira sauce*

*Fillet of grey mullet served with poached asparagus in a pernod beurre blanc*

*Leek and blue cheese strudel served with dressed salad leaves*

*Haunch of venison served with a red onion compôte in a wild mushroom jus*

#### *Dessert*

*A selection of home-made puddings and desserts*

*Freshly ground coffee, hand-made chocolates and sweetmeats*

Ye Olde Nags Head is a 17th Century coaching house situated in the picturesque Peak District village of Castleton, which lies beneath the grey ruins of Peveril Castle at the western end of the glorious Hope Valley.

The restaurant is renowned for its first class cuisine, featuring traditional English Fayre, fresh fish, shell fish and local game when in season, complemented by a good range of wines. From Sunday to Friday a table d'hôte menu (2/3 courses for £14.50 and £18.50 respectively) is offered at lunch and dinner. This changes weekly. The Menu Gourmand shown opposite is available on Saturday evening, and wonderful home-made desserts may include Sticky Toffee Pudding, Glazed Blueberry Brûlée, or Glazed Lime Tart and Passion Fruit Sorbet.

Food may also be taken in the more relaxed atmosphere of the bar, where there is a monthly menu and a blackboard showing daily specials.

Directions: Castleton is about 16 miles west of Sheffield. Approaching on the A625, Ye Olde Nags Head is easily found in the centre of the village.

## USEFUL INFORMATION

**SERVING TIMES:**
Lunch 12pm-2.30pm (every day)
Dinner 7pm-9.30pm (every day)
**SEATING CAPACITY:** 44 in the restaurant, 30 in the bar
**C/C:** V, MC, S, D, AE, DC
**OUTDOOR EATING:** no
**CHILDREN:** welcome

**NUMBER OF WINES:** 50
**HOUSE WINE:** £8.75
**RESERVATIONS:** advisable
**OFF-STREET PARKING:** yes
**NO SMOKING** in the restaurant
**ACCOMMODATION:** 8 rooms
(single fr £46.50, double fr £69.50)

# BROCKENCOTE HALL

### Tel: (01562) 777876

Chaddesley Corbett, near Kidderminster, Worcestershire, DY10 4PY

## MENU AT £24.50

**Marinated Salmon Teriyaki**
*served with a Crunchy Vegetable Salad*
*and a Soy Dressing*

**Pan-fried Pigeon Supremes**
*served with Black Pudding, Spiced Apple and*
*a Natural Jus acidulated with Cider Vinegar*

**Potted Rabbit**
*deep-fried in a light Cornflour Batter,*
*served with Belly Pork, confit of Garlic*
*and a Seasonal Salad*
*enhanced in a Tomato Dressing*

~ ~ ~

**Pot-au-Feu of Seasonal Game**
*served with Root Vegetables, Horseradish*
*and Salt Flowers*

**Devon Skate Wing**
*pan-fried and served with buttered Spinach*
*Leaves, crunchy Capers, Parsley*
*and Red Wine Butter Sauce*

**Fine Slices of Barbary Duck Breast**
*served with Griotte Cherries,*
*a Confit of Potato Pearls*
*and a Sherry Vinegar flavoured Jus*

**Roasted Back of Cod Fillet**
*topped with a Mushroom Mousse,*
*served with Creamed Leeks*
*and a Ginger and Lemon Grass Emulsion*

~ ~ ~

**Passion Fruit Crème Brûlée**
*served with a Brunoise of Exotic Fruit*
*in a Ginger Syrup*

**Individual Caramelised Apple Tart**
*served with a Cinnamon Ice Cream*

## MENU AT £42.50

**Pan-fried Duck Foie Gras**
*served with a Duo of Apple and Raisins*
*and a Cinnamon flavoured Brioche*

**An Open Raviole of Warm Oysters**
*served with fine strips of Braised Chicory*
*and Shellfish and Tarragon flavoured Fumet*

**A Wild Duck Feuilleté**
*served with a Compôte of Shallots*
*and a Blackcurrant flavoured Jus*

**Loch Fyne Scallops**
*poached in their Liquor, served with*
*Solferinos of Celeriac*
*and a Celeriac and Scallop Emulsion*

~ ~ ~

**Roast Aberdeen Angus Beef Fillet**
*served with Glazed Shallots, Wild Mushrooms*
*and a Port Cream Sauce*

**Pan-fried Fillet of Turbot**
*and Loch Fyne Scallops, served with Braised*
*Fennel and a Mussel and Saffron Sauce*

**Roast Noisettes of Venison**
*served with a Poached Pear in Red Wine*
*Syrup and a Natural Jus flavoured with*
*Juniper Berries*

**Fillet of Sea Bass**
*served with a Basil Creamed Potato*
*and an Olive Oil, Tomato and Herb Sauce*

~ ~ ~

**A Light Bitter Chocolate Delight**
*with a crunchy White Chocolate Ice Cream*

**A Poached Pear in Vanilla Liquor**
*served with a Pistachio Ice Cream*
*and an Amaretto Sabayon*

Brockencote Hall is a traditional English country house hotel of great charm and character. It stands within 70 acres of beautiful landscaped grounds which form part of an estate dating back to the 17th Century. The grounds' attractive features include a dovecote, gatehouse, lake and many fine specimen trees.

The elegant restaurant owes its success to a menu of traditional French cuisine and a tempting choice of lighter dishes and vegetarian options (which have not been mentioned on the seasonal table d'hôte menu featured opposite). The slightly simpler menu in the left-hand column is also served at lunch and costs £19.50 per person. The prices of both menus include coffee.

Directions: Brockencote Hall is situated just outside the small village of Chaddesley Corbett, which lies approximately 4 miles to the south-east of Kidderminster on the main A448 Kidderminster-Bromsgrove road. The hotel is set well back from the road and is clearly signposted.

## USEFUL INFORMATION

**SERVING TIMES:**
Lunch 12pm-1.30pm (Sun-Fri)
Dinner 7pm-9.30pm (every day)
**CLOSED:** Saturday lunch
**SEATING CAPACITY:** 50
**C/C:** V, MC, S, AE, DC
**NO SMOKING** in the restaurant
**OFF-STREET PARKING:** yes

**NUMBER OF WINES:** 150
**HOUSE WINE:** £11.40
**RESERVATIONS:** advisable
**CHILDREN:** welcome
**OUTDOOR EATING:** no
**ACCOMMODATION:** 17 rooms
(B&B single £85, double £115)

# THE ARKLE

### Tel: (01244) 324024

The Chester Grosvenor, Eastgate, Chester, Cheshire, CH1 1LT

---

*Three Course Menu £45*   <u>*Dinner*</u>   *Two Course Menu £38*

*Soup of Jerusalem artichokes with creamed spinach and a poached quail egg*
*Canneloni of calf's sweetbread with Dublin Bay prawns*
*and a Mediterranean fish sauce*
*A pressing of Landes duck liver with Sauterne jelly*
*and toasted brioche (supp £8.50)*
*Pan seared scallops with a carrot purée, chicory and a light vanilla sauce*
*Confit of egg plant with plum tomatoes, Scottish lobster*
*and a fennel dressing (supp £6.50)*
*Parfait of wild duck with hot smoked breast of wild duck and a salad of chestnuts*

---

*Pot roasted Bresse pigeon with savoy cabbage and thyme juices*
*Carved loin of venison with egg pasta, caramelised turnips,*
*red wine celery and a juniper scented sauce*
*A composition of fillet and braised shin of veal with a gruyère and truffle risotto*
*Fillet of beef topped with a crust of horseradish and parsley,*
*crushed parsnips and oxtail*
*Cutlets of Welsh lamb with fennel gnocchi, oven dried tomatoes,*
*pesto tortellinis and sweet garlics*
*Poached breast of guineafowl with a pressing of leeks, wild mushrooms*
*and a truffle infused stock*
*Casserole of seafood and shellfish with ginger, star anise,*
*seaweed and seasonal vegetables*

---

*An indulgence of chocolate*
*Calvados rice condé with caramelised apples and hot lemon costolies*
*Marinated apricot soufflé with a butterscotch sauce and amaretto ice cream*
*Iced parfait of white chocolate and griottine cherries*
*with a glazed sabayon of clementine*
*Lime tart with pistachio studded snow eggs and a citrus syrup*
*English plum and date pudding with a compôte of spiced plums*
*and a cinnamon ice cream*
*Specially selected mature British and French farmhouse cheeses*

*Coffee and Sweetmeats £4.50*

The Arkle is The Chester Grosvenor's award-winning gourmet restaurant, named in honour of Anne, Duchess of Westminster's famous steeplechaser. It is renowned for its imaginative food, outstanding service and a serious wine list, one of the most extensive in the country with over 800 bins from around the world.

The menu changes seasonally and the emphasis is on using the very best fresh local produce in an innovative way. The à la carte dinner menu featured on the facing page is supplemented by a *menu gourmande*, priced at £40.00 and which changes nightly. The three-course luncheon menu provides excellent value at £22.50 per person.

Directions: The Chester Grosvenor is situated in Eastgate Street in the centre of the historical city of Chester.

## USEFUL INFORMATION

**SERVING TIMES:**
Lunch 12pm-2pm (Tues-Sun)
Dinner 7pm-9.30pm (Mon-Sat)
**CLOSED:** Mon lunch & Sun dinner
**SEATING CAPACITY:** 40
**C/C:** V, MC, AE, DC
**OFF-STREET PARKING:** 24-hour
NCP car park is available
**OUTDOOR EATING:** no
**NO SMOKING** in the restaurant

**NUMBER OF WINES:** 800
**HOUSE WINE:** £11.50
**RESERVATIONS:** advisable
**CHILDREN:** welcome
**DRESS CODE:** gentlemen prefer
to wear a jacket and tie
**ACCOMMODATION:** 85 rooms
(B&B fr £150 per room per night,
based on two people sharing)

# LA BRASSERIE
### Tel: (01244) 324024
The Chester Grosvenor, Eastgate Street, Chester, Cheshire, CH1 1LT

## STARTERS

Stilton & Guinness Soup  £4.25
Deep fried spring roll of Cornish crab with red pepper rouille  £6.75
Pasta shells with air dried tomato, pesto & pecorino cheese  £4.75
Black pudding sausage with champ potatoes & mustard  £4.95
Mussels with white wine, shallots, parsley & cream  £6.25
Six chilled native oysters with lemon & shallot vinegar  £8.50
Herb marinade chicken with a bacon salad  £6.25
Potato cakes topped with marinated herrings & chive yoghurt  £5.25

## VEGETARIAN

Gruyère & semolina gnocchi with a sweet tomato & oregano sauce £5.75
Choux pastry ring with creamed leaf spinach, wild mushrooms
    & a poached egg  £6.75
Glamorgan sausages with a leek & grain mustard cream  £6.75

## MAIN COURSES

Cumberland sausage with mashed potatoes and onion gravy  £6.75
Breast of guineafowl with Dijon mustard potatoes & basil-grilled
    plum tomatoes  £8.75
Grilled cutlet of veal with a panfried lemon & herb risotto  £12.75
Peppered calf's liver with Thai noodles & Kaffir lime leaf sauce  £14.25
Braised shank of lamb with Toulouse sausage & haricot beans  £10.75
Ribeye steak with Café de Paris butter  £12.00
Roast breast of duck with savoy cabbage, pancetta bacon
    & green peppercorns  £11.25
Traditional chou croûte  £10.50

## FISH

Grilled whole lemon sole with tartare sauce  £12.75
Tempura of haddock with French style garden peas  £9.25
Hot smoked salmon fillet with spinach cream & mussels  £10.75
Brochette of monkfish & king prawns with an Indonesian spiced rice
    & lemon grass sauce  £12.25
Seared sea scallops with tomatoes, capers & black olives  £14.75

*Today's market vegetables  £1.75    Your choice of potatoes  £1.75*

La Brasserie is a bustling, French-styled restaurant attached to The Chester Grosvenor Hotel in the city centre. It was opened in 1988 after the total refurbishment of the hotel and offers a more casual alternative to the gourmet dining enjoyed at The Arkle (please refer to our separate entry).

Open every day from 7am for breakfast through to last orders for dinner at 10.30pm, it provides a seasonal menu simmering with innovative and adventurous ideas for a leisurely meal out. But the informality of the place means that you are just as welcome to pop in for a quick drink and a pastry, or a salad with a glass of wine.

Directions: La Brasserie is situated at the front of The Chester Grosvenor Hotel on Eastgate Street, in the centre of the historic Chester.

### USEFUL INFORMATION

**SERVING TIMES:**
7am-10.30pm (every day)
**SEATING CAPACITY:** 120
**C/C:** V, MC, AE, DC
**OFF-STREET PARKING:** no
**NO SMOKING** area available
**OUTDOOR EATING:** no

**NUMBER OF WINES:** 52
**HOUSE WINE:** £11.50
**RESERVATIONS:** advisable
**CHILDREN:** welcome
**ACCOMMODATION:** 85 rooms
(B&B fr £150 per room per night, based on two people sharing)

# CRABWALL MANOR

### Tel: (01244) 851666

Parkgate Road, Mollington, Chester, Cheshire, CH1 6NE

## A LA CARTE LUNCH AND DINNER MENU

*Tomato consommé, served cold with sweet basil  £4.50*
*Pressed terrine of duck leg confit and potato*
*served with home-made piccalilli  £5.50*
*Frothy white bean soup with giroles  £4.75*
*Cannelloni of scallops and a sauternes sauce  £7.00*
*Paupiette of smoked salmon filled with smoked salmon mousse*
*and garnished with asparagus  £6.50*
*Millefeuille of red mullet and braised cabbage*
*accompanied by a warm gazpacho sauce  £5.50*
*Chicken and leek boudin with a duxelle of mushrooms*
*and a sherry reduction sauce  £4.00*
*Tartlet of griddled onions with red pepper and a salad of mâche  £4.50*

*Loin of venison roasted and served with a tagliatelle of wild mushrooms  £24.00*
*Roast best end of lamb with a tian of Mediterranean vegetables*
*and a thyme flavoured jus  £22.00*
*Grilled delice of cod garnished with sweet and sour courgette tomato confit*
*and tomato reduction sauce  £21.00*
*Supreme of guinea fowl with celery and a smoked bacon sauce  £22.00*
*Medallions of beef fillet with red wine sauce and french fried potatoes  £24.00*
*Paupiette of lemon sole filled with creamed leeks*
*and a veloute flavoured with white truffle oil  £22.00*
*Roasted duck breast set on a Jerusalem artichoke purée*
*and wilted greens with orange zest  £23.50*

*Gâteau Marjolaine encompassing vanilla flavoured marscapone*
*and chocolate mousse  £6.00*
*Iced terrine of coconut parfait and fresh pineapple  £5.00*
*Roast pear with red wine sauce and a cinnamon flavoured crème fraîche  £4.75*
*Baked apple tart tatin with a caramelised sauce  £6.00*
*Coffee crème brûlée topped with a chocolate sabayon  £4.50*
*French style lemon tart glazed and served with an orange syrup  £4.50*

*A selection of farmhouse cheese  £4.00*

*Coffee and petits fours £3.25*

Crabwall Manor is a traditional castellated manor house hotel with its origins dating back to the 10th Century. The estate has the rare distinction of having had only two changes of ownership in 800 years. The present Grade II listed building had the addition in the 17th Century of a fine red brick frontage with its battlemented top.

As you would expect from this luxurious hotel, their kitchens have a reputation for creative and innovative cooking, modern British in style. Light, mouthwatering sauces are combined with the finest market-fresh produce. To complement your meal, there is an extensive wine list which boasts some 600 bins, including some of the most distinguished labels from around the world.

Directions: Crabwall Manor is situated approximately 2 miles to the north-west of the city centre on the A540 Chester to Hoylake road.

### USEFUL INFORMATION

**SERVING TIMES:**
Lunch 12pm-2pm (every day)
Dinner 7pm-9.30pm (every day)
**SEATING CAPACITY:** 100
**C/C:** V, MC, S, D, AE, DC
**NO SMOKING** in the restaurant
**OUTDOOR EATING:** no
**OFF-STREET PARKING:** yes

**NUMBER OF WINES:** 600
**HOUSE WINE:** £13.00
**RESERVATIONS:** advisable
**DRESS CODE:** jacket and tie
**CHILDREN:** welcome
**ACCOMMODATION:** 48 rooms
(B&B single £107.50, double £136)

# PAPARAZZI
### Tel: (01244) 400029
29 Grosvenor Street, Chester, Cheshire, CH1 2DD

## A SMALL SELECTION FROM OUR SEASONAL MENU

### *Pasta - all home-made and freshly cooked to order*
**Fettucine Delicate** with strips of avocado, smoked salmon and parmesan **£4.95**
**Spaghetti Marinara** made with the best selected seafoods **£6.50**
**Linguini Al Nero di Squid** squid ink pasta tossed in butter with garlic **£6.95**
**Risotto with Truffles** House special **£9.50**
**Gnocchi Verde Alla Bolognese** potato & spinach dumplings **£4.25**
**Risotto with Strawberries** with mascarpone, parmesan & strawberries **£5.50**
**Ravioli di Zucca** pumpkin filled pasta parcels with sage butter **£5.90**

### *Starters*
**Antipasto Misto** Italian cold hors d'oeuvres **£6.50**
**Carpaccio** wafer-thin raw fillet steak with extra virgin olive oil **£4.95**
**Rognoni Tostatti** lambs kidneys flamed in cognac with cream & mustard **£4.50**
**Mozzarella Salad** fresh Mozzarella, tomato & oregano salad **£4.50**

### *Fish*
**Fresh Whole Lobster** simply grilled in garlic butter **£18.50**
**Pesce Alle Ligure** red snapper with white wine, lemon & black olives **£9.95**
**Grilled Fillet of Shark** with gremoulade **£10.50**

### *Specialities of the House*
**Polpette Alla Casalinga** home-made meat balls with slices of fresh polenta **£9.50**
**Pan Fried Chicken Breast** with proscuitto & gruyère cheese **£9.95**
**Chicken Cacciatora** in a sauce of tomato, anchovy & black olives **£8.95**
**Rack of Lamb** marinated, then roasted in a mustard & breadcrumb crust **£10.50**
**Vegetable Tian** layers of courgette & aubergine in spicy tomato sauce **£6.50**
**Roasted Duck Breast** with wild berry sauce **£12.95**
**10oz Grilled Fillet Steak** garnished with tomato & Café de Paris butter **£14.50**
**Lombata di Vitello** medallions of veal pan-fried with sage & rosemary **£13.50**
**Capretto a Rosto** roasted joint of baby goat with a rich port & orange sauce **£14.50**
**Fagiano in Salmi** half pheasant in a sauce of red wine, spices & herbs **£13.50**
**Trippa Alla Fiorentina** tripe with tomatoes, white wine, herbs & parmesan **£7.95**
**Fecatu All'agru e Duci** calves liver pan-fried with a sweet & sour sauce **£9.95**

Paparazzi is a brasserie-style Italian restaurant that has quickly built up a loyal following since its opening in July 1996. The Gothic-style building, formerly a bank, has been stunningly converted.

Taking centre stage in the open-plan dining area is an integrated kitchen, where the team of cooks provide a background of live entertainment to accompany your meal. For those of us who haven't grown up yet, it's worth ordering a steak just to watch the flames shoot up all over the place!

Another unusual feature is a walk-in wine cellar, where you are invited down the steps into the converted bank vault to choose your bottle from the extensive selection of predominantly Italian wines. The whites, incidentally, are kept in the safe where the temperature is apparently ideal for chilling them.

Directions: Paparazzi is situated opposite the Magistrates Courts in the city centre.

## USEFUL INFORMATION

**SERVING TIMES:**
12pm-11pm (every day)
**SEATING CAPACITY:** 100
**C/C:** V, MC, S, D, AE, DC
**OFF-STREET PARKING:** yes

**NUMBER OF WINES:** 142
**HOUSE WINE:** £9.95
**OUTDOOR EATING:** no
**RESERVATIONS:** advisable, but
compulsory at the weekends

# ROWTON HALL
### Tel: (01244) 335262
Whitchurch Road, Rowton, Chester, Cheshire, CH3 6AD

---

*TABLE D'HOTE DINNER*
*£18.50*

*Country Vegetable Soup*

*Niçoise Salad*
*Tuna, Tomato and Green Beans tossed in Olive Oil*

*Parisienne of Melon with Sweet Vermouth*

*Deep Fried Cheese with Cranberry Sauce*

~ ~ ~ ~

*Crusted Roast Leg of Lamb*
*with Redcurrant and Rosemary Sauce*

*Escalope of Turkey Parisienne*

*Peppered Ragoût of Fillet Beef, Rice Pilaf*

*Poached Rolled Delice of Salmon with Seafood Farci*
*in a Pink Peppercorn Sauce*

*Vegetable Lasagne*

*Vegetables and Potatoes of the Day*

~ ~ ~ ~

*Selection of Sweets from the Trolley*

*Cheese and Biscuits*

~ ~ ~ ~

*Coffee*

Rowton Hall is an 18th Century country house hotel which stands in eight acres of gardens and pastureland with far-reaching views across the Cheshire Plains to the hills of Wales. The building itself still retains many original features including a Robert Adam fireplace and an ornamental carved staircase.

The Langdale Restaurant offers first-class dining in elegant surroundings. In addition to the set price dinner featured opposite, which changes nightly, there is an extensive à la carte menu available. The daily luncheon table d'hôte is good value, with two courses priced at £10.50 per head and three courses £12.50, both of which include coffee.

Directions: Rowton Hall is situated in the village of Rowton which lies approximately 3 miles to the south-east of Chester city centre. The hotel is signposted from the main A41 Chester to Whitchurch road.

### USEFUL INFORMATION

**SERVING TIMES:**
Lunch 12pm-2pm (every day)
Dinner 7pm-9.30pm (Mon-Sat)
7pm-9pm (Sunday)
**SEATING CAPACITY:** 100
**C/C:** V, MC, S, D, AE, DC
**OFF-STREET PARKING:** yes
**DRESS CODE:** smart casual

**NUMBER OF WINES:** 90
**HOUSE WINE:** £8.95
**RESERVATIONS:** advisable
**CHILDREN:** welcome
**OUTDOOR EATING:** no
**ACCOMMODATION:** 42 rooms
(B&B single fr £72, double fr £88)

# THE CHOLMONDELEY ARMS
## Tel: (01829) 720300
Cholmondeley, Malpas, Cheshire, SY14 8BT

### STARTERS

| | |
|---|---|
| GARLIC BREAD | £1.65 |
| FRESHLY MADE SOUP OF THE DAY with french or granary bread | £2.50 |
| HOT CRAB PATE with brown toast and butter | £4.25 |
| GARLIC MUSHROOMS WITH BACON with french or granary bread | £4.50 |
| JULIAN'S SAFFRON PRAWNS | £4.50 |
| COARSE COUNTRY TERRINE chicken, pork and veal with layers of ham with toast and butter, gherkins and olives | £4.25 |
| GINNEY'S BLINIS two rye and whole wheat pancakes with smoked salmon and sour cream | £4.95 |
| WHITEBAIT with french bread and butter | £4.25 |

### MAIN COURSES

| | |
|---|---|
| PLOUGHMAN'S LUNCH cheshire, cheddar or stilton with salad, pickles, french or granary bread | £4.40 |
| THE CHOLMONDELEY OPEN prawns, egg, cucumber, tomato and mayonnaise on granary bread | £6.60 |
| ROAST HAM OR BEEF SALAD with mustard and horseradish | £7.25 |
| PRAWN SALAD with mayonnaise and french dressing | £7.25 |
| THE SCHOOL LUNCH a hot baguette containing a large spicy sausage garnished and served with a barbecue sauce | £4.20 |
| DEVILLED LAMB'S KIDNEYS on granary toast served with salad | £6.95 |
| OMELETTE AND SALAD plain; fines herbs; bacon; cheese; mushroom | £4.75 |
| LASAGNE AND SALAD | £6.95 |
| STUFFED PANCAKES two pancakes with a choice of filling, grilled with cream and parmesan and served with salad | £5.95 |
| HOT MADRAS BEEF CURRY with rice, poppadoms and chutney | £7.25 |
| HOME-MADE PIE OF THE DAY | £7.25 |
| CASTLE CUTLETS three lamb cutlets grilled with Dijon mustard, garlic and herbs | £8.50 |
| LARGE GRILLED GAMMON STEAK with pineapple or fried egg | £7.95 |
| BREADED AND DEEP FRIED FILLET OF PLAICE and tartare sauce | £7.75 |
| STEAKS: RIBEYE, SIRLOIN, FILLET with garlic or parsley butter | 10.75/10.95/12.25 |

### PUDDINGS

*all £3.50*

BAKEWELL TART AND CREAM, MERINGUES AND CREAM, CHOCALATE ROULADE, SYRUP TART AND CREAM, HOT BAKED SYRUP SPONGE AND CREAM, CHOCOLATE HAZLENUT CHARLOTTE, AMERICAN CHEESECAKE, ICED SOUFFLE GRAND MARNIER, MERINGUE GLACE, CHOCOLATE BANANA SPLIT, HOT FUDGED BANANAS, HOT GRAND MARNIER PANCAKE

The Cholmondeley Arms was the village school until 1982. Six years later it was converted into an elegant pub restaurant by Guy and Carolyn Ross-Lowe. The high ceilings, exposed beams, wooden tables and chairs give this pub a really warm and relaxed atmosphere. Throw in the superb food and it is hardly surprising that its reputation has gone from strength to strength.

The basic menu (shown opposite) is the same at lunch and dinner. It includes a good selection of sandwiches (from £3.25) and a range of children's meals (all priced at £3.95). A blackboard featuring about six starters, twelve main courses and a couple of desserts, shows the day's specials, which may include Salmon Fishcakes with Hollandaise Sauce (£7.50) or Thai Green Curry with Rice & Salad (£8.35). In addition to the delicious home-made puddings there is a wide selection of home-made sorbets and ices (£2.95).

For those who are too full to face the drive home, accommodation is available in the schoolmaster's house next door.

Directions: Heading north from Whitchurch to Tarporley on the A49, The Cholmondeley Arms is found on the right, just past Bickley Moss.

### USEFUL INFORMATION

**SERVING TIMES:**
Lunch 12pm-2.15pm (every day))
Dinner 7pm-10pm (Sun-Fri)
        6.30pm-10pm (Saturday)
**SEATING CAPACITY:** 100
**C/C:** V, MC, S, D
**OUTDOOR EATING:** yes

**NUMBER OF WINES:** 53
**HOUSE WINE:** £8.95
**RESERVATIONS:** advisable
**OFF-STREET PARKING:** yes
**CHILDREN:** welcome
**ACCOMMODATION:** 6 rooms
(single £32, double £38)

# THE CROWN INN
### Tel: (01588) 650613
Wentnor, Shropshire, SY9 5EE

## TODAY'S SPECIALS

### STARTERS

Game Soup  £2.10     Garlic Mushrooms with Cream  £2.95
Pheasant Pâté  £3.25     Avocado Mousse  £3.25
Grilled Sardines with a Peppery Lemon Glaze  £2.95

### VEGETARIAN DISHES

Crisp Tacos  £6.95
stuffed with an aubergine mixture, topped with cheese, on tomato sauce
Chilli Fiesta  £6.95
a medley of fresh vegetables with kidney beans in a chilli tomato sauce
Mushroom Stroganoff  £6.95
mushrooms in a creamy cheese sauce, with paprika and tagliatelle

### MAIN COURSES

Fillet of Red Bream  £8.50
with a delicate fennel and pastis sauce
Ocean Crumble  £7.50
smoked fish, white fish and prawns in parsley sauce with cream and a hint of
cheese, topped with a cheesey wholemeal breadcrumb finish
Poacher's Pie  £9.25
pheasant, grouse, pigeon and turkey in a creamy mushroom sauce
Locally Smoked Pork Steak  £9.25
served with a smooth mango sauce
Prime 8oz Rump Steak au Poivre  £9.25
with a creamy cracked pepper and mushroom sauce
Prime 8oz Fillet Steak  £10.95
grilled and garnished with tomatoes, mushrooms and onion rings

### DESSERTS

Crème Brûlée  £2.65     Fresh Fruit Lattice Tart  £2.65
Banoffee Cheesecake with Toffee Sauce  £2.65
Layered Triple Fruit Mousse  £2.65

The Crown Inn is a traditional 17th Century country pub with exposed beams and log fires. Although it is well off the beaten track, the good home-cooked food draws a loyal following from miles around.

Sir Hugh Wontner, famous for founding the Savoy Group, was a direct descendant of the builder of this pub in 1640. It is alleged in local folklore that a drunken scribe was later responsible for jumbling the letters of his surname to create the name of the village, Wentnor.

You can choose to eat in either the bar area or one of the two separate dining rooms, the smaller of which was originally the hen-house. The menus for both remain the same, written out daily on the blackboards.

Various ploughmans (from £4.75) and sandwiches (from £1.50) are available at lunchtimes, together with daily specials such as Cumberland Sausages (£5.50), Wholetail Battered Scampi and Chips (£6.50), Grilled Gammon Steak (£7.95) and a Pasta Dish of the Day (£6.95).

Directions: The Crown Inn is situated in the small village of Wentnor which lies approximately 4 miles to the west of Church Stretton and 5 miles to the north-east of Bishop's Castle. The village is signposted from the A49 and the A489.

### USEFUL INFORMATION

**SERVING TIMES:**
Lunch 12pm-2pm (every day)
Dinner 7pm-9pm (every day)
**SEATING CAPACITY:** 60
**C/C:** V, MC, S, D
**OUTDOOR EATING:** yes
**OFF-STREET PARKING:** yes

**NUMBER OF WINES:** 21
**HOUSE WINE:** £7.95
**RESERVATIONS:** advisable
**CHILDREN:** welcome
**ACCOMMODATION:** 4 rooms
(B&B single £22.50, double £40)

# PECKS RESTAURANT

### Tel: (01260) 275161

Newcastle Road, Moreton, nr Congleton, Cheshire, CW12 4SB

**A Selection of Hors d'Oeuvres**

~~~

**Leek & Potato Soup with Toasted Almonds**
**Smoked Bacon & Butterbean Soup**

~~~

**Peppered Chicken Salad with Celeriac Remoulade**
**Oyster Mushroom & Porcini Timbale with Hollandaise Sauce**
**Grilled Fillet of Cobble Haddock with a Cheese Crumb**
**Crust & Coriander Sauce**

~~~

**Roast Leg of Pork with Apple & Potato Rosti & Mustard Sauce**
**Crisp Duckling with Port Wine & Roasted Green Peppers**
**Ragoût of Beef with Kumquats and Caraway on Spiced Rice**
**Oatcake Canneloni filled with Ricotta Cheese, Pinenuts & Basil**
**on a Trivet of Tomato Concasse**
*All served with*
*Two Vegetable & Two Potato Dishes*

~~~

**A Selection of Delicious Home-made Sweets**

~~~

**A Selection of English and Continental Cheeses**

~~~

**Fresh Coffee & Petits Fours**

There is something slightly decadent, and perhaps a little arrogant, about a one sitting restaurant that offers 'Dinner at Eight', but at Pecks it is entirely justified. Established in 1984, this elegant and sophisticated restaurant offers superb contemporary French and English cuisine, which ensures that guests return again and again.

The monthly set menu, which includes seven courses (£22.50 Tuesday to Thursday, £25.50 Friday to Saturday), is a culinary experience of some distinction. Indulgent desserts, full of rich Belgian chocolate, alcohol and full fat double cream, are all home-made and there is always a very good selection, with Rum and Raisin Cheesecake being a house speciality. The restaurant also has an excellent policy of not imposing a corkage charge on your own wine.

Directions: Heading south from Congleton on the A34, Pecks Restaurant is found on the left after about 2 miles, just beyond the village of Astbury.

### USEFUL INFORMATION

**SERVING TIMES:**
One sitting at 8pm (Tues-Sat)
and on the Sundays of Bank Holidays
**CLOSED:** Every lunchtime and
Sunday and Monday evening
**SEATING CAPACITY:** 100
**C/C:** V, MC, S, D, AE, DC

**NUMBER OF WINES:** 30
**HOUSE WINE:** £8.50
**NO SMOKING** during dinner
**RESERVATIONS:** compulsory
**OUTDOOR EATING:** no
**OFF-STREET PARKING:** yes
**DRESS CODE:** smart

# THE SWETTENHAM ARMS

### Tel: (01477) 571284

Swettenham Village, nr Congleton, Cheshire, CW12 2LF

### *A selection from the Blackboard*

#### *Starters all £3.95*

*Avocado, Smoked Salmon & Cream Cheese*
*Sautéed Lambs' Kidneys in Red Wine*
*Deep-fried Devilled Whitebait with a Lemon & Chive Dip*
*Deep-fried Mushrooms with a Remiche Dip*
*Sautéed Button Mushrooms in Garlic Butter*
*Deep-fried Brie with a Strawberry Coulis*
*Deep-fried Mozzarella with a Mango Coulis*
*Salmon & Ginger Samosas in a Hot & Sweet Sauce*
*Mango & Prawns in a Marie Rose Sauce*
*Melon & Sorbet with a Fruit Coulis*
*Tiger Prawns in Garlic Butter*

#### *Snacks all £4.95*

*Home-made Lasagne with Bolognaise Sauce*
*Tomato Pasta with Tomato, Onion & Basil*
*Hot Fried Szechuan Beef with Rice and Salad*
*New Zealand Mussels in a White Wine & Parsley Sauce*

#### *Main Dishes all £7.95*

*Casserole of Rabbit in Cider & Mustard*
*Turkey, Leek & Ham Pie*
*Baked Marinated Lamb Henry*
*Casserole of Venison in Red Wine with Juniper Berries*
*Sugar Baked Ham with a Sweet & Sour Sauce*
*Poached Chicken Breast filled with Spicy Crab with Lemon Sauce*
*Roast Topside of Beef with Yorkshire Pudding*
*Broccoli, Brie & Hazelnut Pie*
*Baked Whole Grey Mullet with Tomato*

The tiny village of Swettenham, made up of a few cottages, a parish church and a wonderful pre-17th Century inn, is tucked away at the end of a quiet country lane. Originally a nunnery, The Swettenham Arms has been transformed in recent years by owners Frances and Jim Cunningham (whose other pubs, The Dog Inn and The Old Packet House, are featured elsewhere in this guide), and now enjoys a somewhat livelier atmosphere and an enviable reputation for its food.

An extensive choice of dishes, including at least twenty main courses, appear daily on a blackboard and a sample is shown opposite. For those after a lighter meal, a Sandwich Menu is also available.

Directions: Easily found in the village of Swettenham, which is signposted off the A54 between Holmes Chapel and Congleton.

## USEFUL INFORMATION

**SERVING TIMES:**
Lunch 12pm-2.30pm (every day)
Dinner 7pm-9.30pm (every day)
**SEATING CAPACITY:** 100
**C/C:** V, MC, S, D
**OFF-STREET PARKING:** yes

**NUMBER OF WINES:** 37
**HOUSE WINE:** £7.20
**RESERVATIONS:** advisable
**OUTDOOR EATING:** yes
**NO SMOKING** area available
**CHILDREN:** welcome

# THE CHOLMONDELEY RIVERSIDE
### Tel: (01952) 510900
Cound, Cressage, nr Shrewsbury, Shropshire, SY5 6AF

*A Sample*
### SPECIALS MENU

### STARTERS

Mussel Soup or Leek Soup £2.65
Gratin of Monkfish & Prawns £4.50
Smoked Chicken, Crispy Bacon & Pinenuts in a Walnut Dressing £4.25
HoHo Mushrooms, cooked with Red Peppers, Ginger & Soy £4.50
Cold Spicy Prawns with a Mustard & Olive Oil Dressing £4.50

### MAIN COURSES

Steak & Kidney Pie £7.25
Chicken, Cheese & Bacon Pie £7.25
Cholmondeley Fishcakes with a Hollandaise Sauce £7.25
Slow Cooked Shoulder of Lamb, with Flageolets Beans, Tomatoes,
Shallots, Rosemary & Garlic £8.50
Duck Breast, grilled with a Port, Spring Onion & fresh
Ginger Sauce £9.50
Aubergine, stuffed with Vegetables & Rice, grilled with
Gruyère & Salad £7.25
Chicken Breast in a Mushroom, Dijon Mustard & Cream Sauce £8.50
Creole Jambalaya - Ham, Chicken, Chorizo Sausage, Prawns
& Rice in a Cajun Tomato Sauce £8.50
Filet Mignon with a Pepper, Cream & Brandy Sauce £13.50
Fresh Fish of the Day £7.75
Chicken Breast, stuffed with Spinach & Mushrooms with a
Tomato & Basil Sauce £8.50

### FROM THE CHAR GRILL
*from £7.25*
Squid, with a Hot Chilli, Olive Oil & Lemon Sauce
Smoked Fish Kebab with a Horseradish Sauce
Courgette, Pepper & Onion Kebab

Following a major refurbishment, The Cholmondeley Riverside Inn at Cound has opened very recently and is a sister restaurant to the well-known Cholmondeley Arms, near Whitchurch (also featured in this guide). Enjoying a beautiful setting on the banks of the River Severn, the emphasis is on fine food and quality wine. Early indications are that this will be another resounding success!

There is a regular menu which features popular dishes and lighter meals, complemented by a char grill and a specials blackboard. This changes weekly and an example of what you may expect is shown opposite. Delicious home-made puddings, such as Bread and Butter Pudding, are all £3.50.

Directions: Easily found a few miles south of Shrewsbury on the A458 Bridgnorth road.

### USEFUL INFORMATION

**SERVING TIMES:**
Lunch 12pm-2.15pm (every day)
Dinner 7pm-10pm (Sun-Fri)
    6.30pm-10pm (Saturday)
**SEATING CAPACITY:** 100
**C/C:** V, MC, S, D
**OUTDOOR EATING:** yes

**NUMBER OF WINES:** 53
**HOUSE WINE:** £8.95
**RESERVATIONS:** advisable
**OFF-STREET PARKING:** yes
**CHILDREN:** welcome
**ACCOMMODATION:** 6 rooms
(single fr £35, double fr £40)

# THE WHITE LION INN
### Tel: (01270) 500303
Main Road, Weston, Nr Crewe, Cheshire, CW2 5NA

*~ selections from the à la carte menu ~*

*~ Starters ~*

**Fresh Asparagus Spears £4.50**
Poached asparagus spears served with hot butter or Hollandaise sauce
**Arbroath Smokies Mornay £4.60**
Flaked fish with a rich cheese sauce
**Mediterranean Prawns £6.95**
Large prawns served in garlic butter with diced spring onions
**Vegetable Quiche £3.95**
Home-made quiche served hot on a bed of salad

*~ Meat, Poultry, and Fish Dishes ~*

**Rack of Lamb £10.95**
Lamb cutlets served on a coulis of redcurrants
**Venison Bordelaise £11.75**
Haunch of venison flattened and served with a shallot and red wine sauce
**Roast Duckling with Apple £10.95**
Duckling served with a puréed apple sauce and savoury stuffing
**Game Dish of the Day £11.25**
Fresh seasonal game bird of the day prepared by the chef
**Scallops in Lobster Sauce £12.50**
King scallops poached in a lobster sauce
**Sea Bass Celeriac £12.75**
Sea Bass pan-seared and served on puréed celeriac

*~ Vegetarian Dishes ~*

**Spinach Rolls Mornay £9.95**
Sautéed diced vegetables wrapped with spinach leaves topped with cheese sauce
**Asparagus and Mushroom Pancakes £9.95**
Diced asparagus and mushrooms in a pancake topped with a white wine sauce

*~ Sweets ~*

**Hot Dessert of the Day £3.25, Desserts from the trolley £3.25**
**A selection of Ice Creams £3.50**

The White Lion Inn was originally a Tudor farmhouse, and the inscription 1652 is the earliest date given to this listed building.

All the food here is prepared to order, using the very best of fresh, local produce, and diners may choose to eat in either a relaxed bar or a more refined adjoining restaurant.

In the restaurant, the extensive evening à la carte menu changes seasonally, and a small selection from it is shown opposite. For groups of eight or more, there are good value set dinners available (£16.95 for 3 courses). The Luncheon Menu (£12.95 for 3 courses) also offers a very good choice of dishes. The Sunday lunch menu (£12.95 for 3 courses) includes a traditional roast of the day. In the bar, the menu is less expensive and caters for those after a quick snack as well as a more substantial meal.

Directions: Leaving the M6 at junction 16, follow the A500 towards Nantwich. At the second roundabout turn right and follow the signs to Weston.

### USEFUL INFORMATION

**SERVING TIMES:**
Lunch 12pm-2pm (Sun-Fri)
Dinner 7pm-9.30pm (Mon-Sat)
Food served in the bar every day
**CLOSED:** in the restaurant for Saturday lunch and Sunday dinner
**SEATING CAPACITY:** 70 in the restaurant, 70 in the bar
**C/C:** V, MC, S, D, AE, DC
**OFF-STREET PARKING:** yes

**NUMBER OF WINES:** 103
**HOUSE WINE:** £8.50
**RESERVATIONS:** advisable at weekends
**CHILDREN:** welcome (a separate snug area is provided)
**NO SMOKING** in the restaurant
**OUTDOOR EATING:** yes
**ACCOMMODATION:** 16 rooms (single £49, double £59)

# THE HOWARD ARMS
## Tel: (01746) 712200
Ditton Priors, near Bridgnorth, Shropshire, WV16 6SQ

### DINNER

### £24.00

Duck liver pâté with spiced green tomatoes
Rillettes of pheasant with garlic vinaigrette
Smoked salmon and crab cream
Tomato, carrot and lemon soup
Galia melon with Parma ham
Stilton cream quiche
Moules au gratin
Game soup

Pheasant breast on caramelised apple with curry sauce
Roast duck hymettus, walnut and herb stuffing
Sweet and sour hare with a hint of chocolate
Smoked haddock with chive butter sauce
Grilled Dover sole (£5 supp)
Fillet steak chasseur
Stuffed Aubergine

Pudding
or
Cheese, celery and biscuits

Coffee and petits fours

The Howard Arms is a traditional 15th Century country pub/restaurant, well off the beaten track in the heart of the beautiful Shropshire countryside. The interior is full of period charm with open log fires, low exposed beams and cosy seating areas.

Dining here certainly falls into two quite distinct categories - the village inn and the restaurant. The small pub at the side of the building does not stand on gastronomic ceremony, offering simple good-value bar meals, while the main restaurant area comes alive in the evenings with an innovative menu created by Jane Marsh (sweet and sour hare with a hint of chocolate!).

The restaurant does open for lunch on Sundays, with the traditional three-course menu priced at £15.00. The main courses will normally include a choice of two roast meats, supplemented by one fish and one vegetarian dish.

Directions: The Howard Arms can be found in the centre of the village of Ditton Priors, approximately 9 miles to the south-west of Bridgnorth. The village is signposted from both the B4368 (Bridgnorth-Craven Arms road) and the B4376 (Bridgnorth-Ludlow road).

## USEFUL INFORMATION

**SERVING TIMES:**
Lunch 12pm-2pm (Sunday only)
Dinner 7.15pm-9.30pm (Tues-Sat)
**CLOSED:** lunch (Mon-Sat),
Sunday evening & all day Monday
**SEATING CAPACITY:** 30
**C/C:** V, MC, S, D

**NUMBER OF WINES:** 90
**HOUSE WINE:** £9.90
**RESERVATIONS:** essential
**NO SMOKING** in the restaurant
**OFF-STREET PARKING:** yes
**CHILDREN:** welcome
**OUTDOOR EATING:** no

# COUNTRY FRIENDS RESTAURANT
### Tel: (01743) 718707
Dorrington, nr Shrewsbury, Shropshire, SY5 7JD

### MENU

**2 Courses £23 ~ 3 Courses £26 ~ 4 courses £29.50**

Crispy Salmon with a Spicy Oriental Sauce
Sole and Prawn Cream with Rosemary Sauce
Spinach Fettucine with Smoked Salmon
Marinated Quail with Peanuts
Calf's Liver with Celeriac Purée and Balsamic Vinegar
Twice-baked Blue Cheese Soufflé with Pear Salad

~

Chicken Breast with Wild Mushroom Ravioli and Madeira Sauce
Venison with a Shallot Purée and Damson Sauce
Duck Breast on a bed of Lentils and Bacon
with a Red Wine Sauce
Fillet Steak with Boudin Blanc and a Mustard Sauce
Ravioli of Goats' Cheese with Red Pepper Sauce
Fresh Fish from the Market

~

White Chocolate Soufflé with Chocolate Chip Ice Cream
Pear Timbale with Caramel Sauce
Summer Pudding with Elderflower Ice Cream
Trio of Chocolate
Lemon Flan with a Lime and Sauternes Sauce

~

British Cheese

~

Coffee
(included in price)

Country Friends is a well-established restaurant with an enviable reputation throughout Shropshire. The half-timbered building dates from 1673, although one wing is reputed to be at least 100 years older. "The rest was mucked about with by the Victorians," according to chef/proprietor Charles Whittaker, "it's a real hotch-potch."

The same cannot be said of the cooking, which is deserving of the praise it receives from fellow restaurateurs in the local area. The menu opposite changes regularly and is used for both lunch and dinner. Light lunches are also available, such as Baked Mushrooms with Bacon (£3.00), Fish Quenelles with a Herb Sauce (£3.75), Stilton Soufflé with Salad (£5.50), Calf's Liver served on a bed of Lentils and Pancetta (£4.75), Brioche filled with Chicken and Mushrooms in a Madeira Sauce (7.80), Home-made Pasta with Salmon (£8.50), or Fish Cakes served with Spinach and a Poached Egg (£8.00).

Directions: Country Friends Restaurant is situated in the centre of the village of Dorrington, which lies approximately 6 miles to the south of Shrewsbury on the A49 Shrewsbury-Leominster road.

## USEFUL INFORMATION

**SERVING TIMES:**
Lunch 12pm-2pm (Tues-Sat)
Dinner 7pm-9pm (Tues-Sat)
**CLOSED:** all day Sun & Mon
**SEATING CAPACITY:** 40
**C/C:** V, MC, S, D
**OFF-STREET PARKING:** yes

**NUMBER OF WINES:** 80
**HOUSE WINE:** £10.95
**OUTDOOR EATING:** no
**RESERVATIONS:** advisable
**NO SMOKING** in the restaurant
**ACCOMMODATION:** 3 rooms
(D,B&B single £65, double £102)

# JULIAN'S BISTRO
### Tel: (01785) 851200
21 High Street, Eccleshall, Staffordshire, ST21 6BW

## TO START / MAIN MEAL

| | |
|---|---|
| Confit of Duck with Ginger & Honey & Warmed New Potatoes | £4.50/£8.25 |
| Hot Sliced Salmon with a Creamy Champagne Sauce | £3.95/£7.95 |
| Crunchy Pistachio Chicken with a Lime Crème Fraîche | £4.25/£8.95 |
| Ratatouille Tart with Melting Goat's Cheese | £3.50/£7.95 |
| Penne Pasta with Wild Mushrooms and a Light Nutmeg Mascarpone Sauce | £3.85/£7.95 |
| Crab and Fennel Cake with Caper and Cucumber Sauce | £3.50/£7.50 |

All the above served with home-made wholemeal and white bread

## TO REFRESH YOUR PALATE

Elderflower and Lemon Granite £1.75          Champagne Sorbet £1.95

## TO FOLLOW

| | |
|---|---|
| Chicken Filled with Wild Mushrooms on Truffle Mash and Champagne Sauce | £7.95 |
| Glazed Gammon on Rosemary Mash with Puy Lentils, Savoy Cabbage and Prunes | £8.25 |
| Fillet Steak with Creamed Potato, Black Pudding and Onion Gravy and Crispy Leeks | £10.95 |
| Caramelised Duck Breast Coated with a Peach and Apricot Brandy Sauce | £8.95 |
| Casseroled Shank of Lamb with a Tomato, Basil and Light Garlic Stew | £8.95 |
| Creamed Parsnips, Braised Lentils and Spinach Rolled in Filo Pastry with melting Crème Fraîche | £7.50 |
| Red Bream on Pasta with Warm Peanut and Chilli Dressing | £7.50 |

All served with potato and vegetables or a tossed salad

## PUDDINGS

| | |
|---|---|
| A Slice of Sheridan Parfait with a Chocolate Sauce | |
| Warm Chocolate and Pecan Pie with Bourbon Mascarpone | |
| Sharp Lemon Tart with Vanilla Sauce and Poppy Seeds | |
| Baked Banana with a Warm Fudge Sauce | |
| Selection of Fine Cheeses with Walnut Bread and Grapes | ALL |
| Selection of Ices and Sorbets | £2.85 |

Julian's is a delightful bistro restaurant in the pretty village of Eccleshall. Exposed beams, sanded floors and pastel shades have helped to create a warm and relaxing atmosphere in which to enjoy some excellent food.

The evening à la carte menu changes every six to eight weeks, and daily specials are shown on a blackboard. This is also where the day's lunch menu appears, when the emphasis is very much on fish dishes fresh from Birmingham Market. For those after something lighter there is an all day menu featuring snacks like Creamy Flat Mushrooms on a Toasted Brioche (£2.50) and sandwiches such as Crispy Duck and Cranberry Compôte (£3.50), made on delicious home-made bread.

The theme evenings (Caribbean, Medieval, Tapas etc) are very popular, as are Gourmet Quiz Nights (£19.95 for 7 courses and 2 wines) when each table has to answer the chef's questions on the food presented. The prize is a bottle of champagne!

Directions:  Eccleshall lies between Newport and Stoke-on-Trent on the A519, and Julian's Bistro is easily found in the middle of the high street.

## USEFUL INFORMATION

**SERVING TIMES:**
Lunch 12pm-3pm (every day)
Dinner 6.30pm-10pm (every day)
Coffee and light snacks all day
**SEATING CAPACITY:** 50
**C/C:** V, MC, S, D
**NO SMOKING** in the restaurant
but allowed in the bar

**NUMBER OF WINES:** 16
**HOUSE WINE:** £7.50
**RESERVATIONS:** advisable, but
compulsory on Fri & Sat evenings
**CHILDREN** welcome
**OUTDOOR EATING:** no
**OFF-STREET PARKING:** no

# THE MINER'S ARMS
## Tel: (01433) 630853
Water Lane, Eyam, Derbyshire, S30 1RG

### *Restaurant Evening Menu*

Cream of Winter Vegetable Soup £2.75
Tomato and Pesto Cappelleti with a fresh Tomato Sauce £3.50
Avocado Salad with warm Chicken Livers £3.95
Melon and Parma Ham £3.75
Smoked Salmon stuffed with Crab Meat and Prawns £3.95

Grilled Sirloin Steak £9.95
Confit of Duck £8.75
Steak and Pheasant Pie £8.50
Fillet of Pork with Stilton and Cider Sauce £9.75
Grilled Fillet of Lemon Sole with Walnut Butter £8.95
King Scallops with a Lemon and White Wine Sauce £10.50
Vegetable and Nut Stir Fry £7.50

All the above dishes are served with a selection of
fresh vegetables and potatoes

Selection of Home-made Desserts £3.50

Selection of fine Cheeses £2.75

Coffee and Mints £1.50

The Miner's Arms, a 17th Century inn dating back to 1630, nestles at the bottom of a quiet country lane just off the main square in Eyam. This friendly inn with a beamed ceiling and stone fireplace is reputed to have several ghosts, the most famous being Sarah and Emily, two young girls who perished in a fire here several centuries ago.

The Miner's Arms has a very good reputation for food, which is all freshly prepared using local produce wherever possible. The style is traditional English with some French influences, and a typical menu is shown opposite. This is only offered in the restaurant and changes every three weeks.

At lunchtime there is a bar menu which includes old favourites like Ploughmans (from £3.75) and Sandwiches (from £2.10), as well as more imaginative choices such as Braised Beef in Stout Sauce (£5.50). There is also a blackboard menu featuring six special dishes, and a traditional 3 course roast lunch is offered every Sunday.

Directions: Easily found in the village of Eyam, which lies about 12 miles west of Chesterfield and is signposted off the A623.

## USEFUL INFORMATION

**SERVING TIMES:**
Lunch 12pm-2pm (Tues-Sat)
        12pm-1.30pm (Sunday)
Dinner 7pm-9pm (Tues-Sat)
**CLOSED:** Sunday evening and
Monday. Bar meals only at lunchtime
**SEATING CAPACITY:** 60
**C/C:** V, MC, S, D
**CHILDREN** welcome at lunch

**NUMBER OF WINES:** 20
**HOUSE WINE:** £7.25
**RESERVATIONS:** advisable for
the restaurant in the evening
**OFF-STREET PARKING:** yes
**OUTDOOR EATING:** at lunch
**ACCOMMODATION:** 7 rooms
(single £25, double £50)

# THE MARSH

## Tel: (01568) 613952
Eyton, Leominster, Herefordshire, HR6 0AG

## *Dinner Menu*

Jerusalem Artichoke and Scallop soup
Blue Cheese Timbale with a Fig and Nut dressing
Glazed Eggs on a bed of Leeks with Watercress sauce
Fresh Crab Terrine with Chive Butter sauce

\* \* \*

Saddle of Venison with Green Peppercorn sauce,
Potato and Parsnip Croquette, Brussel Sprouts
Oven baked Sea Bass
with sautéed Potato and Red Pepper, spiced Aubergine relish
Tagliatelli with Tomato, Garlic and Wild Mushrooms
Roast Herefordshire Duck Breast with Duck Leg and Mushroom Filo
parcels, Carrots and stuffed Cabbage in a Lemon sauce

\* \* \*

Calvados Parfait with Caramelised Apples and Cider sauce
Gingerbread Pudding with Rhubarb and Banana
Chocolate and Mascarpone Mousse with a Coffee sauce
A selection of Cheese with Biscuits
*(as an additional course £4.00 extra)*

**Price:**
**£24.75 per person**

The Marsh is an attractive 14th Century timbered house set amidst peaceful gardens of one and a half acres. In the Dining Room chef Jacqueline Gilleland enjoys sharing her pleasure in producing delectable dishes.

Over 40 herbs grow in the garden and many are used to flavour and enhance each meal. The variety of fresh ingredients, including vegetables and fruit from their own grounds, make dining at The Marsh an enjoyable experience. In addition to the table d'hôte dinner menu featured on the facing page, an excellent Sunday lunch is available, priced at £19.95. After lunch a wealth of local treasures awaits to be discovered - great houses, famous gardens, pretty villages and breath-taking walks across open countryside.

Directions: The Marsh is located 2 miles to the north-west of Leominster, 5 minutes from the A44 and A49. Approach Leominster from the northern end of the A49 by-pass. After the level crossing, turn right onto the B4361 to Richards Castle. In fl mile turn left signposted Eyton and Lucton. Continue along the lane until reaching the common and The Marsh is on the right.

### USEFUL INFORMATION

**SERVING TIMES:**
Lunch 12.30pm-2pm (Sunday)
Dinner 7.30pm-9pm (every day)
**CLOSED:** lunch (Mon-Sat)
**SEATING CAPACITY:** 24
**C/C:** V, MC, AE, DC
**OUTDOOR EATING:** no
**NO SMOKING** in the restaurant

**NUMBER OF WINES:** 70
**HOUSE WINE:** £9.50
**RESERVATIONS:** compulsory, especially between Nov and March
**OFF-STREET PARKING:** yes
**ACCOMMODATION:** 4 rooms
(short breaks from £160 per person inc 2 nights B&B and set dinner)

# THE CHEQUERS INN
### Tel: (01433) 630231
Froggatt Edge, nr Calver, Derbyshire, S30 1ZB

---

### TO START

**FENNEL AND RICOTTA MOUSSE**
*baked in a red pepper sat on a green pepper coulis*
**LARGE GREENLIP MUSSELS**
*cooked in a white wine and saffron sauce garnished with leeks*
**CHICKEN AND CRAB PARCELS**
*chicken and crab force meat with sun-dried tomatoes*
*wrapped in filo pastry served on a tomato and basil sauce*
**BREAST OF WOOD PIGEON**
*thinly sliced warm breast of wood pigeon with summer leaves*
*served with a pinenut and balsamic dressing*
**BRESAOLA OF BEEF**
*thin slices of Italian dried beef served with a home-made sweet vegetable pickle*
**MELON AND WATER ICE**
*fan of melon on a raspberry coulis accompanied by a refreshing water ice*
**DEEP FRIED CAMEMBERT**
*served with a warm blackcurrant sauce*

### INTERMEDIATES

**SMOKED BACON AND STILTON SALAD**
*with a garlic dressing sat on a watercress salad*
**COMPOTE OF CITRUS FRUITS**
*set in a light vermouth*
**HOME-MADE SOUP OF THE DAY**

### MAIN COURSES

**PAN-FRIED VENISON STEAK**
*garnished with straw potatoes on a fresh cranberry sauce*
**ROULADE OF CHICKEN**
*with spinach and brie wrapped in bacon with a red wine and tarragon sauce*
**FILLET OF BRILL (£2.50 extra)**
*rolled set on a lobster bisque accompanied by a timbale of wild rice and assorted shellfish*
**STRIPS OF LAMB AND SCALLOPS**
*lightly pan-fried with Chinese style vegetables and water chestnuts*
*served on a bed of linguine pasta*
**MEDALLIONS OF PORK**
*set on a potato and carrot rosti with a prune and apricot sauce*
**FRESH PARTRIDGE (£2.50 extra)**
*part boned whole bird roasted, served with a light Cumberland sauce*
**BEEF WELLINGTON (£3.95 extra)**
*prime beef fillet wrapped in a puff pastry lattice with a mushroom herb pâté*

### VEGETABLES IN SEASON

The Chequers Inn was originally four houses, which were rebuilt in the 18th Century, and are now a traditional country inn with open fires and wonderful views across the Peak National Park.

Food is served in both the restaurant and bar, with menus comprising of a wide variety of European and British dishes, including local game in season, all complemented by an interesting wine list.

The table d'hôte dinner menu shown opposite (£15.95 for 4 courses, or £11.95 for 2 courses) changes every three months, but there are daily specials on offer as well. The Innkeeper's Fare menu features both traditional pub food such as home-made Steak and Kidney Pie (£5.95), and more exotic choices like Chinese Five Spice Salmon (£6.95). An excellent selection of daily specials are displayed on a blackboard. Sunday lunch is a 3 course set menu at £10.95.

Directions: Leaving Baslow on the A623, turn right on to the B6001, and immediately right again on to the B6054 to Froggatt. After about a mile you will see the Chequers on your right.

## USEFUL INFORMATION

**SERVING TIMES:**
Lunch 12pm-2pm (every day)
Dinner 7pm-9pm (in the restaurant)
    6pm-9.30pm (in the bar)
Food served all day Sunday
**SEATING CAPACITY:** 28 in the restaurant, 60 in the bar
**C/C:** V, MC, S, D
**OFF-STREET PARKING:** yes

**NUMBER OF WINES:** 70
**HOUSE WINE:** £6.95
**RESERVATIONS:** compulsory for the restaurant
**NO SMOKING** in the restaurant
**OUTDOOR EATING:** yes
**CHILDREN:** restaurant only
**ACCOMMODATION:** 6 rooms
(single £44, double £55)

# THE MAYNARD ARMS

## Tel: (01433) 630321

Main Road, Grindleford, Derbyshire, S30 1HP

### A selection from the Padley Restaurant Table d'Hôte Menu

**TERRINE OF PRESSED VEGETABLES**
Served on a bed of radicchio with a green bean salsa
**PEARLS OF MELON AND MANGO**
Dressed on fine leaves flavoured with ginger and cardamom vinaigrette
**DUCKLING AND SHITAKE MUSHROOM PASTIE**
Duckling and mushrooms in cream, wrapped in a puff pastry case with apricot marmalade
**FRESH GRILLED MACKEREL**
Fillet of mackerel with a warm gooseberry sauce
**DEVON DRIED VENISON**
Thin slices on a bed of à la rosso lettuce with tomato chutney
**SMOKED HAKE**
Warm pieces of hake on a green bean salad with poached egg and a herb cream
**AUBERGINE TIMBALE**
With sautéed mushrooms and goats cheese set on a tomato relish

### *INTERMEDIATES*

**FRESHLY HOME-MADE SOUP**
**FRESH FRUIT SORBET**
**FRESH SCALLOPS**
Cooked in butter with bacon and garlic, dressed with fine seaweed (£2.95 extra)
**LEEK AND APPLE FRICASSEE**
Sautéed with a creamy herb sauce placed on a crisp crouton (£1.95 extra)

### *MAIN COURSES*

**TAGLETTINI**
Tossed in butter with leaf spinach, topped with goats cheese in a creamed salmon sauce
**FRESH RAINBOW TROUT**
Boned fillets of trout stuffed with smoked ham, with garlic, onion and chive butter
**CANNON OF LAMB**
Saddle of lamb rolled with a wild mushroom and pâté stuffing, with a mushroom jus-lie
**BALLANTINE OF DUCK**
Breast of duck filled with orange and tarragon mousse with a light orange sauce
**BRAISED OXTAIL**
Tender pieces of oxtail with fresh vegetables served with new potatoes
**MEDALLIONS OF PORK**
Dressed on a bed of courgette and ginger marmalade with a sweet apple sauce
**SEARED CHICKEN**
Chicken breast shallow fried and flavoured with thyme, accompanied by Jasmine rice

### A SELECTION OF HOME-MADE PUDDINGS
or
### ENGLISH AND CONTINENTAL CHEESES

The Maynard Arms Hotel was built in the late 19th Century, and enjoys a superb position overlooking the Peak National Park.

Food may either be taken in the elegant Padley Restaurant, where there is an excellent table d'hôte menu (£15.95 for 4 courses, £12 for 2 courses) which changes seasonally, or in the more relaxed atmosphere of the Longshaw Bar. Here the menu offers a good choice of grills and sandwiches, as well as more interesting dishes such as Lamb Wellington (£6.25) or Vegetable and Nut Crumble (£4.45). Both menus are supplemented by daily and weekly specials, which always include one fresh fish dish. Sunday lunch is £11.50.

Directions: Grindleford is about ten miles south-west of Sheffield. The hotel is easily found just off the A625, on a hill overlooking the village.

## USEFUL INFORMATION

**SERVING TIMES:**
Lunch 12pm-2pm (Mon-Sat)
Dinner 7pm-9.30pm (in the restaurant)
        6pm-9.30pm (in the bar)
Food served all day Sunday
**SEATING CAPACITY:** 55 in the restaurant, 60 in the bar
**C/C:** V, MC, S, D, AE
**NO SMOKING** in the restaurant

**NUMBER OF WINES:** 60
**HOUSE WINE:** £8.95
**RESERVATIONS:** advisable in the restaurant; not available in the bar
**OUTDOOR EATING:** limited
**OFF-STREET PARKING:** yes
**ACCOMMODATION:** 10 rooms (single £59, double £69)

# CALVELEY ARMS
## Tel: (01829) 770619
Whitchurch Road, Handley, nr Tattenhall, Cheshire, CH3 9DT

## TODAY'S
## BLACKBOARD SPECIALS

### STARTERS

Smoked Salmon with Bread & Butter  £3.75
Fresh Figs & Parma Ham  £3.95
Marinaded Juniper Salmon  £3.25

### MAIN COURSES

Baked Sea Bass with Fennel  £10.50
Red Bream Fillet with a Sauce Maltaise  £6.85
Cod Steak Provençale  £6.50
Whole Grilled Plaice with Buttered Cucumber
and Pickled Samphire  £6.75
Lemon Sole with Anchovy, Parsley & Caper Butter  £7.95
Pan-fried Monkfish with Garlic, Bacon & Cream  £9.95
Medallions of Pork Fillet with Peppered Sauce  £7.25
Roasted Pheasant with Cranberry Gravy  £6.95
Fillet Steak Rossini  £10.25
Honey-roasted Ham with Cumberland Sauce  £6.50
Smoked Duck Breast with Port Sauce & Black Cherries  £10.50

### DESSERTS

Fresh Fruit Meringue served with Cream  £2.25
Tropical Brandy Snap Basket  £2.25
Bakewell Tart served with Cream  £2.25
Bread & Butter Pudding  £2.25

Cheeseboard  £2.75

The Calveley Arms is a 16th Century, half-timbered former coaching inn with exposed beams, a real log fire, a large beer garden and even a boules court. It is still very much a country pub that serves good food, rather than a restaurant that sells beer. There is just the one dining area and they specialise in fresh fish and game in season.

The food here is all cooked to order using fresh local produce and the specials on the blackboard (featured opposite) change daily. A bar menu is also available, with dishes such as Guacamole & Potato Skins (£2.50), Hot Avocado & Stilton (£3.50), Dim Sum (£3.50), Steak & Kidney Pie (£4.50), Breaded Aubergine Fritters (£4.95), Breton Chicken (£6.25), Teriyaki Salmon (£7.50), Lamb Cutlets on a sizzle platter (£5.95) or Pasta Carbonara (£5.25).

Directions: the Calveley Arms is located in the village of Handley, which lies 6 miles to the south-east of Chester, just off the A41 Chester-Whitchurch road.

## USEFUL INFORMATION

**SERVING TIMES:**
Lunch 12pm-2.30pm (every day)
Dinner 6pm-9.30pm (Mon-Sat)
7pm-9.30pm (Sundays)
**SEATING CAPACITY:** 52
**OUTDOOR EATING:** yes

**NUMBER OF WINES:** 18
**HOUSE WINE:** £7.00
**RESERVATIONS:** advisable
**C/C:** V, MC, D
**OFF-STREET PARKING:** yes

# GEORGE HOTEL
## Tel: (01433) 650436
Hathersage, Derbyshire, S30 1BB

### TO START

**A clear tomato soup**
a classic soup, flavoured with dill and vegetables diamonds
**Wild mushroom terrine**
served with a warm ragoût of woodland mushrooms in a pastry pillow
**Avocado pear tempura**
pieces of pear cooked in a crisp Japanese batter served with sweet pepper sauce
**Warm salad**
liver, bacon and mushrooms set on French leaves dressed with
balsamic vinegar and olive oil
**Soft boiled egg**
served in a pastry case with crayfish sauce

### INTERMEDIATE COURSE

**Redcurrant and rosepetal sorbet**
home-made and served with sliced apple
**Gratin of seafoods**
fresh fish glazed under a mousseline sauce

### MAIN COURSE

**Monkfish and prawn sausage**
home-made and served with pasta and a green peppercorn sauce
**Castlegate wing rib steak**
chargrilled to your liking, served with a Burgundy and pepper oil
sauce, new potatoes and salad
**Breast of Deben duck**
the skin caramelised and served pink with a casserole of vegetables and potatoes
**Fillet of salmon**
poached and served with a cardamom sauce, new potatoes and vegetables
**Chargrilled vegetables**
courgette, aubergine, pepper and mushroom marinated in olive oil,
herbs and pepper served with a grilled cheese dip
**Lumaconi pasta**
filled with onion cooked in balsamic vinegar and topped with a five
cheese sauce served with vegetable salad

### A SELECTION OF HOME-MADE DESSERTS

Dating from the 16th Century and set in the pretty village of Hathersage in the Peak District National Park, the George Hotel has recently undergone a change of ownership (now belonging to Eric Marsh and Nick Buckingham of the Cavendish Hotel). Tasteful design by Liz Marsh, retaining wooden beams and open fires, has resulted in a friendly and intimate atmosphere.

As to be expected the food is very good. The basic table d'hôte menu shown opposite (2,3 or 4 courses at £13.95, £16.95 and £19.95 respectively) is served all day, and is complemented by a blackboard of daily specials. Desserts are all home-made and may include Sticky Toffee Pudding or Banana Wontons.

Directions: Hathersage is about 8 miles south-west of Sheffield. The George is easily found in the centre of the village on the A625.

### USEFUL INFORMATION

**SERVING TIMES:**
Food 10am-10pm (every day)
**SEATING CAPACITY:** 60
**C/C:** V, MC, S, D, AE, DC
**OUTDOOR EATING:** no
**CHILDREN** welcome
**NO SMOKING** in the restaurant

**NUMBER OF WINES:** 30
**HOUSE WINE:** £9.50
**OFF-STREET PARKING:** yes
**RESERVATIONS:** advisable
**ACCOMMODATION:** 19 rooms
(single £59, double £79)

# THE SCOTSMAN'S PACK INN

## Tel: (01433) 650253

School Lane, Hathersage, Sheffield, Derbyshire, S30 1BZ

### Appetisers

*Prawn Cocktail £3.60*
*Soup of the Day £1.80*
*Garlic Mushrooms £2.95*
fresh mushrooms sautéed in garlic butter
with toast and salad garnish
*Green Lipped Mussels in Garlic £2.95*
in cream and white wine served with
brown bread and butter
*Brussels Pâté £2.60*
served with toast and salad garnish

### Fish and Vegetarian

*Golden Fried Haddock in Batter £5.50*
*Batter Crisp Whole Tail Scampi £6.20*
succulent Scampi tails cooked in a
light crisp batter
*Lemon Sole Breton £7.95*
boneless lemon sole fillet with
crabmeat and scallops
*Swaledale Trout £6.20*
grilled in butter and served with crispy salad
*Salmon Aurore £6.30*
a salmon fillet poached in a light aurore
sauce with Greenland prawns
*Vegetarian Lasagne £5.50*
pasta with green peppers, courgettes,
tomatoes, onions & fresh mushrooms topped
with cheese
*Vegetable Balti and Naan Bread £5.65*
an exciting blend of exotic spices added to
fresh vegetables
*Spicy Tomato Pasta £5.50*
penne shaped pasta in a rich tomato, red
pepper and mushroom sauce

### Fresh Salad Platter

Delicious crispy, fresh green salad with:
*Prawns £5.95*
*Roast Ham £5.50*
*Ploughman's Lunch £5.50*

### Steak and Meat

*Home-made Chicken & Ham Pie £5.60*
tender chunks of chicken and ham combined
with sautéed onions and mushroom sauce
topped with short crust pastry
*Lambs Liver and Onion £5.50*
*Steak au Poivre £9.20*
*Grilled Sirloin Steak £8.50*
with onion rings, tomatoes and mushrooms
*Mixed Grill £8.60*
steak, sausage, lamb chops, liver, gammon,
kidney, tomatoes and mushrooms
*Generous Gammon Steak £7.10*
with pineapple, egg, mushrooms & tomatoes
*Turkey Escalope Cordon Bleu £6.30*
a turkey breast cooked in a light white wine
and cream sauce layered with mushrooms,
ham and cheese
*Barbecued Pork Steaks £5.95*
*Lamb Cutlets £6.20*
lamb cutlets in a redcurrant sauce

### Continental Specialities

*Lasagne Verdi £5.50*
egg pasta with spinach interlayed with
mornay & bolognaise sauce & parmesan
*Moussaka £5.50*
a traditional moussaka with layers of minced
lamb, aubergines, courgettes & potatoes
with a creamy sauce of cheese & yoghurt
*Lamb Balti £5.60*
*Chicken Balti £5.60*
pieces of tender chicken, fresh fruit and
vegetables in a subtle blend of spices in our
own medium balti sauce

**All the main courses are served, where
appropriate, with a choice of either
potatoes, french fries or rice, and seasonal
vegetables or fresh salad.**

Rebuilt in 1926, this friendly inn enjoys a good location on the edge of a pretty village in the heart of the Peak District National Park. The Scotsman's Pack gets its name from before the 18th Century, when it was a regular watering hole for the "packman" or travelling drapers, who visited every farm and village in the area offering their goods and carrying news. Packmen from Scotland sold their tweeds here to the local farmers.

The bar menu which offers both regular pub food as well as more substantial dishes, is supplemented by a blackboard with daily specials like Duck Breast in Cumberland Sauce (£8.10) or Thai Style Prawns (£8.00). Home-made stir fries are particularly popular here, as is the Sunday lunch at a very reasonable £5.75.

Directions:  Hathersage is on the A625 about 8 miles from Sheffield. The Scotsman's Pack is signposted off the main road which runs through the village.

### USEFUL INFORMATION

**SERVING TIMES:**
Lunch 12pm-2pm (every day)
Dinner 6pm-9pm (every day)
**CLOSED:** for food on Christmas Day
**SEATING CAPACITY:** 20 in the
dining room, 68 in the bar
**C/C:** not accepted
**CHILDREN:** welcome until 8pm
**OFF-STREET PARKING:** yes

**NUMBER OF WINES:** 8
**HOUSE WINE:** £7.25
**RESERVATIONS:** advisable at
weekends
**NO SMOKING** area available
**OUTDOOR EATING:** yes
**ACCOMMODATION:** 4 rooms
(single £35, double £55)

# BRIDGE END RESTAURANT

### Tel: (01663) 747321

7 Church Street, Hayfield, Derbyshire, SK12 5JE

### STARTERS

Soup of the day £2.50
Bridge End salad; a jumble of salad leaves, sundried tomatoes,
olives and peppers, with a hazelnut oil dressing £4.00
Grilled asparagus with shaven parmesan and a truffle oil dressing £4.50
Goats cheese tart; a crisp tart filled with onions and fromage frais,
topped with goats cheese and grilled £4.20
Warm salad of duck, bacon lardons and apples tossed with baby spinach £4.50
Benjamin Smokies; smoked haddock, prawns and salmon simmered
in cream, topped with cheese and grilled £5.50
Crab cakes served on a bed of creamy cabbage £5.00

### MAIN COURSES

Hot smoked fillet of beef, garnished with a creamy onion tart,
on a thyme jus £15.50
Grilled hake with a roasted red pepper dressing £13.00
Breast of chicken roasted with garlic, baby onions, and mushrooms
on a tarragon sauce £14.00
Roast haunch of venison, on a redcurrant jelly sauce with
glazed baby apples £14.80
Filo pastry parcels, filled with ricotta cheese, sundried tomatoes, pinenuts
and olives on a tomato and garlic sauce £10.00
Saddle of rabbit, served on a beetroot sauce £14.50
Duck breast, served with sautéed potatoes on a herb butter sauce £13.50
*All main courses are served with a selection of fresh vegetables or a salad*

### DESSERTS

Sweetened mascarpone served with strawberries and passion fruit £4.00
"The Unabridged" a selection of desserts in miniature, including
sable, sorbet and parfait £6.00
Apricot and raspberry sorbet, served in a tuille biscuit on a fruit coulis £3.80
Hot chocolate pudding, served with coffee and chocolate anglaise £3.80
Nougatine parfait; a white chocolate parfait, studded with hazelnuts, pistachios,
cherries and honey, lined with star anise and poppy seeds
on a passion fruit coulis £4.00
Fresh fruit sable; sable biscuit with layers of crème patissière and
fruit, on a fruit coulis £4.00
Apricot and almond tart, served with apricot sauce £3.80

Although the main section of the dining area is mid 19th Century, Bridge End Restaurant dates back to 1760 when it formed part of weavers' cottages. Beautifully renovated about eight years ago, it is warm and inviting, with pastel shades complementing the sanded floors and pine farmhouse furniture.

The à la carte menu shown opposite changes weekly, and the modern English cuisine is freshly prepared using local produce when available. Absolutely everything, from bread to after dinner chocolates, is home-made and quite delicious.

Every month there is a music evening when one may enjoy jazz or classical music, and a gourmet night (set menu featuring 4/5 courses for £23). These are always very popular so please book early to avoid disappointment!

Directions: About 5 miles north of Chapel-en-le-Firth on the A624, turn right into Hayfield village and the restaurant is 100 yards along on the right.

## USEFUL INFORMATION

**SERVING TIMES:**
Dinner 7.30pm-10pm (Tues-Sat)
**CLOSED:** lunchtime and all day
Sunday and Monday
**SEATING CAPACITY:** 50
**C/C:** V, MC, S, D, AE, DC
**OUTDOOR EATING:** no
**CHILDREN:** welcome

**NUMBER OF WINES:** 60
**HOUSE WINE:** £12.50
**RESERVATIONS:** advisable
**OFF-STREET PARKING:** yes
**NO SMOKING** before coffee
**ACCOMMODATION:** 4 rooms
(B&B single £30, double £40)

# THE WALTZING WEASEL
## Tel: (01663) 743402
New Mills Road, Birch Vale, Derbyshire, SK22 1BT

| *TYPICAL RESTAURANT MENU* | *TYPICAL BAR MENU* |
|---|---|
| **STARTERS** | **STARTERS** |
| *Soup of the day* | *Soup of the day £2.50* |
| *Cheese Soufflé* | *Garlic Mushrooms £4.00* |
| *Smoked Tuna* | *Smoked Tuna £4.50* |
| *Chilled Melon* | *Shrimps on Toast £4.00* |
| *Warm Fresh Fruit Salad* | *Egg Mayonnaise £2.50* |
| *Marinated Anchovies* | *Marinated Anchovies £4.50* |
| *Crayfish Tails* | *Crayfish Tails £5.50* |
| *Game Pâté* | *Game Pâté £4.00* |
| **MAIN COURSES** | **MAIN COURSES** |
| *Lobster Salad* | *Lobster Salad £12.50* |
| *Braised Rabbit* | *Peak Pie £8.50* |
| *Sirloin Steak* | *Sirloin Steak £12.50* |
| *Steak and Kidney Pie* | *Steak and Kidney Pie £8.50* |
| *Roast Duck* | *Chicken Curry £6.95* |
| *Beef in Whisky* | *Ham and Eggs £6.75* |
| *Grilled Halibut in Lemon Butter* | *Seafood Tart £8.75* |
| *Scotch Salmon* | *Vegetable Tart £6.75* |
| *Barnsley Chop* | *Barnsley Chop £10.50* |
| *Grilled Lemon Sole* | *Grilled Lemon Sole £10.50* |
| *Summer Chicken* | *Dressed Crab and Salad £8.75* |
| *All served with a selection of fresh vegetables* | *All served with a selection of fresh vegetables* |
| **PUDDINGS** | **PUDDINGS** |
| *Treacle Tart* | *Treacle Tart* |
| *Bread and Butter Pudding* | *Bread and Butter Pudding* |
| *Fresh Fruit Pavlova* | *Fresh Fruit Pavlova* |
| *Ice Cream or Sorbet* | *Ice Cream or Sorbet* |
| *Fruit Crumble* | *Fruit Crumble* |
| *Chocolate Mousse* | *Chocolate Mousse* |
| *Summer Pudding* | *Ice Cream* |
| *2 Courses £20.50   3 Courses £24.50* | *All £3.00* |

Dating back to the 18th Century, The Waltzing Weasel is a traditional country inn which enjoys excellent views of Kinder Scout and across the Peak District. Catching just the right balance between local pub and stylish restaurant, the atmosphere is friendly and the home-made food a little bit special.

At lunchtime the menu comes in the form of a sumptuous carvery, which includes both hot and cold dishes all laid out handsomely in the restaurant. In the evening one may choose between a daily blackboard bar menu and a restaurant table d'hôte which changes seasonally.

Directions: Leaving Hayfield on the A6015, The Waltzing Weasel is found on the right after about a mile.

### USEFUL INFORMATION

**SERVING TIMES:**
Lunch 12pm-2pm (every day)
Restaurant: Dinner 7pm-9pm (every day)
Bar: Dinner 7pm-9.30pm (every day)
**SEATING CAPACITY:** 35 in the restaurant, 60 in the bar
**C/C:** V, MC, S, D, AE
**OUTDOOR EATING:** yes

**NUMBER OF WINES:** 45
**HOUSE WINE:** £8.95
**RESERVATIONS:** advisable
**OFF-STREET PARKING:** yes
**CHILDREN:** welcome
**ACCOMMODATION:** 8 rooms
(single from £45, double from £65)

# NUTHURST GRANGE

### Tel: (01564) 783972

Nuthurst Grange Lane, Hockley Heath, Warwickshire, B94 5NL

*Main Course with Coffee £22.50*
*Two Courses with Coffee £32.50*
*Three Courses with Coffee £42.50*
*Four Courses with Coffee £46.50*

\* \* \* \* \*

*Pumpkin and Minestrone Soup*
*Galantine of Guinea Fowl with Pistachio Nuts*
*Smoked Chicken with a Chilli and Ginger Dressing*
*Melon, Mango and Pawpaw with Citrus Yoghurt*
*Breast of Pigeon with Mixed Beans, Sesame Seeds and Honey*

*Fish Soup with Cayenne Pepper and Mussels, Rouille Croutons*
*Baked Marinated Salmon with Coriander and Saffron*

*Fillet of Scotch Beef with Burgundy Wine and Pickled Walnuts*
*Breast of Duck with Grand Marnier and Green Peppercorns*
*Best End of English Lamb with a Port Wine and Rosemary Sauce*
*Saddle of Venison, Bubble and Squeak, Gin and Juniper Berry Sauce*
*Whole Roasted Boneless Quails, with Grapes and Madeira Wine*
*Turbot with a Lightly Curried Crabmeat Sauce*
*Grilled Dover Sole, off the bone with Champagne and Dill Sauce*
*Lobster Salad with Pink Grapefruit and New Potatoes*

*Passion Fruit Parfait*
*Apple and Sultana Crumble*
*Pear and Almond Tart*
*White and Dark Chocolate Mousse with Marinated Figs*
*Steamed Lime Sponge with Vanilla Sauce*
*Glazed Fruits with Rice Pudding*
*Selection of Cheeses*

*Coffee and Petits Fours*

Nuthurst Grange is a traditional country house hotel that nestles in seven and a half acres of landscaped gardens and woodlands. Chef/proprietor David Randolph with his team of cooks compiles imaginative menus featuring only the freshest local produce. The cuisine embraces the best of both classical and modern French/British cooking. The canapés served with your pre-meal drink, the selection of bread rolls, and the biscuits and petit fours served with your coffee are all made in the kitchen.

In addition to the gourmet menu on the facing page, there is a more rustic alternative priced at £26.90 for three courses and coffee. Luncheon is à la carte, with dishes such as Sardines with Walnut Toast, Black Olive and Anchovy Butter (£4.50) as a starter, or Chargrilled Tuna Salad with Tomato, Quails Eggs, Beans and Basil (£9.50) to follow. Sunday lunch, with one traditional roast meat, is also very popular - £16.90 for three courses and coffee.

Directions: Nuthurst Grange is situated just south of Hockley Heath off the A3400 Birmingham to Stratford road, approximately 1 mile to the north of Junction 16 of the M40. Please note that this junction is for southbound traffic only. If you are heading north, follow the airport sign onto the M42 and exit at Junction 4.

### USEFUL INFORMATION

**SERVING TIMES:**
Lunch 12pm-2pm (Sun-Fri)
Dinner 6.30pm-9.30pm (every day)
**CLOSED:** Saturday lunch
**SEATING CAPACITY:** 50, but with extra capacity in the function rooms
**C/C:** V, MC, S, D, AE, DC
**OUTDOOR EATING:** yes

**NUMBER OF WINES:** 200
**HOUSE WINE:** £10.90
**RESERVATIONS:** advisable
**NO SMOKING** in the restaurant
**CHILDREN:** welcome
**OFF-STREET PARKING:** yes
**ACCOMMODATION:** 15 rooms
(B&B single £99, double £125)

# THE YELLOW BROOM
### Tel: (01477) 534048
Twemlow Green, nr Holmes Chapel, Cheshire, CW4 8BL

### *A selection from the A La Carte*

#### *Entrées*

**MARINIERE DE LEGUMES ET CRUSTACES A L'HUILE D'OLIVE £7.95**
*Marinated fresh vegetables and seafood in an olive oil dressing*
**TERRINE DE FOIE GRAS PARFUME AU RIESLING £10.50**
*A foie gras terrine flavoured with Riesling*
**EVENTAIL DE CANARD FUME ACCOMPAGNE D'UNE SALADE DE
PATES FRAICHES ET TAPENADE £7.95**
*A fan of smoked duck with a linguini salad and a tapenade dressing*
**TIAN DE SAUMON FUME A LA MOUSSE DE CITRON £8.50**
*Layered Scottish smoked salmon and lime mousse accompanied by a cucumber dressing*
**PETIT SABLE DE BIQUETTE GRILLE ET UNE SALADE DU CHEF £5.85**
*A slice of goat's cheese, grilled and served with a seasonal salad*
**PITHIVIERS D'ESCARGOTS A L'AIL, BEURRE NANTAIS £6.70**
*A large puff pastry envelope filled with snails and garlic butter*

#### *Poissons*

**BROCHETTE DE POISSONS GRILLES FINES HERBES £14.10**
*Seafood skewer served with a prawn risotto*
**BRANDADE DE MORUE AUX COQUILLES ST JACQUES £10.75**
*Finnan haddock steamed with sliced potatoes and fresh scallops*
**SUPREME DE SAUMON A LA VAPEUR, COMPOTE D'ECHALOTES £10.85**
*Steamed salmon served with a light melted butter and compote of shallots*

#### *Viandes et Grillades*

**PAVE DE VEAU POELE AUX CONFITS DE POMES WILLIAMS £11.30**
*Lightly pan fried calf liver served with apple confit*
**CANON DE VOLAILLE AUX AMANDES ET EPINARDS A LA CREME £11.20**
*Supreme of chicken filled with spinach and almonds with a cream sauce*
**FILET DE BOEUF EN CROUTE AUX CHAMPIGNONS SAUVAGES £15.80**
*Fillet of beef cooked in puff pastry with wild mushrooms*
**NAVARIN DE CHEVREUIL AU PORTO GARNI DE CHOUX ROUGES £11.60**
*Venison casserole braised in port wine served with pickled red cabbage*
**FILET D'AGNEAU DAUPHINOIS £12.85**
*A fillet of lamb with a mousseline of chicken and truffle on a bed of rosti potato*
**SELLE DE LAPIN ROTI PROVENCALE £9.95**
*Braised saddle of rabbit dusted with basil and rosemary and served with ratatouille*
**COULIBIAC DE LEGUMES £8.95**
*Seasonal vegetables and rice, wrapped in fine herb pancake served with a fresh tomato sauce*

Set in beautiful and tranquil Cheshire countryside, The Yellow Broom is a popular restaurant renowned for its innovative French cuisine. The elegant interior contributes to a relaxed ambiance, with pastel colours and lightly stained exposed beams conjuring up a warm feeling of Provence in summer.

The à la carte menu, a selection from which appears opposite, changes seasonally, but always features a fish dish of the day (Dover Sole and Lobster when available). This is complemented by an excellent weekly table d'hôte menu (4 courses and coffee £22.50) and a traditional roast every Sunday (3 courses £12.50).

Directions: Twemlow Green is about 2 miles north-east of Holmes Chapel and junction 18 of the M6. The Yellow Broom is on the A535 by the turning to Swettenham.

## USEFUL INFORMATION

**SERVING TIMES:**
Lunch 12pm-2pm (Sunday)
Dinner 7pm-9.30pm (Tues-Sat)
**CLOSED:** for lunch (except Sunday)
Sunday evening and all day Monday
**SEATING CAPACITY:** 45
**C/C:** V, MC, S, D

**NUMBER OF WINES:** 40
**HOUSE WINE:** £9.95
**DRESS CODE:** smart casual
**RESERVATIONS:** advisable
**OUTDOOR EATING:** no
**OFF-STREET PARKING:** yes
**CHILDREN:** welcome on Sunday

# THE ROBIN HOOD INN

## Tel: (0114) 289 0360

Lydgate, Holmesfield, Derbyshire, S18 5WB

### APPETISERS

GARLIC & HERB MUSHROOMS in a
cream sauce served with salad garnish
and French bread £3.50
YORKSHIRE PUDDING with
rich onion gravy £2.25
PRAWN COCKTAIL served with a marie
rose sauce, bread & butter £3.65
HOME-MADE SOUP served with freshly
baked French bread & butter £2.25
HOME-MADE PATE made with wine &
brandy, with salad garnish & toast £3.50
DEEP FRIED POTATO WEDGES served
with garlic dip & salad garnish £2.75

### GRILLS

SIRLOIN STEAK 10oz £10.95
FILLET STEAK 8oz £11.95
Both served with either a Black Pepper &
Brandy or Chasseur sauce £1.95
MIXED GRILL steak, pork, lamb chop,
Cumberland sausage & liver £9.95
GAMMON STEAK 10oz served with
either pineapple or fried egg £8.95
*All the above are served with chips, peas,
mushrooms, onion rings, tomato & garnish*

### MAIN COURSES

LASAGNE layers of pasta in a ground
beef & tomato sauce, bechamel sauce &
topped with cheese, served with
salad or chips £5.75
CHILLI CON CARNE ground beef &
red kidney beans in a spicy tomato sauce
served with rice & French bread £5.75
HOME-MADE STEAK, ALE &
MUSHROOM PIE served with chips and
fresh vegetables £5.95
TANDOORI CHICKEN served with
chips, onion rings & salad garnish £6.50
LAMB CUTLETS served with potatoes &
fresh vegetables £7.50

### MAIN COURSES

ROBIN HOOD QUICHE ham, onion,
tomato, cheese quiche served with
lyonnaise potatoes & salad £5.45
DEEP FRIED SCAMPI TAILS served
with chips, peas & salad garnish £5.95
DEEP FRIED HADDOCK in a golden
batter served with chips, peas and
a salad garnish £5.95
STILTON & WALNUT QUICHE served
with lyonnaise potatoes & salad £5.95

### SALADS

HONEY GLAZED HAM £6.95
SMOKED SALMON & PRAWN £8.95
TUNA £5.95    CHICKEN BREAST £6.95
PATE £5.95
TRADITIONAL PLOUGHMANS £4.95

### SWEETS

HOT CHOCOLATE FUDGE CAKE
BREAD & BUTTER PUDDING
FRUIT CRUMBLE
*All £2.50 and served with fresh cream*
BRANDY SNAPS £2.35
SYRUP SPONGE £2.50
RASPBERRY SURPRISE £2.95
CHEESE AND BISCUITS £3.50

*The items below are not available on a
Saturday night*

JACKET POTATOES from £2.95

SANDWICHES from £2.95

HOT ROAST BEEF BAGUETTE or
a STEAK SANDWICH each £4.75

ROBIN HOOD STAPLE DIET home-
made soup served with bacon in freshly
baked French bread £3.95

A grade II listed building dating back to the early 18th Century, The Robin Hood Inn enjoys a wonderfully isolated location in the Peak District, where on a clear day the views stretch for 40 miles. Exposed beams, open fires and original stone floors give this inn a delightful olde worlde charm, and it is a very pleasant place to enjoy good home-made food.

There is one main menu available at lunch and dinner, and it is supplemented by a fine selection of about 20 blackboard specials, which may include dishes such as Lamb Steak in an Orange and Redcurrant Sauce (£9.50) or Stuffed Beef Olives with a Herb and Red Wine Sauce (£9.50). The fish dishes here, like Fresh Whitby Cod (£5.95) and Grilled Salmon Steak (£9.25), are particularly popular.

Directions:   About 6 miles south of Sheffield on the A621, take the B6054 signposted to Holmesfield. The Robin Hood Inn is easily found on the left after about a mile.

### USEFUL INFORMATION

**SERVING TIMES:**
Lunch 12pm-2.30pm (Mon-Fri)
Dinner 6pm-9.30pm (Mon-Fri)
Food served 12pm-9.30pm (Sat-Sun)
**SEATING CAPACITY:** 90
**C/C:** V, MC, S, D
**OUTDOOR EATING:** yes

**NUMBER OF WINES:** 18
**HOUSE WINE:** £10
**CHILDREN:** welcome
**OFF-STREET PARKING:** yes
**RESERVATIONS:** advisable from
Friday to Sunday

# THE CROWN INN

### Tel: (01299) 270372

Hopton Wafers, near Cleobury Mortimer, Shropshire, DY14 0NB

**A Small Selection from "The Hopton Poacher" Menu ...**

Fillets of Smoked Trout on Mixed Leaves with Poppy Seeds £4.75
Tagliatelle Verdi with Piquant Tomato Sauce & Parmesan £4.00
Feta Cheese Salad with Olives, Dressed in Walnut Oil £4.50
Tandoori Chicken Salad £4.75

Cumberland Sausages & Mash with a Rich Onion Gravy £7.25
Steak & Kidney Pie Braised in Irish Stout £7.50
Pan-fried Venison Rissoles served with Cranberry Sauce £8.00
Brochette of King Prawns served on Crushed Garlic Potatoes £11.75
Stir-fried Vegetables with Mandarin Sauce £7.25
Spiced Lamb Meatballs on a bed of Noodles with Rosemary Sauce £7.75
Plate of Deep-fried Seafoods with Lemon & Tarragon Mayonnaise £7.25

**... and our Restaurant Dinner Menu**

**£24.00** *(including coffee)*

Mozzarella, Tomato & Basil Salad with Crisp Smoked Bacon
Courgette & Sweetcorn Pancake with Cashel Blue
Salad of Diced Pear & Grilled Smoked Salmon
Wild Mushroom & Truffle Cappelletti
Hot Mixed Seafoods in a Crisp Pancake with Piquant Tomato Sauce

Pork Medallions with Wholegrain Mustard & Grape Sauce, Black Noodles
Roast Rack of Lamb with a Blackcurrant and Rosemary Sauce
Lemon & Garlic Supreme of Chicken, pan-fried with Pine Kernels
Grilled Polenta & Smoked Haddock with a Salad
Braised Duck Breast with Apple & Green Peppercorn Sauce
Prime Herefordshire Steak, garnished & grilled to your choice

Lemon Curd and Cream Cheese
with Amaretto Biscuit and Baileys Custard
Apple and Cinnamon Crumble
Dark Chocolate Delice
Peach and Brandy Trifle

The Crown at Hopton is a traditional 16th Century country inn full of character and period charm, with open log fires and exposed beams covered with hop vines. There are two quite separate dining areas: the restaurant (with a three-course table d'hôte that changes every six weeks or so) and *The Hopton Poacher* (more informal, brasserie-style, with individually priced dishes from a seasonal menu supplemented by daily specials on the blackboard).

The mainstays of chef Peter Francis' excellent cooking are modern English and European dishes, with the accent on fresh produce and local game in season, occasionally supplemented by choices from further afield.

Directions: The Crown Inn is situated just outside the village of Hopton Wafers about 2 miles west of Cleobury Mortimer on the A4117 Ludlow-Bewdley road.

### USEFUL INFORMATION

(HP) refers to Hopton Poacher    (R) refers to the restaurant

**SERVING TIMES:**
Lunch (HP) 12pm-2.30pm (every day)
(R) 12pm-2.30pm (Sunday, other days by prior arrangement only)
Dinner (HP) 6.30pm-9.30pm (every day)
(R) 7.30pm-9.30pm (every day)
**SEATING CAPACITY:** 40 in each
**C/C:** V, MC, S, D
**OFF-STREET PARKING:** yes

**NUMBER OF WINES:** 65
**HOUSE WINE:** £8.75
**NO SMOKING** in the restaurant
**OUTDOOR EATING:** yes
**RESERVATIONS:** (R) advisable, (HP) for Sunday lunch only
**CHILDREN:** welcome
**ACCOMMODATION:** 8 rooms (B&B single £45, double £75)

# DA VINCI'S

**Tel: (01952) 432250**

26 High Street, Ironbridge, Telford, Shropshire, TF8 7AD

## ~ ANTIPASTI ~

| | |
|---|---|
| Antipasto Di Leonardo | £10.95 |
| *A selection of cured ham & salami served with Italian pickles (2 people)* | |
| Fegatini Marsala | £4.25 |
| *Chicken livers sautéed with marsala wine & sage* | |
| Tonno E Fagioli | £3.95 |
| *Barlotti bean & tuna fish salad with onion garnish* | |
| Carciofi Ripieni | £4.25 |
| *Grilled artichokes with home-made goats' cheese* | |

## ~ PASTA E MINESTRA ~

| | |
|---|---|
| Linguine Alle Vongole | £6.25 |
| *Linguine with clams* | |
| Spaghetti Peppino | £6.25 |
| *Spaghetti in tomato, bacon & chilli sauce* | |
| Tortelloni Dei Sogni | £6.25 |
| *Stuffed pasta in a cream, ham & mushroom sauce* | |
| Gnocchi Al Ragu | £6.25 |
| *Potato dumplings with a rich meat sauce* | |

## ~ SECONDI ~

| | |
|---|---|
| Bistecca Fiorentina Di Filippo | £16.95 |
| *Charcoal grilled T-bone steak drizzled with olive oil* | |
| Filetto Borgia | £10.95 |
| *Split fillet in a rich red wine & porcini sauce* | |
| Vitello Del Principe | £9.25 |
| *Pan-fried veal in a white wine, cream & mushroom sauce* | |
| Pollo Marco | £8.75 |
| *Chicken & coriander seeds, in a white wine & cream sauce* | |
| Salmone In Cartoccio | £8.75 |
| *Oven baked salmon with wine & herbs* | |
| Pesce Spada Di Enzo | £11.95 |
| *Swordfish steak, marinated in lemon juice, garlic & oregano, grilled* | |
| Melanzane Al Forno | £7.95 |
| *Char-grilled aubergine baked with tomato & mozzarella* | |
| Frittata Di Rita | £7.75 |
| *Italian style omelette stuffed with seasonal vegetables & served with a light tomato sauce* | |

Da Vinci's is an intimate Italian restaurant that has quickly built up an enviable reputation for good food and friendly service since it opened in Ironbridge in the summer of 1996. Dining is on two floors, the most popular room being downstairs in the brickwork 'wine cellar'.

The decor upstairs is slightly eccentric - the stripped wooden flooring has been painted with an oak tree that develops into a vine, hung with portrayals of various game birds and fruit. So when you telephone to reserve a table (the restaurant is often fully booked up 10 days in advance), why not ask to be seated on the pheasant? Or perhaps the kangaroo? (Don't ask!)

The à la carte menu, a small selection of which is featured opposite, changes every 3 to 4 months and is supported by a choice of daily specials on the blackboard. Traditional Italian desserts (all £2.95), such as Coppa Del Bosco, are there to tempt you, as well as a number of sweets on the à la carte. The meal can be rounded off with a selection from a fabulous cheese board that normally includes a choice of 6 or 7 different Italian cheeses.

Directions: Da Vinci's can be found at the top of the High Street in the centre of the town.

## USEFUL INFORMATION

**SERVING TIMES:**
Lunch 12pm-2pm (Thur-Sun)
    12pm-2pm (Sat,Sun Jan-Easter)
Dinner 7pm-10pm (Wed-Sun)
**CLOSED:** all day Mon & Tues,
and Wed lunch
**SEATING CAPACITY:** 30
**C/C:** V, MC, S, D

**NUMBER OF WINES:** 25
**HOUSE WINE:** £8.50 (litre)
**RESERVATIONS:** advisable, but
compulsory at weekends
**OUTDOOR EATING:** no
**NO WHEELCHAIR ACCESS**
**OFF-STREET PARKING:** no

# THE GOLDEN BALL INN
### Tel: (01952) 432179
Newbridge Road, Ironbridge, Shropshire, TF8 7BA

## HOME-MADE BLACKBOARD SPECIALS

Bacon, Tomato & Bean Soup £1.75

Calzone (Closed Pizza) £3.50
extra fillings: beef, pepperoni, ham (50p each)
pineapple, chilli, onion, mushroom, peppers, olives (30p each)

Chicken Enchilada £4.95
spicy pieces of chicken wrapped in tortillas, topped with cream,
Mexican chilli sauce & cheese, served with fries or salad

Tuna Lasagne served with fries or potatoes & salad garnish £4.95

Tagliatelle Carbonara £4.95
ribbons of pasta cooked with smokey bacon & mushrooms
in a cheese & cream sauce with a hint of garlic

Mushroom & Pepper Croustade £4.95
cooked in a garlic & herb cream, served in a hollowed roll

Chicken Strudel served with fries or potatoes and fresh vegetables £5.95

Steak & Ale Pie served with fries & seasonal vegetables £4.50

Chilli con Carne served with rice £4.75

Lamb Vindaloo served with rice & poppadums £5.95

Bacon & Potato Pie with fresh vegetables & salad garnish £4.95

~ ~ ~ ~ ~ ~ ~ ~ ~ ~

Banana Caramel Crêpes £2.25

Grilled Honey Peaches with Yoghurt £2.25

Jam Sponge Pudding £2.25

Bakewell Tart £2.25

The Golden Ball Inn is a traditional 17th Century country inn, full of period charm and character. The oldest pub in Ironbridge, licensed in 1728, it stands on what used to be the village green at Madeley Wood and thus pre-dates the town itself. Oak beams, quarry tiles, stripped wooden floors and open log fires welcome you to the three separate dining areas.

The food is eclectic - a mix of standard English bar food combined with mainly Italian, Mexican and Indian dishes. The *Chicken Enchilada* here is so popular that it has been featured on their blackboard for over 4 years!

The blackboard specials change regularly (except for the *enchilada!*) and offer exceptionally good value for money. On Sundays, a traditional roast is available in addition to the standard bar menu and costs just £4.50 for the main course.

Directions: The Golden Ball Inn is set back from the main road. Halfway down the Madeley Road heading towards Ironbridge, turn left into Jockey Bank and follow the signs to their large car park.

## USEFUL INFORMATION

**SERVING TIMES:**
Lunch 12pm-2.30pm (every day)
Dinner 6pm-9.30pm (Mon-Sat)
　　　7pm-9.30pm (Sunday)
**SEATING CAPACITY:** 80
**C/C:** V, MC, S, D
**NO SMOKING** area available
**OFF-STREET PARKING:** yes

**NUMBER OF WINES:** 14
**HOUSE WINE:** £7.50
**RESERVATIONS:** advisable
**CHILDREN:** welcome
**OUTDOOR EATING:** yes
**ACCOMMODATION:** 5 rooms
(B&B single fr £30, double fr £40)

# RESTAURANT BOSQUET
## Tel: (01926) 852463
97a Warwick Road, Kenilworth, Warwickshire, CV8 1HP

### A La Carte Menu

#### Starters
Terrine de Homard et Asperges, Beurre de Laitue de Mer £7.00
*Warm terrine of lobster and asparagus served with a seaweed butter sauce*
Soupe de Haricot Blanc et Tomate au Magret de Canard Fumé £5.80
*Tomato and bean soup with smoked duck breast*
Galette de Foie Gras de Canard aux Figues Epicées, Sauce Vin Doux £7.50
*Foie gras served on a slice of pastry covered with a compôte of spicy figs*
Salade des Ecrevisses, Asperges et Pigeon £7.00
*Salad of pigeon, crayfish and asparagus with truffle oil and balsamic vinaigrette*
Coquilles St. Jacques, Sauce au Safron et l'Encre £7.00
*Pan-fried scallops served on a bed of fennel and saffron purée*
*with a saffron and ink sauce*

#### Main Courses
Côte de Boeuf au Vin Rouge et Echalottes £15.00
*Rib-eye steak served with a red wine sauce and shallots*
Selle d'Agneau aux Epices et Abricots £15.00
*Saddle of lamb served with a spicy apricot sauce and vegetable cous cous*
Selle de Chevreuil au Genievre et Chocolat £15.00
*Saddle of venison served with a juniper berry and chocolate sauce,*
*garnished with red cabbage and game chips*
Pigeonnaux Rôti £15.00
*Roast squab pigeon served on a bed of lentils and root vegetables with sherry sauce*
Turbot Rôti aux Onions et Lard Fumée £15.00
*Roast turbot with onions and bacon*

#### Desserts & Cheeses
Gratin de Fruits au Sabayon de Muscat £6.00
Sorbets Maison £4.50
Marquise au Chocolat £4.50
Millefeuille de Framboises £6.00
Parfait de Poire £4.50
Tarte au Citron £4.50
Assiette de Chocolat £6.50
Feuilleté de Fraises £6.00
Fromages de France £5.00

Restaurant Bosquet is a Victorian terraced townhouse restaurant that has become extremely popular over the years for the excellence of its French cuisine, expertly prepared by Chef Patron Bernard Lignier and served to your table by his wife Jane.

The feel is very much that of a private dinner party (albeit seated at separate tables) as the restaurant itself is basically the sitting room of the owners' private home. The only real concession to its true identity is a small bar area in the corner of the room.

The classical French cuisine on the à la carte menu featured opposite is backed up by a three-course fixed price menu available on weekday evenings, priced at £22.00 per person. The large wine list, made up exclusively of French wines, is also excellent.

Directions: Restaurant Bosquet is on the Warwick Road in the town centre.

## USEFUL INFORMATION

**SERVING TIMES:**
Dinner 7pm-9.30pm (Tues-Sat)
**CLOSED:** every lunch and Sunday
& Monday evening
**SEATING CAPACITY:** 26
**OFF-STREET PARKING:** a public
car park is available nearby

**NUMBER OF WINES:** 100
**HOUSE WINE:** £11.50
**RESERVATIONS:** advisable
**C/C:** V, MC, S, D, AE
**CHILDREN:** welcome
**DRESS CODE:** smart
**OUTDOOR EATING:** no

# SIMPSON'S
### Tel: (01926) 864567
101/103 Warwick Road, Kenilworth, Warwickshire, CV8 1HL

## 2 Courses at £19.50
## 3 Courses at £23.50

### Starters
Veloute of Sweetcorn with Chicken
Salmon & Brill Terrine with Caesar Salad
Marinated Aubergine with Cracked Wheat Salad
Seared Foie Gras with Rocket Salad, Caramelised Oranges
and Hazelnut Dressing (£3.50 supplement)
Crispy Mackerel with Potato Salad & Truffle Cream
Confit of Duck with Braised Red Cabbage & Peppercorn Sauce
Goats Cheese coated with Cous Cous & Plum Tomato Relish
Sweet Tomato Risotto with Parmesan Crisps

### Main Courses
Kleftico with Fondant Potatoes & Lentil Sauce
Char-Grilled Rib-Eye Steak "Bourguignonne" & Celeriac Mash
Breast of Chicken with Mushroom Ravioli & Creamed Tarragon Sauce
Confit of Pork Belly with Black Pudding Mash and Cider Sauce
Roast Wood Pigeon with Mushy Peas & Foie Gras Sauce
Pan Fried Salmon with Pok Choi & Oriental Sauce
Steamed Cod with an Olive Crust, Fennel & Basil
Leek & Pecorino Tart with Poached Egg Salad

*All main courses have been created to include vegetables as part of the dish*

### Puddings
Lemon & Blueberry Sponge Pudding
Snow Eggs with Raspberries & Vanilla Sauce
Pineapple Tart Tatin with Rum & Raisin Ice Cream
Caramel Crème Brûlée with Banana Sandwich
Apple Fritters with Apricot Parfait
Trio of Chocolate Mousse with Cappuccino Sauce
Pecan Pie with Crème Fraîche
Selection of English & French Farm Cheese

Simpson's is an extremely popular town centre restaurant with an enviable repuation where the food belies its rather ordinary location.

Chef Patron Andreas Antona and his team have created a selection of classical English and European dishes - "fresh interpretations of bourgeois and regional cuisine with a lighter contemporary touch".

The seasonal dinner menu which appears on the facing page is best described as à la carte with a fixed price (£19.50 for two courses, £23.50 for three). Lunch is a *menu rapide* consisting of three courses and priced at £15.00 per person, generally with a choice of three dishes at each course. The service here, whichever time of day you choose to visit, is excellent.

Directions: Simpson's is on the Warwick Road in the centre of Kenilworth. The private car park is located to the rear of the building down a small side street.

### USEFUL INFORMATION

**SERVING TIMES:**
Lunch 12.30pm-2pm (Mon-Fri)
Dinner 7pm-10.30pm (Mon-Sat)
**CLOSED:** Sat lunch & all day Sun
**SEATING CAPACITY:** 70
**C/C:** V, MC, S, D, AE, DC
**NO SMOKING** area available

**NUMBER OF WINES:** 90
**HOUSE WINE:** £9.95
**RESERVATIONS:** advisable
**OFF-STREET PARKING:** yes
**CHILDREN:** welcome
**OUTDOOR EATING:** no

# STONE MANOR

### Tel: (01562) 777555

Stone, near Kidderminster, Worcestershire, DY10 4PJ

## A LA CARTE LUNCH AND DINNER MENU

### Appetisers

Butternut Squash and Ginger Soup  £2.50
New England Seafood Chowder  £4.25
Warm Scallops, Hummus and Mixed Bean Salad  £5.50
Wild Mushroom Pancake topped with a Parmesan Crust  £6.25
Trio of Salmon served with their own Sauces  £7.50
Scallion and Artichoke, Walnut Pastry Tartlet, with a Chive Dressing  £3.95
Black Forest Ham and Sweet Melon, dressed with crushed Pepper  £5.25
Game Terrine wrapped in Pastry, served with a Cumberland Sauce  £4.50
Thai Prawn Salad, tossed in a Coconut and Lemongrass Dressing  £7.25

### Fish

Pan fried Fillet of Scottish Salmon, served on a spicy Vegetable Sauce  £13.25
Medallion of Monkfish with a Herb Crust and Red Pepper Sauce  £12.25
Fillet of Red Seabream topped with Lemon, Herb Butter and Pine Kernels  £10.95
Grilled Whole Lemon Sole accompanied by Dill Pesto  £14.50

### Main Courses

Venison Loin Fillet, served on a Beetroot and Orange Glaze  £18.50
Breast of Chicken filled with Leeks, with a Riesling and Sage Sauce  £12.25
Italian Rabbit Ragoût  £12.95
Fillet of Beef poached in Claret, served with a Shallot Sauce  £16.95
Crispy Roast Duckling, flamed with brandy, with your choice of sauce  £17.25
Roast Leg of Lamb filled with Rosemary, and a Honey and Lemon Sauce  £13.75
Roasted Sweet Potatoes; Chilli Jam and Coriander  £9.50
Green Fettucine tossed in Butter, fresh Parmesan, Tomatoes and Cream  £8.50
Filo Pastry Parcel filled with Spinach and Cottage Cheese  £8.50
Fillet Steak, chargrilled to your preference, with a grilled Tomato  £16.95

### Flambé Dishes

Breast of Chicken pan fried with Ham & Mushrooms, flamed with Brandy  £13.75
Pork Fillet with Onions, Mushrooms & Caraway, flamed with Vodka  £14.25
Fillet of Beef pan fried with Onions & Mushrooms, flamed with Calvados  £19.75
King Prawns cooked in a Lobster Cream Sauce, flamed with Brandy  £17.50

Selection of fresh seasonal vegetables / salad and potatoes  £3.00

Stone Manor is country house hotel built in 1926 with a black-and-white timber façade and set in 25 acres of gardens and countryside. Many of the building's timber structures were re-sited from the last Fighting Man of War to go into battle under sail, HMS Arethusa.

Fields Restaurant offers fine dining from a seasonal à la carte menu, an example of which is featured opposite, supplemented by two fixed price menus which are changed daily. The three-course luncheon costs £14.50 (or two courses for £12.50) while the table d'hôte dinner menu is set at £17.50 per person for three courses (two courses £15.50).

Flambé dishes are a house speciality, which of course means that you should be able to find Crêpes Suzette on the dessert menu.

Directions: Stone Manor is located 2 miles east of Kidderminster on the main A448 Bromsgrove to Kidderminster road.

### USEFUL INFORMATION

**SERVING TIMES:**
Lunch 12pm-2pm (Mon-Sat)
      12.30pm & 1.45pm (Sunday)
Dinner 7pm-10pm (Mon-Sat)
      7pm-9pm (Sunday)
**SEATING CAPACITY:** 80
**C/C:** V, MC, S, D, AE, DC
**NO SMOKING** in the restaurant

**NUMBER OF WINES:** 80
**HOUSE WINE:** £9.85
**RESERVATIONS:** advisable
**CHILDREN:** welcome
**OUTDOOR EATING:** yes
**OFF-STREET PARKING:** yes
**ACCOMMODATION:** 52 rooms
(from £49.50 to £110 room only)

# BELLE EPOQUE
### Tel: (01565) 633060
60 King Street, Knutsford, Cheshire, WA16 6DT

## STARTERS

**Belle Epoque's Home-Made Pizza**
*Topped with Roasted Red Onions, Chillies, Smoked Bacon , Oregano, Mozzarella £4.25*

**Watercress Pancakes**
*Filled with Naturally Smoked Haddock, infused with Tomato and Tarragon £3.95*

**Spicy Chorizo Sausage**
*Braised with Haricot Beans, Red Wine and Thymes £4.50*

**Fishcakes**
*A selection of fresh and Smoked Fish flavoured with Coriander in a fresh Tomato Sauce £3.95*

**Strips of Chicken Breast**
*Sautéed with Rosemary, Garlic, Chillies and Mango £4.25*

**House Smoked Salmon Fillet**
*Coriander and Onion Salsa £4.25*

**Tiger Prawn Tails**
*Feisty Pepper and Chilli Relish £7.95*

**Timbale of Duck**
*Braised Duck infused with Aromatic Chinese Spices and Mushrooms £4.50*

**Cornish Mackerel Fillet**
*Braised, Char Grilled Bulb Fennel £4.25*

**Bury Black Pudding**
*Topped with crispy Onion Rings, Onion and Cumin Purée £3.95*

**Finest Tripe**
*Baked with Root Vegetables, Onions and Cheshire Cheese £3.95*

**Belle House Salad**
*Salad Leaves, Bacon Lardons, Melon, and Herb Croutons, with a Balsamic and Olive Oil Dressing £4.25*

**Confit of Tomato and Spinach**
*Layered with Char Grilled Vegetables, and Baked with Basil £3.95*

**Chicken Liver Parfait**
*Pear and Marjoram Dressing, with Soda Bread £4.25*

## MAIN COURSES

**Home-made Sausage and Mash**
*Pork Sausage made in our Kitchens, flavoured with Garlic and Sage, served with Belle Epoque's Baked Beans and Onion Gravy £7.95*

**Char Grilled Fillet of Monkfish**
*Cucumber and Dill Purée*

**Roast Chicken Breast**
*Baked with Shards of Garlic, Light Madeira Gravy, Potato and Parsley Purée £9.95*

**Cod Fillet**
*Mustardy Cheese Sauce, spiked with Spring Onions, with Herb Mash £8.95*

**Layers of Herb Pancake**
*Filled with Aubergine, Peppers and a Rich Mushroom Duxelle, topped with Goats Cheese £7.95*

**Escalope of Turkey Breast**
*Wrapped in Parma Ham and Sage, with a Marsala Sauce £9.25*

**Traditional Hot Pot**
*Local Lamb cooked with Carrots, Leeks and Onions, topped with Potatoes £8.25*

**Seared Scottish Salmon Fillet**
*Sweet Tomato Vinaigrette £9.95*

**Fish and Chips**
*Fresh Haddock in a Yeast Batter, with Proper Chips and Mushy Peas £8.95*

**Steak, Mushroom and Oxtail Pie**
*Finest British Beef in Shortcrust Pastry, served with Mash £8.50*

**Fresh Tuna Fillet**
*Char Grilled, Roqette Oil studded with Red Pepper £11.95*

**Lamb's Liver and Bacon**
*Placed on Wilted Onions and Sage, deglazed with Balsamic Vinegar £7.95*

**Sirloin of Best British Beef**
*Au Poivre Sauce and served with Dauphinoise Potatoes £13.95*

To celebrate the 21st Anniversary of Belle Epoque, a rose was named after it. Perhaps the honour is hardly surprising, as this 1907 listed building in Italian style, which has been in the Mooney family for 23 years, is now a beautiful restaurant decorated in deep green and adorned with many original art nouveau pieces. What is more, the food is excellent.

The dinner menu, an example of which is shown opposite, changes seasonally. Desserts are all home-made, including ice creams and sorbets, and may include Chocolate and Praline Parfait or Pear Brulée Tart (£3.50 each).

The lunch menu, which again changes seasonally, offers slightly lighter dishes such as Pasta Spirals with Smoked Salmon Purée spiked with Dill and Lime (£4.50), or an Open Sandwich of Home Cooked Ham, Char Grilled Peppers and Salad with a Pineapple Vinaigrette (£5.50).

Directions: Easily found on King Street in the middle of Knutsford, which is two miles east of junction 19 of the M6.

### USEFUL INFORMATION

**SERVING TIMES:**
Lunch 12pm-2pm (Mon-Fri)
Dinner 7pm-10.30pm (Mon-Sat)
**CLOSED:** Saturday lunch, all day Sunday and Bank Holidays
**SEATING CAPACITY:** 70
**C/C:** V, MC, S, D, AE, DC
**OUTDOOR EATING:** yes
**CHILDREN** over 7 welcome

**NUMBER OF WINES:** 80
**HOUSE WINE:** £9.95
**NO SMOKING** in one restaurant
**RESERVATIONS:** advisable in the week, and compulsory at weekends
**OFF-STREET PARKING:** no
**ACCOMMODATION:** 7 rooms (single £40, double £50)

# THE DOG INN
## Tel: (01625) 861421
Well Bank Lane, Over Peover, Cheshire, WA16 8UP

### *STARTERS*
*All £3.95 unless otherwise stated*

Home-made Soup of the Day, served with crusty roll and butter
Deep Fried Whitebait with Salad; Melon with Prawns and Salad
Fanned Melon with Strawberries
Deep Fried Mushrooms in Beer Batter with Garlic Dip
Garlic Mushrooms in a Cream and Garlic Sauce
Sweet Herring and Salad; Deep Fried Brie with Fresh Cranberry Sauce
Duck and Port Pâté with Toast; Rollmop Herring with Salad
Bury Black Pudding served with Mustard
Smoked Mackerel and Salad; Egg Mayonnaise with Prawns and Salad
Barbecue Chicken Wings; Half Pint of Unpeeled Prawns with Garlic Dip
Avocado with Prawns Marie Rose
King Prawns in Garlic Butter and Salad £4.95
Hot Buttered Corn on the Cob; Smoked Trout and Salad
Lamb Lasagne with Salad £4.95
Grilled Sardines in a Light Mustard Sauce
Smoked Salmon with Salad; Welsh Rarebit with Bacon

### *MAIN COURSES*
*All £7.95 unless otherwise stated*

Roast Leg of Lamb with Mint Sauce
Roast Topside of Beef with Yorkshire Pudding
Roast Cheshire Turkey with Stuffing
Chicken Fillet in a Mushroom and Brandy Sauce
Roast Loin of Pork with Apple Sauce
Haddock and Prawn au Gratin; Ham Shank with Parsley Sauce
Plaice Fillet with a Cream and Grape Sauce
Turkey and Mushroom Pie; Old English Steak and Ale Pie
Poached Salmon with Cucumber Sauce
Halibut with Cheese served on a bed of Spinach
Spinach and Mushroom Lasagne; Baked Ham and Pineapple Mornay
Leek, Stilton and Mushroom Pancake; Smoked Salmon and Prawn Pancake
Braised Steak in a Red Wine Sauce; Rabbit with Herbs and Mustard
Half of Roast Duckling in a Plum Sauce £8.95
Roast Rack of Lamb with Apricots and Ginger £8.95
Deep Fried King Cod with Tartare Sauce; Jumbo Scampi with Salad

Lost in the heart of beautiful Cheshire countryside, this delightful 18th Century inn has become very popular over the last few years. Owned and run by Frances and Jim Cunningham (their two other pubs, The Swettenham Arms and The Old Packet House, are featured elsewhere in this guide), The Dog Inn is renowned for serving imaginative food, in an informal and traditionally "pubby" atmosphere.

The blackboard menu, a sample of which appears opposite, changes daily but always features 22 main courses. For those after something lighter, there is also a Sandwich Menu.

Directions: About 3 miles south of Knutsford, follow the signs to Over Peover from either the A537 or A50. Apparently it is very easy to find, but I got terribly lost. You stand warned!

### USEFUL INFORMATION

**SERVING TIMES:**
Lunch 12pm-2.30pm (every day)
Dinner 6.30pm-9.30pm (every day)
**SEATING CAPACITY:** 90
**C/C:** V, MC, S, D
**OFF-STREET PARKING:** yes
**CHILDREN:** welcome

**NUMBER OF WINES:** 37
**HOUSE WINE:** £7.20
**RESERVATIONS:** advisable
**OUTDOOR EATING:** yes
**NO SMOKING** area available
**ACCOMMODATION:** 3 rooms
(single £47.50, double £67.50)

# THE BOOT IN LAPWORTH
### Tel: (01564) 782464
Old Warwick Road, Lapworth, Warwickshire, B94 6JU

Parsnip, Coriander & Carrot Soup  £2.75
Chargrilled Bruschetta topped with Smoked Salmon, Scallops
& Crème Fraîche  £5.55
Penne Pasta with roast Garlic, Tomato Chilli
& shaved Parmesan  £3.95 / £7.95
Duck Leg Confit with Rocket & Red Onion Cous Cous  £4.45
Toasted Bagel with Black Pudding, roast Tomato,
Goats' Cheese & Basil Oil  £3.95
Chargrilled Tuna Salad with chargrilled Baby Potatoes
& Red Onion Jam  £4.25 / £8.25
Lamb Kofta skewered on Lemon Grass with Cumin Yoghurt &
Chilli Jam  £4.45 / £8.95

Pork, apple & leek sausages
with smashed new potatoes  £7.95
Polenta gnocchi
with a mozzarella, tomato & basil coulis  £7.95
Baked chicken breast
stuffed with pinenuts, sundried tomatoes, spinach & ricotta
on fresh tomato sauce & buttered potatoes  £8.65
Haddock & salmon fishcakes
with Asian spices & raita & frites  £7.95
Chargrilled calves' liver
with Alsace bacon, onion jam & mash  £10.95
Roast rump of lamb marinated in lemon oil & Mediterranean
spices with fennel dauphinoise potatoes  £9.95
Chargrilled rump steak
with Café de Paris butter & frites  £9.95
Chargrilled veal steak with lemon sage & masala
& buttered potatoes  £10.95

Sticky toffee pud  £3.25
Apple & cinnamon tart tatin  £3.25
Ginger & pear pudding in honey syrup  £3.25

"A tremendously fab, posh country pub set in the delightful windy roads of Warwickshire" is proprietor Paul Salisbury's inimitable description of his pub/restaurant. I shall try to be rather more delicate and simply say that *The Boot* is a traditional country pub with a distinct London feel to it (helped by the fact that the majority of the staff are either from Australasia or South Africa).

The atmosphere is certainly casual, but the food and service are excellent and word has already spread - the place is buzzing. The cuisine is primarily "Pacific Rim", with the menu opposite supplemented by daily specials such as Pan Fried Squid with Salsa Verde and Cous Cous (£4.25) or Grilled Escalope of Salmon with Herb Mash and Thai Red Oil (£9.75).

But a word of caution: try to arrive in style - horseback and helicopters seem to be in vogue here at the moment!

Directions: The Boot can be found in the small village of Lapworth on the Old Warwick Road (now the B4439) which runs parallel to the M40. To get to the village, turn off the A3400 in Hockley Heath and the pub is about one mile down the lane on your left.

## USEFUL INFORMATION

**SERVING TIMES:**
Lunch 12pm-2.30pm (every day)
Dinner 7pm-9.30pm (every day)
**SEATING CAPACITY:** 70 in the restaurant, 60 in the bar area
**C/C:** V, MC, S, D

**NUMBER OF WINES:** 50
**HOUSE WINE:** £8.35
**RESERVATIONS:** advisable, but compulsory at weekends
**OFF-STREET PARKING:** yes
**OUTDOOR EATING:** yes

# LES PLANTAGENETS
### Tel: (01926) 451792
15 Dormer Place, Leamington Spa, Warwickshire, CV32 5AA

## MENU à £18.50

### Potage Cultivateur
Freshly made vegetable soup

### Moules Farcies
Fresh mussels cooked with garlic butter and ricard

### Cassolette de Rognons Grand-Mère
Lambs kidneys cooked with mushrooms, bacon and baby onions
flambéed with brandy and finished with red wine and cream

### Poire d'Avocat au Gambas et Rouille
Fan of avocado served with king prawns and garlic mayonnaise

### Pavé de Boeuf au Poivre
Roast Scotch sirloin of beef with black pepper, Flambée Cognac
and reduced with red wine

### Tresse de Sole et Saumon au Beurre Nantais
Sole and salmon strips baked with shallots
and served with butter and wine sauce

### "Fricassée de Poulet à l'Angevine"
Breast of chicken stuffed with a purée of mushrooms
flambéed with brandy and finished with a Loire wine and cream

### Mignon de Porc au "Calva"
Fillet of pork cooked with apples flambéed in Calvados
served with red cabbage

### Legumes du Marché    ou    Quelques Feuilles
Seasonal vegetables                          Mixed Salad

### Fromages ou Desserts

Les Plantagenets is an oasis of Gallic sentiment in the heart of Leamington Spa. The staff are all French, the menu is in French, the piped music is French, the superb cheeseboard comprises around 30 different varieties of cheese (yes, they're *all* from France) and, to be honest, you sometimes need an interpreter to book. Needless to say, this town house restaurant serves exquisite French cuisine to the highest standard.

Chef Patron Rémy Loth changes his menu every three to four months, or "whenever I feel like it". In addition to the fixed price menu opposite, there is a concise à la carte menu to choose from. Lunchtimes are orientated towards the businessman, with the popular two-course table d'hôte priced at £6.95 and three courses costing just £8.95.

Directions: Les Plantagenets can be found in Leamington Spa Old Town opposite the Pump Rooms.

### USEFUL INFORMATION

**SERVING TIMES:**
Lunch 12pm-2pm (Mon-Fri)
Dinner 7.30pm-10pm (Mon-Sat)
**CLOSED:** Sat lunch & all day Sun
**SEATING CAPACITY:** 40
**C/C:** V, MC, D, AE
**OUTDOOR EATING:** no

**NUMBER OF WINES:** 129
**HOUSE WINE:** £10.50
**RESERVATIONS:** advisable
**OFF-STREET PARKING:** no
**CHILDREN:** welcome
**NO WHEELCHAIR ACCESS**

# COLLEY'S YARD

### Tel: (01543) 416606

26 Bird Street, Lichfield, Staffordshire, WS13 6PR

### STARTERS

Salad of mixed Seafood with a Lemon Balm & Cracked Pepper Dressing £6.50
Roasted Asparagus with Virgin Oil and shavings of Fresh Parmesan £4.50
Chilled Melon Soup £2.50
Hedgerow Salad with Shredded Duck, Sundried Tomato Croutons
and Ginger Dressing £5.00
Red Onion & Blue Cheese Tartlets with a warm Tomato & Cherry Sauce £4.50
Herbed Yorkshire Puddings with Wild Mushrooms, Roasted
Baby Onions and Garlic £5.50
Crab and Avocado Salad with an Elderflower Sauce £5.50
Breast of Chicken bound in Lime Mayonnaise with Baby Vegetables
on Rocket Leaves £4.50
Colley's Yard Soup, please ask for today's special £2.50

### MAIN COURSES

Fillet of Fresh Tuna with a light Scallop and Summer Herb Sauce £12.50
Loin of Lamb in a Pastry Lattice with Apple Mint Sauce £11.50
A trio of Fish Cakes, Crab, Salmon & Hake with a warm
Cucumber and Dill Sauce £11.50
Roast Duckling with Pears poached in Claret £11.50
Pan Fried Sea Bass served on a bed of caramelised Red Cabbage £12.50
Loin of Venison with Wood Mushrooms and Shallots £12.50
A sauté of Pork Fillet with Honey and Pink Grapefruit £10.50
A Fillet of Scotch Beef with Saffron Glazed Potatoes £13.50
Sliced Breast of oven roast Chicken filled with a Leek & Bacon Soufflé £10.50
An assortment of slow roasted Stuffed Peppers with a
Lentil and Coriander Sauce £9.50
Individual Aubergine & Cherry Tomato Tartlets with a Red Pepper Sauce £8.50
Penne Pasta served with our own Pesto Sauce with Sundried Tomatoes,
finished with shavings of Parmesan £7.50
A selection of Fresh Market Vegetables and Potatoes £1.95

### SWEETS £4.25 each

Trio of Sorbets set upon a Hazelnut Meringue with Orange & Lemonade Sauce
Red Fruits with a Lemon Scented Custard
Chocolate Fetish
Minster Pool "Choux" Swans with an Irish Coffee Cream
Baked Brioche and Butter Pudding with Vanilla and Nutmeg
Mascarpone Hearts with Sugar Frosted Berries
Caged Wild Strawberries with Crème Fraîche
A selection of Organic Cheese from the board, and Biscuits

Colley's Yard is situated in a quiet street in the centre of Lichfield. The style and cuisine of this restaurant is a pleasant mix of English and Mediterranean, and it is a very popular place to eat. Wooden floors and tables, and a lovely courtyard out the back (a great place to listen to live jazz in the summer), have helped to create a relaxed and friendly atmosphere. For those who don't suffer from seasickness, there is even a swinging table downstairs in the 'cave'.

The food here is very good. The à la carte menu, an example of which appears opposite, changes seasonally and is complemented by daily specials and a fortnightly set menu (3 courses £11.95) available at lunch and dinner during the week.

Directions: Easily found in Bird Street in the centre of Lichfield, a short walk from the cathedral.

### USEFUL INFORMATION

**SERVING TIMES:**
Lunch 12pm-2.30pm (every day)
Dinner 7pm-10pm (Mon-Sat)
**CLOSED:** Sunday night
**SEATING CAPACITY:** 85
**C/C:** V, MC, S, D, AE
**OUTDOOR EATING:** yes

**NUMBER OF WINES:** 47
**HOUSE WINE:** £8.95
**RESERVATIONS:** advisable
**NO SMOKING** area available
**OFF-STREET PARKING:** no
**CHILDREN:** welcome

# SWINFEN HALL HOTEL
### Tel: (01543) 481494
Swinfen, Nr Lichfield, Staffordshire, WS14 9RS

*A selection from the* **House Menu** *3 courses £22.00*

*A Terrine of Chargrilled Mediterranean Vegetables*
*Served with a Pesto dressing*
*Spinach and Ricotta Cheese Tart*
*On a tomato and leek salad*
*Smoked Duck Consommé Flavoured with Tarragon*
*Served with a confit of duckling*
*Poached Mussel Broth with Shallots and Parsley*
*Finished with fresh cream*
*A Carpaccio of Fresh Tuna*
*With a seaweed salad and herb vinaigrette*

~~~~~~~~~~

*Breast of Free Range Chicken*
*On a bed of creamed leeks flavoured with truffles*
*Roasted Chump of Welsh Lamb and Root Vegetables*
*With a rosemary flavoured "Rösti"*
*Baked FIllet of Codling with a Fondue of Tomatoes*
*Served on a bed of fresh pasta in a saffron cream*
*Tournedos of Prime Aberdeen Beef with a Soufflé of Wild Mushrooms*
*On a rich ruby port jus (supplement £5.50)*
*Grilled Supreme of Scottish Salmon*
*Served with glazed baby onions and a Pinot Noir sauce*

~~~~~~~~~~

*Warm Chocolate and Agen Prune Pudding Soufflé*
*With a delicate fudge sauce*
*Raspberry and Amaretto Fool*
*A light refreshing cream dessert served on Amaretto Biscuits*
*A Rich Dark Chocolate Cheesecake*
*With a White Chocolate Sauce*
*Home-made Pancakes filled with Apples and Winter Berries*
*Accompanied by a Kirsch ice cream*
*Individual Jaffa Cake Pudding*
*Served on an orange syrup*

The grand entrance hall, with its balustraded Minstrels Gallery, provides an impressive welcome to Swinfen Hall, which was completed in 1757 and is now an elegant hotel and restaurant.

The Four Seasons Restaurant, split on two levels, is panelled in oak from floor to ceiling and is celebrated for both its beautiful carvings, attributed to Grinling Gibbons, and its original and exciting cuisine. In addition to the evening House Menu shown opposite, there is a good value lunchtime table d'hôte (3 courses £14.95) and a lounge menu with lighter dishes like sandwiches (from £2.95) and seasonal salads (from £7.95). The Sunday lunch is a traditional roast (3 courses £13.95) with desserts specially selected by the pastry chef.

Directions: Leaving Lichfield on the A38, Swinfen Hall is signposted on the left after about 2 miles. For those after a healthy portion of porridge, bear left to Swinfen Prison!

### USEFUL INFORMATION

**SERVING TIMES:**
Lunch 12.30pm-2pm (Sun-Fri)
Dinner 7.30pm-9pm (Mon-Fri)
      7.30pm-9.30pm (Saturday)
**CLOSED:** Sat lunch & Sun dinner
**SEATING CAPACITY:** 60
**C/C:** V, MC, S, D, AE
**CHILDREN** welcome

**NUMBER OF WINES:** 85
**HOUSE WINE:** £14.50
**NO SMOKING** in the restaurant
**OFF-STREET PARKING:** yes
**RESERVATIONS:** advisable
**OUTDOOR EATING:** yes
**ACCOMMODATION:** 19 rooms
(single £75, double £90)

# THRALES RESTAURANT

### Tel: (01543) 255091

40-44 Tamworth Street, Lichfield, Staffordshire, WS13 6JJ

## A LA CARTE

### TO START

*Fresh mussels with white wine, cream, garlic and onions £4.95*
*Marinade of fresh salmon with dill and sweet mustard sauce £4.95*
*Home-made soup of the day £2.95          Garlic bread £1.50*
*Mixed seafood terrine with gazpacho sauce £4.95*
*Fresh salmon lasagne with chives £4.50*
*Fantail of Galia melon with parma ham £4.95 or passion fruit coulis £3.75*
*Baked mushroom filled with stilton, wrapped in bacon £3.95*
*Tomato and mozzarella samosa with fresh basil and parmesan £4.25*
*Prawn and mushroom thermidor in a filo pastry basket £4.95*
*Mousseline of chicken stuffed with snails in garlic butter £4.75*

### MAIN COURSES

*Fresh fish of the day, see blackboard £9.95*
*Scotch sirloin steak:  Plain £11.50          Scotch fillet steak:   Plain £13.50*
*With garlic butter & parsley £12.50          With garlic butter & parsley £14.50*
*Glazed with stilton & herbs £12.50          Glazed with stilton & herbs £14.50*
*Lamb kleftico with rosemary gravy & baked macaroni in a cheese sauce £9.95*
*Lamb and onion pie with a rosemary pastry £8.95*
*Half a roast corn fed chicken with pancetta, a leek & sweetcorn pancake £10.95*
*Salmon fishcake with fresh dill and tartare sauce £11.95*
*Tournedos of venison on a pâté croûte with wild mushrooms £13.95*
*Old English sausage with bubble and squeak and onion gravy £8.95*
*Rack of lamb with a fresh herb crust and rosemary gravy £13.95*
*Breast of duck with an orange salad, apple sauce, and gravy £13.00*

*Selection of fresh vegetables £2.50  Home-made chips £1.50  Mixed salad £2.00*

### VEGETARIAN

*Breaded, deep fried avocado with a celery and nut salad £9.95*
*Baked leek and mushroom pancake gratinated with gruyère £9.95*
*Cashew nut paella £9.95*

### SWEETS

*Selection of home-made sweets from our menu £3.95 or cheese & biscuits £4.25*
*Coffee and mints £1.50*

Thrales began life rather inauspiciously as an abattoir and butcher's shop in the early 18th Century, but has become one of the area's finest restaurants. Exposed beams and brickwork complement a casual and relaxed atmosphere, where one may enjoy a brasserie style of cuisine. For those after an intimate evening, there are even a few tables in their own rooms!

In addition to the seasonal à la carte menu shown opposite, there are blackboards with weekly specials, which reflect the best of local produce and a mix of dishes from around the globe. Winter specials may include Fresh Crab Beignets with a Ginger and Tomato Coulis (£4.50), and Double Breast of Pheasant with a Celeriac and Parsnip Dauphinoise (£12.50).

During the week there is a good value set menu at £11.50 for three courses (each course has three choices), and the Sunday lunch at £11.95 includes a good choice of starters, a fish course, as well as the traditional main courses. This is very popular and reservations are essential.

Directions: Thrales is easily found on Tamworth Street in the centre of Lichfield.

## USEFUL INFORMATION

**SERVING TIMES:**
Lunch 12pm-1.30pm (every day)
Dinner 7pm-9.30pm (Mon-Sat)
**CLOSED:** Sunday evening
**SEATING CAPACITY:** 85
**C/C:** V, MC, S, D

**NUMBER OF WINES:** 50
**HOUSE WINE:** £9.25
**RESERVATIONS:** advisable
**CHILDREN:** welcome
**OUTDOOR EATING:** no
**OFF-STREET PARKING:** yes

# THE COURTYARD
### Tel: (01584) 878080
Quality Square, Ludlow, Shropshire, SY8 1AR

## *DINNER MENU*

**Roasted Pumpkin Soup  £2.20**
**Salmon Fillet in a Paper Parcel  £4.50**
*with Coriander and Lime*
**Baked Goat's Cheese with Cashew Nuts  £4.50**
*and Bramble Chutney*
**Crab and Lemongrass Tart  £4.75**

**********

**Fillet of Beef with Garlic Mash  £11.50**
*Mushrooms and Guinness Sauce*
**Fillet of Lamb with Creamed Leeks  £9.50**
*on a Port and Rosemary Sauce*
**Pork Fillet with Sage and Onion Stuffing  £8.75**
*on a Madeira Sauce*
**Chicken Breast with Morels  £8.95**
*and a Sherry Cream Sauce*
**Brill  £11.50**
*with a Mussel and Saffron Sauce*
**Potato Pancakes  £6.50**
*with Spicy Chick Peas and Tomatoes*

**********

**Crème Brûlée  £3.50**
*with Star Anise*
**Orange Pancakes with Apples and Sultanas  £3.50**
*and Cinnamon Ice Cream*
**Chocolate Hazelnut Tart  £3.50**
*served with Clotted Cream*

**********

**Selection of Cheeses  £3.50**

The Courtyard is an anomaly. It resembles a restaurant (but is far less formal with a great atmosphere generated by its open plan kitchen), a café (though the food is far too good), a brasserie, a coffee house, a bistro and tea rooms. The only thing I can say for certain is that it is not a country pub.

Coffee and cakes are served from 10am until 3pm. Lunch is then available every day except Sunday and is written up on the blackboard. Dishes might include Broccoli & Cheddar Soup (£1.95), Toasted Muffin with Poached Eggs & Basil Hollandaise (£3.50), Baked Crab with Lime & Ginger (£5.50), Salmon & Leek Crumble (£5.95), Smoked Chicken Hashcakes (£5.95) and Crème Brûlée with Cranberries & Orange (£2.90).

The dinner menu, an example of which appears on the opposite page, changes monthly but is only served on Thursday, Friday and Saturday evenings. Despite its slight identity problem, the Courtyard has become extremely popular and you will need to telephone them in advance to make a reservation.

Directions: Hidden away in Quality Square, off the main Market Square.

### USEFUL INFORMATION

**SERVING TIMES:**
Lunch 12pm-2pm (Mon-Sat)
Dinner 7pm-9pm (Thurs-Sat)
**CLOSED:** dinner (Sun-Wed) and
Sunday lunch
**SEATING CAPACITY:** 30
**C/C:** none accepted

**NUMBER OF WINES:** 22
**HOUSE WINE:** £8.50
**RESERVATIONS:** very advisable
**OUTDOOR EATING:** yes
**OFF-STREET PARKING:** no
**CHILDREN:** welcome
**NO SMOKING** area available

# THE MERCHANT HOUSE
### Tel: (01584) 875438
Lower Corve Street, Ludlow, Shropshire, SY8 1DU

## Menu
*£26 per person*

saffron and asparagus risotto
grilled red mullet fillet with dill and crème fraîche
pheasant and chestnut soup with soft spices
warm lobster in salads with sesame dressing

-----

grilled turbot with mustard and cucumber sauce
saddle of venison with fresh goat's cheese gnocchi
rack of lamb and sweetbreads with potato and olive cake
bourride of free range chicken
*braised in saffron and red pepper stock, then thickened with garlic mayonnaise*

-----

raspberry crème brûlée
trio of chocolate desserts
caramel and apple tart
iced prune and armagnac parfait
cheese - Vacherin, Gorgonzola and Wigmore

-----

coffee - tea - tisane  £2.50

The Merchant House is a Jacobean building at the northern end of Ludlow, home to Shaun and Anja Hill who cook and serve respectively for a maximum of twenty-four diners on five evenings and two lunchtimes each week.

Shaun Hill is renowned as one of this country's most creative cooks and The Merchant House as one of our top restaurants. The food is an eclectic mix, based on sound cooking techniques and personal taste rather than any particular country's cuisine. The unifying feature is a core of excellent ingredients, organic where feasible and carefully chosen where not.

The menu has a fixed price and generally gives a choice of four dishes at each course. These change daily according to market availabilities and will feature whatever fish, meat and vegetables were best that day. Service attempts to be both informal and reasonably efficient. There are no dress codes or similar pomposities to contend with.

It is worth noting that reservations are compulsory. If you simply turn up unannounced, you will not be offered a table even if there is one available.

Directions: The Merchant House is situated 400 yards to the north of the town centre. Lower Corve Street itself forks off Corve Street at the bottom of the hill.

## USEFUL INFORMATION

**SERVING TIMES:**
Lunch 12.30pm-2.30pm (Fri & Sat)
Dinner 7pm-9.30pm (Tues-Sat)
**CLOSED:** lunch (Sun-Thur) and
all day Sunday & Monday
**SEATING CAPACITY:** 24
**C/C:** V, MC, S, D, AE

**NUMBER OF WINES:** 70
**HOUSE WINE:** £12.50
**RESERVATIONS:** compulsory
**NO SMOKING** in the restaurant
**OUTDOOR EATING:** no
**OFF-STREET PARKING:** no

# OAKS RESTAURANT

### Tel: (01584) 872325

17 Corve Street, Ludlow, Shropshire, SY8 1DA

## £20

### Roast Dumpling of Chicken
with Morels in Gewurtztraminer Sauce

### Breast of Wood Pigeon
with Boudin Blanc and Onion Ravioli on Balsamic Vinegar Dressing

### Grilled Fillet of Dover Sole
on a Purée of Sugar Snap Peas with Tomato Butter Sauce

### Toasted Hazelnut Pâté
with Artichoke Salad and Parmesan Tuiles

*****

### Roast Loin of Bodenham Venison
on Celeriac Dauphinoise with Braised Chestnuts and Caramelised Port Sauce

### Sauté Breast of Guinea Fowl
on Roast Tomatoes and Fennel

### Trelough Duck served in Foie Gras Sauce
with a Confit of Duck Leg on Winter Vegetables

### Steamed Escalope of Turbot
on Wild Mushrooms and Leeks with Scallop Sauce

*****

### Toffee Mousse with Caramelised Bananas and Banana Sorbet

### Brandy Chocolate and Cherry Torte

### Baked Plum and Almond Pastry with Vanilla Sauce

### Cheese
Stinking Bishop - Shropshire Blue - Reblochon
(Cheese as an extra course £4.50)

*****

### Coffee and Petits Fours  £1.95

Oaks Restaurant occupies the ground floor of a 17th Century building that was once a coaching inn called *The Eagle*. The name derives from the very special 17th Century oak-panelling that adorns the restaurant.

The restaurant is run by chef/proprietor Ken Adams, a charming man with strong views about the quality of the produce used in his cooking. The fixed price menu changes daily and is accompanied by a list of the suppliers of the fresh food used in the dishes, an unusual feature to say the least.

Ken tries to use organic produce wherever possible (free-range, hand-reared Berkshire Pork from Mr. R. Tudge!) and the fish on the menu will have been caught the previous night and driven up from Cornwall. The results of this attention to detail are excellent, dishes with traditional ingredients cooked in a modern style, though not necessarily modern English.

"For example, I will not mix fish with vanilla," he says. Please tell me if he ever does!

Directions: Oaks Restaurant is conveniently situated just down the hill from the famous Feathers Hotel in the centre of the town.

### USEFUL INFORMATION

**SERVING TIMES:**
Lunch - bookings only (for 4 or more)
Dinner 7pm-9.30pm (Tues-Sun in the
    summer, Tues-Sat in the winter)
**CLOSED:** Sun evening in the winter,
every lunchtime & all day Monday
**SEATING CAPACITY:** 30

**NUMBER OF WINES:** 60
**HOUSE WINE:** £9.95
**RESERVATIONS:** compulsory
**OUTDOOR EATING:** no
**NO SMOKING** in the restaurant
**C/C:** V, MC
**OFF-STREET PARKING:** yes

# CHIANG RAI
### Tel: (0161) 237 9511
16 Princess Street, Manchester, M1 4NB

## Starters

**Tod Man Pla £5.45**
Spicy fish cakes with lime leaf
**Yam Talay £6.95**
Hot & sour seafood salad
**Nam Prik Ong £4.95**
Spicy northern dip with crispy prawn crackers
**Tempura £5.45**
Prawns or crab claws with vegetables, deep fried in batter
**Gratong Gai £4.95**
Batter cases with curried chicken and vegetable filling
**Tod Man Khao Pohd £4.45**
Sweetcorn cakes with fresh cucumber pickle
**Satay Het Hom £5.45**
Mushroom satay, marinated and grilled on skewers served with peanut sauce & fresh pickle
**Yam Wun Sen £5.95**
Hot & sour vermicelli salad
**Po Pia Tod £4.45**
Thai vegetarian spring rolls

## Soups

**Po Taek £5.95**
Hot and sour seafood
**Gai Tom Ka £4.95**
Chicken, coconut cream & galangal soup
**Tom Yam Het £4.45**
Hot and sour mushroom soup
**Gaeng Jud Taeng Gwa £4.25**
Clear soup with cucumber and egg
**Gaeng Jud Wun Sen £4.25**
Clear soup with vermicelli

## Main Dishes

**Nua Nam Man Hoy £6.95**
Beef stir-fried with oyster sauce
**Preow Wan £6.45**
Sweet and sour pork or chicken with vegetables
**Poysien £6.95**
Seven ingredients stir-fried with vermicelli, chicken and prawn
**Gaeng Pa £6.95**
Beef, pork or chicken in jungle style curry with krachai
**Gung Pad Krapow £7.95**
Spicy prawns stir-fried with basil and chilli
**Pla Preowan £9.50**
Deep fried fish, sweet & sour sauce
**Pla Samui £9.50**
Samui island style hot and sour fish with ginger and pineapple
**Makua Pat Prik £5.95**
Fresh aubergine with chilli and basil in yellow bean sauce
**Man Jian £5.95**
Fried potato with ginger and mushroom sauce
**Tao Hou Pat Pack £5.95**
Spicy stir-fried beancurd with chilli and vegetables
**Gaeng Kari £5.95**
Potato curry, flavoured with galangal and lemon grass
**Laab Na £6.95**
Beef, pork or chicken in blackbean sauce over soft noodles
**Pad Thai £6.95**
Thai style special fried noodles with beancurd, dried prawns, ground peanuts and bean sprouts

Chiang Rai is a basement restaurant which enjoys a convenient location in the centre of Manchester. Popular, busy and friendly, the order of the day here is authentic, high quality Thai cuisine served at a very reasonable price.

There is an extensive à la carte with a vegetarian menu supplement, and a small selection of dishes are featured opposite. Good value set menus are also available (£42.60 for two, and £85.50 for four), and business lunches are proving to be very successful (choose from set meals priced between £5 and £9 for two courses and coffee).

The owners and staff pride themselves on their in-depth knowledge of Thai cuisine, and you are encouraged to let them select and prepare a special surprise meal for you to enjoy. This is a great way to discover new favourites!

Directions: Easily found in the centre of Manchester, just off St Peter's Square in Princess Street.

## USEFUL INFORMATION

**SERVING TIMES:**
Lunch 12pm-2pm (Mon-Sat)
Dinner 6pm-11pm (every day)
**CLOSED:** Sunday lunch
**SEATING CAPACITY:** 75
**C/C:** V, MC, S, D, AE, DC

**NUMBER OF WINES:** 29
**HOUSE WINE:** £8.95
**CHILDREN:** welcome
**OFF-STREET PARKING:** no
**RESERVATIONS:** advisable
**OUTDOOR EATING:** no

# SIMPLY HEATHCOTES
## Tel: (0161) 835 3536
Elliot House, 151 Deansgate, Jackson Row, Manchester, M3 3WD

## appetizers & starters
Starters are available as main course portions

**BOWL OF OLIVES £2.00**

**PLATTER OF OLIVES, TAPENADE, HOUMOUS, ROUILLE £3.50**

**Brandade of Salt Cod 'on Toast'**
*with poached egg and shallot butter £4.50*

**Cream of Cauliflower Soup**
*with stilton crust and truffle oil £3.50*

**Bubble and Squeak**
*with pan-fried chicken livers,, lentil dressing £4.50*

**Pressed Terrine of Pigs Cheek**
*beetroot chutney and sauce gribiche £4.50*

**Risotto of Wild Mushrooms**
*with parmesan crisps and thyme £4.50*

**Salad of Lancashire Cooked Breakfast**
*black pudding, mushrooms, haricot beans and poached egg £4.50*

**Salad of Crab**
*with celery and apple, walnut sauce £5.50*

**Tagliatelle of Tomato Confit**
*with aubergine caviar, aubergine crisps and chardonnay dressing £4.50*

**Salad of Pan-fried Mackerel**
*with celeriac, mussels and mustard £4.50*

**Potted Duck**
*with green beans, artichokes and toasted brioche £4.50*

## main courses
All main courses are accompanied by their own garnish

**Breast of Goosnargh Corn-fed Chicken**
*with buttered cabbage, glazed with Lancashire cheese £13.00*

**Pan-fried Cod**
*with kedgeree and curry oil £11.50*

**Char-grilled Calves Liver**
*onion tart, mashed potatoes and red wine sauce £14.50*

**Baked Ruby Snapper**
*with bouillabaisse and rouille £14.50*

**Baked Lobster "En Papillote"**
*with fennel, star anise and orange, curly endive and chicory salad £25.00*

**Char-grilled Rib-eye of Beef**
*with parsley glaze, garlic mashed potatoes and leeks £14.00*

**Roast Breast of Duck**
*with pan-fried foie gras, spiced pear, sherry vinegar and shallot sauce £16.00*

**Roast Best End of Lamb**
*with faggots and peas, fondant potatoes, mint gravy £16.00*

**Baked Vegetarian Polenta**
*"croque monsieur", candied red peppers and deep-fried spinach £11.00*

**Braised Pork Shank**
*with crushed potatoes, butter beans and sage sauce £12.50*

**Pan-fried Halibut**
*with lemon, butter and capers £11.50*

Simply Heathcotes is a stylish new restaurant which, in a matter of months, has become *the* place to eat and be seen eating in Manchester. The post-modern interior establishes a wonderful atmosphere of fashion and dynamism, with bright colours, polished floors, high ceilings and Philippe Starck furniture all helping to excite the senses.

As one expects of Paul Heathcote, the cuisine here is superb. In the evening there is a seasonal à la carte (shown opposite) which also features delicious desserts such as Caramelised Apple Cheesecake and Bread and Butter Pudding (each £5.50). A pre-theatre table d'hôte (3 courses £18.50) is served between 6pm and 7pm and offers a choice of three dishes with each course.

At lunch there is a very good value table d'hôte (2 or 3 courses for £9.50 and £11.50 respectively) and this changes daily.

Directions: Easily found in the centre of Manchester, a short walk away from St. Peter's Square and the G-Mex Centre.

## USEFUL INFORMATION

**SERVING TIMES:**
Lunch 11.45am-2.30pm (Mon-Sat)
Dinner 6pm-11pm (Mon-Sat)
All day 12pm-9pm (Sunday)
**SEATING CAPACITY:** 150
**C/C:** V, MC, S, D, AE
**DRESS CODE:** smart casual

**NUMBER OF WINES:** 40
**HOUSE WINE:** £10.25
**OFF-STREET PARKING:** no
**CHILDREN:** welcome
**RESERVATIONS:** advisable
**OUTDOOR EATING:** no

# THE FRENCH RESTAURANT
### Tel: (0161) 2363333
Holiday Inn Crowne Plaza Midland, Peter Street, Manchester, M60 2DS

## SAMPLE MENU

### AMUSE GOURMANDS

~~~~~

### CANAPES

~~~~~

### DELICATE PAN FRIED SCALLOPS
with truffle, mixed leaves, shaved parmesan and marjoram

~~~~~

### BABY TURBOT MEUNIERE
served with gallet potato and fennel

~~~~~

### BREAST OF GRESSINGHAM DUCK AND CONFIT LEG
with oyster mushrooms, cabbage and potato gallette

~~~~~

### POACHED PEAR
with vanilla flavoured brioche and a caramel sauce

~~~~~

### COFFEE AND SWEETMEATS

~~~~~

### £32.50 PAR PERSONNE

The Holiday Inn Crowne Plaza Midland is an elegant Edwardian hotel situated in the centre of Manchester. It has three restaurants covering a range of styles and tastes, from the modern French cuisine of the formal French Restaurant, to the Trafford Room with its generous buffet and carvery, and finally the brasserie food of the more relaxed Wyvern Bar.

Head Chef Bernard Faraut has helped to establish The French Restaurant as one of the finest in the country. In addition to the Menu Gastronomique (featured opposite) which changes weekly, there is an extensive à la carte.

Directions: Easily found in the centre of Manchester on the corner of St. Peter's Square, a short walk from the train station and the G-MEX Exhibition Centre.

### USEFUL INFORMATION

**SERVING TIMES:**
Dinner 7pm-11pm (Mon-Sat)
**CLOSED:** Sunday
**SEATING CAPACITY:** 50
**C/C:** V, MC, D, AE, DC
**NO SMOKING** area available
**CHILDREN:** welcome
**OUTDOOR EATING:** no

**NUMBER OF WINES:** 160
**HOUSE WINE:** £13.50
**OFF-STREET PARKING:** no
**RESERVATIONS:** advisable, and compulsory Friday and Saturday
**DRESS CODE:** smart
**ACCOMMODATION:** 303 rooms (B&B single & double from £135)

# THE MOSS NOOK RESTAURANT
## Tel: (0161) 437 4778
Ringway Road, Moss Nook, Manchester, M22 5WD

### *First Courses*

*Quickly pan-fried chicken livers with crispy bacon and apples flamed
with calvados, served on a warmed salad £8.25*

*A selection of salmons, each served cold with individual sauces £9.25*

*Fresh asparagus & lobster salad served cold with a raspberry vinaigrette £12.95*

*Quickly sautéed fresh scallops set around crispy fried cabbage with
a red pepper coulis £11.95*

*Mild goats cheese, toasted and set on a slightly warmed salad £8.95*

*Foie gras sliced, pan-fried and served on a lightly sauced thin croûton £12.95*

*Asparagus wrapped in fresh salmon and served hot with a béarnaise sauce £9.25*

*Goujons of chicken breast, marinated in yoghurt, coriander and turmeric,
served hot on salad leaves with a garlic and honey sauce £8.75*

### *Main Courses*

*Traditionally roasted breast of duckling served with roast garlic,
onions and a light apple sauce £18.95*

*Grilled fillet of British beef, topped with mousse de foie gras
with a madeira and truffle sauce £19.25*

*Rack of local lamb, coated with a herb and almond crust,
served pink, with a red wine sauce £18.95*

*Simply grilled loin of veal, with a tomato and tarragon sauce £18.95*

*Roast breast of chicken, filled with mushrooms on a creamy morille sauce £17.95*

*Grilled loin of venison, served pink, with a sultana and pepper sauce £19.50*

*Grilled medley of fish and shellfish served with basmati rice
and béarnaise sauce £18.95*

A mere stone's throw from runway seven of Manchester Airport, The Moss Nook Restaurant enjoys an enviable reputation as a culinary oasis in somewhat unlikely surroundings. The interior is ornate, yet inviting, with a rich burgundy decor, lace tablecloths and gentle lighting all helping to establish a tone of understated luxury which never becomes impersonal.

The cuisine is Modern English with touches of classical French. A seasonal à la carte (shown opposite) is supplemented by a luncheon menu (5 tasting courses £16.95), and the now famous "Menu Surprise" (8 tasting courses from canapes to coffee £29.50) which is offered in the evening. Excellent home-made sweets may feature temptations such as Chocolate and Chestnut Parfait or Toffee and Nut Tart with Ice Cream.

Directions: Moss Nook is 1 mile from Manchester Airport. Leaving the M56 at junction 5, approach the roundabout and follow signs for Wilmslow / Moss Nook. The restaurant is one mile along on the left.

## USEFUL INFORMATION

**SERVING TIMES:**
Lunch 12pm-2pm (Tues-Fri)
Dinner 7pm-9.30pm (Tues-Sat)
**CLOSED:** Saturday lunch and
all day Sunday and Monday
**SEATING CAPACITY:** 65
**C/C:** V, MC, D, AE, DC
**DRESS CODE:** smart preferred

**NUMBER OF WINES:** 100
**HOUSE WINE:** £9.50
**OFF-STREET PARKING:** yes
**RESERVATIONS:** advisable
**OUTDOOR EATING:** yes
**ACCOMMODATION:** a cottage
(£140 for 2, including dinner)

# THE SWAN

### Tel: (01948) 663715

Marbury, Cheshire, SY13 4LS

## STARTERS

Garlic Bread £1.50
Home-made Parsnip and Apple Soup £1.75
Garlic Mushrooms £3.35
Deep Fried Feta Cheese with Cranberry Sauce £2.50
Chef's Liver Pâté £2.95
King Prawns with Garlic Mayonnaise £4.50
Smoked Salmon with a Honey and Mustard Dressing £4.50
Swan Prawn Cocktail £4.50

## MAIN COURSES

Chicken Breast cooked with Apricots and Brandy
in a Cream Sauce £6.50
Braised Steak in a Green Peppercorn Sauce £7.50
Home-made fresh Salmon Fish Cakes £5.85
Seafood Pancake £5.85
Beef cooked in Red Wine with Smoked Bacon and Baby Onions £6.50
Wild Rabbit Casserole with Parsley Dumplings £6.50
Local Game Pie £6.50
Home-made Steak and Kidney Pie £5.95
Minty Lamb Casserole £5.95
Pork Normandy cooked with Apples, Sage and Calvados £6.95
Plaice Roulade, filled with Prawns, Mushrooms and Lemon £7.25
Pigeon Pie £6.50
Spinach and Mushroom Pancakes £5.50
Mushrooms and Pasta in a Stilton Sauce £5.50
Cauliflower and Stilton Flan £5.50

## HOME-MADE DESSERTS £2.50

Coffee and Tia Maria Cheesecake, Boozy Raspberry Brûlée
Chocolate and Almond Torte, Bread and Butter Pudding
Coffee Meringue with Coffee Ice Cream, Sticky Toffee Pudding
Hot Winter Fruit Salad, Chocolate and Rum Pots

Rebuilt in 1884, The Swan at Marbury is a picturesque pub, nestling in beautiful Cheshire countryside, a short walk from the Llangollen branch of the Shropshire Union Canal.

Ann and George Sumner have had The Swan for twenty-five years and specialise in serving delicious home-made food. The menu opposite appears on the blackboard and changes daily. This is supported by a fixed menu. At lunchtime, sandwiches and filled jacket potatoes are also available. There is a separate children's menu as well.

Directions: Marbury is about three miles north of Whitchurch, and is signposted off the A49.

### USEFUL INFORMATION

**SERVING TIMES:**
Lunch 12pm-2pm (Tues-Sun)
Dinner 7pm-9pm (Sun-Fri)
      7pm-10pm (Saturday)
**CLOSED:** Monday lunch, except Bank Holidays
**SEATING CAPACITY:** 60
**C/C:** V, MC, S, D, AE, DC

**NUMBER OF WINES:** 24
**HOUSE WINE:** £8.95
**RESERVATIONS:** advisable at weekends
**NO SMOKING** in one bar
**OFF-STREET PARKING:** yes
**OUTDOOR EATING:** yes
**CHILDREN:** welcome

# GOLDSTONE HALL
### Tel: (01630) 661202
Goldstone, nr Market Drayton, Shropshire, TF9 2NA

## STARTERS

Pheasant and pickled walnut terrine with first cold press
olive oil and balsamic vinegar £6.25
Chicken and lemon grass soup with chillies, ginger
and coriander £3.95
Mussels steamed open with garlic, cream and wine £4.95
Seared chicken livers and smoked bacon in a sherry cream
with black pudding £5.95
Six Loch Fyne oysters with Sevruga caviar and lime £9.95
Home peat smoked chicken with avocado, vine tomatoes
and pine nuts £6.50
Quenelle of pike mousse with Cognac cream £6.75
"From our cellar" spiced beef with beetroot chutneys, green tomato
relish and warm bread £5.50
Roast pigeon with puy lentils and caramelised shallots £5.75

## MAIN COURSES

Seared calf's livers with onions, garlic mash and meat juices £15.75
Roast fillet of beef with Irish stout glaze, crispy leeks,
truffle and oil £18.95
Grilled breast of duckling with prunes, garnacha vinegar
and Cassis £18.25
Lightly baked salmon with a lemon sabayon £16.25
Grilled lobster with garlic and herbs. Half £18.95  Whole £32.50
Aubergine, cherry tomato, roast pepper and avocado charlotte
with pesto cream £13.25
Fried breast of chicken with oyster mushrooms,
thyme and cream £16.95
Sautéed monkfish tail with coarse pepper, tomato
and aniseed nage £17.95
Casserole of venison with quince and rosti potato £17.25

\*\*\*\*\*

Goldstone Hall was built as an English home in 1390 by Hugh de Golstan, and is now an elegant hotel restaurant with an enviable reputation for fine cuisine. It enjoys a rural location on the outskirts of a tranquil Shropshire village, only a short drive from Hawkstone, Hodnet Hall, Ironbridge Gorge and other local delights.

The food served is excellent, and those particularly impressed may be tempted to learn more about the talents of chef Carl Fitzgerald-Bloomer by attending one of the Masterclasses that he holds here (£27.50 including a three course lunch).

The evening à la carte menu, a sample of which appears opposite, changes daily along with a formidable dessert menu, and at lunch the "Squire's Tiffin" menu is offered. The Sunday lunch (3 courses £14.50) is very popular, so be sure to make a reservation.

Directions: Goldstone Hall is about five miles south of Market Drayton. Follow the brown signs to Goldstone Hall Gardens from the A529 or A41.

### USEFUL INFORMATION

**SERVING TIMES:**
Lunch 12pm-2.30pm (every day)
Dinner 7.30pm-10pm (every day)
**SEATING CAPACITY:** 50
**C/C:** V, MC, S, D, AE
**OFF-STREET PARKING:** yes
**OUTDOOR EATING:** yes

**NUMBER OF WINES:** 73
**HOUSE WINE:** £10.35
**RESERVATIONS:** advisable
**CHILDREN:** welcome
**ACCOMMODATION:** 8 rooms
(single £59.95, double £83.50)

# OLD COLEHURST MANOR
### Tel: (01630) 638833
Colehurst, Sutton, Market Drayton, Shropshire, TF9 2JB

## *Elizabethan Evening Menu*

### *Fish Mould*
*An amazing flavoured mould made from fish,*
*cream and wine. 15th Century recipe*
*or*
### *Lentil Mould (Vegetarian)*
*A vegetarian dish adapted from a 15th Century recipe*

*\*\*\**

### *Split Leek Soup*
*Delicious 14th Century leeks in wine,*
*served with home-made bread*

*\*\*\**

### *Olive of Pork*
*Pieces of tender pork stuffed with a medieval forcemeat of*
*herbs and onions, cooked in apple cider*
*or*
### *Forced Mushrooms (Vegetarian)*
*Mushrooms stuffed with a medieval forcemeat*
*of almonds and herbs*

*Served with selected vegetables*

*\*\*\**

### *Honey and Saffron Tart*
*Served to Henry IV at his coronation on 13th October 1399.*
*Accompanied with vanilla cream and honey spice syrup*

*\*\*\**

### *Selection of local cheeses*
### *Platter of fresh fruit*
### *Coffee*
*Served with home-made petits fours*

Old Colehurst Manor is unique. Lovingly and authentically restored from ruin by Bjorn and Maria Teksnes, this beautiful, candle-lit 17th Century home has become an invitation to step back in time. Whether your visit is for a weekend or an evening, you cannot help but be captivated by the romantic sense of history that surrounds you.

All the dishes served here date from the 14th to the 19th Century, and are the result of five years intensive research by Maria. The set menu changes every day and by prior arrangement will cater for any special dietary requirements - apparently vegetarians are not particularly enamoured by the prospect of Charles I's Spit Roast Venison!

The menu featured opposite is part of a full evening of 17th Century splendour, including a mulled wine reception, a half bottle of mead, and entertainment provided by Elizabethan musicians (£52.50 per person).

Directions: About 3 miles south of Market Drayton, follow the brown signs to The 17th Century Experience from the A41.

## USEFUL INFORMATION

**SERVING TIMES:**
Lunch 12pm-2pm (every day)
Dinner one sitting at 8pm (every day)
**SEATING CAPACITY:** 30
**C/C:** V, MC, S, D, AE, DC
**DRESS CODE:** 17th Century preferred!
Dress hire available at £10 pp
**OUTDOOR EATING:** yes

**NUMBER OF WINES:** 120
**HOUSE WINE:** £10
**NO SMOKING** in the Manor
**OFF-STREET PARKING:** yes
**RESERVATIONS:** compulsory
**ACCOMMODATION:** 7 rooms
(B&B £50 to £175)

# RIBER HALL

## Tel: (01629) 582795

Matlock, Derbyshire, DE4 5JU

*A selection from the Dinner Menu*

**TO COMMENCE**

**Fresh Asparagus served with Baked Brie and a Warm Basil Vinaigrette**

**Warm Foie Gras on a bed of Crunchy Fine Beans and a Madeira Sauce
lightly scented with Raspberry Vinegar**

**Riber Hall Salad of Green Leaves with a Confit of Duck in Filo Parcels,
Apples and Pine Kernels with a Pink Peppercorn Jus**

**Smoked and Marinated Salmon with a Grain Mustard Dressing**

**Terrine of Pork Fillet with a Spicy Mushroom and Coriander Chutney**

**MAIN COURSES**

**Fillet of Beef wrapped in Bacon and Herbs topped with Baked Goats
Cheese and served with a Provençale Sauce**

**Roasted Breast of Duck glazed with Honey and served
with a Piquant Kumquat Sauce**

**Chicken Boudin, lightly curried on a bed of Crunchy Vegetables and a
light Calvados and Apple Sauce**

**Tian of Lamb on Spinach Tomatoes and Mushrooms with
Garlic and White Wine Sauce**

**Medallion of Roasted Monkfish on a bed of Samphire and a Trio
of Pepper Coulis**

**Fish Platters set on Creamed Potatoes on a Chive Beurre Blanc**

*Chef's selection of Vegetables or Salad of your choice
is included in the price*

**Three Course Dinner £32
Two Course Dinner £27**

Riber Hall enjoys a wonderfully secluded location on the borders of the Peak District in the picturesque village of Riber. An Elizabethan manor house set in its own grounds with a delightful walled garden, orchard and conservatory, the atmosphere here is one of understated luxury and pure romance.

The restaurant is divided into two beautiful dining rooms, each reflecting different periods in the history of Riber Hall, and the cuisine is appropriately rich, indulgent and quite worthy of its outstanding reputation.

At luncheon a seasonal table d'hôte is offered (2 or 3 courses for £13 and £16 respectively) which features a good selection of five dishes with each course. In the evening there is a seasonal à la carte (shown opposite), complemented by an excellent wine list and mouth-watering desserts such as Baked White Chocolate Cheesecake with Caramelised Apple and a Strawberry Sauce, or Iced Coconut Parfait with a Dark Rum Pastry and a Pineapple Sauce.

Directions:  From Matlock head east on the A615. At Tansley turn right by the Murco filling station into Alders Lane, and proceed 1 mile up a winding lane to a T-junction. Riber Hall drive is straight ahead.

### USEFUL INFORMATION

**SERVING TIMES:**
Lunch 12pm-1.30pm (every day)
Dinner 7pm-9.30pm (every day)
**SEATING CAPACITY:** 40 in the main restaurant, 30 in the other
**C/C:** V, MC, S, D, AE, DC
**OUTDOOR EATING:** no
**NO SMOKING** in main restaurant

**NUMBER OF WINES:** 150
**HOUSE WINE:** £12.75
**RESERVATIONS:** advisable
**OFF-STREET PARKING:** yes
**CHILDREN:** over 10 welcome
**DRESS CODE:** jacket and tie
**ACCOMMODATION:** 11 rooms
(single fr £87.50, double fr £108)

# THE MANOR HOTEL
### Tel: (01676) 522735
Main Road, Meriden, Solihull, West Midlands, CV7 7NH

### *First Course*

*Grilled Tuna with Niçoise Salad and Watercress Oil £7.95*
*Parfait of Chicken and Calves' Livers with Toasted Brioche £4.50*
*Scottish Smoked Salmon with Fresh Lime and Black Pepper £7.95*
*Pork and Smoked Bacon Terrine with Caesar Salad £4.95*
*Prosciutto with Seasonal Melon and Fruits £5.95*
*Gâteau of Avocado Pear with Prawns £4.95*
*Shellfish Bisque Scented with Brandy £3.95*

### *Main Course*

*Lamb Fillet Roasted with Oven-dried Tomatoes and Basil Jus £14.95*
*Rosette of Beef Fillet with a Horseradish Mousse,*
*Potato and Celeriac Rosti and Baby Yorkshire Puddings £16.95*
*Breast of Corn-fed Chicken, Pan Fried with Chargrilled Vegetables,*
*Wild Mushroom Jus £14.50*
*Escalope of Calves' Liver, Pan Fried with Fresh Spinach*
*and Caramelised Red Onions £13.95*
*Breast of Duck Roasted with Star Anise Sauce, Chive Mash*
*and Exotic Fruit Gâteau £14.95*
*Fillet Steak Plain Grilled or Glazed with a Café de Paris Butter £15.95*

*Dover Sole Grilled with a Lemon and Herb Butter £17.95*
*Fillet of Monkfish Pan Fried with Chinese Five Spice,*
*Fennel Mash and Red Wine Sauce £13.95*
*Roast Fillet of Brill with Stir Fry Vegetables and a Plum Sauce £14.95*
*Fresh Salmon Lightly Grilled with King Prawns, a Plum Tomato*
*and Coriander Butter Sauce and Crisp Leeks £14.50*
*Roast Cod Fillet, Mushy Peas, Spiced Tomato and Pulses £13.50*

*Spinach and Egg Tagliatelle with Water Chestnuts, Fresh Asparagus*
*and Mushrooms in a Parmesan Cream £9.95*
*Confit of Mediterranean Vegetables with Mozzarella Cheese and Herb Mash £9.95*
*Fresh Mushrooms Pan Fried with Artichokes and Peppers*
*in a Paprika Cream Sauce with Wild Rice £10.95*

### *A Selection of Desserts*

Set in the village of Meriden, said to be the exact centre of England, The Manor Hotel is a handsome Georgian building that provides a haven of tranquillity away from the Midlands' motorway network. Presided over by Executive Chef Peter Griffiths, the hotel's Regency Restaurant provides a perfect blend of traditional English and French cooking.

In additional to the seasonal à la carte menu featured on the opposite page, the restaurant offers a fixed price menu which changes daily, with the option of two courses (priced at £13.95 for lunch and £14.95 for dinner) or three courses (£16.95 for lunch, £17.95 for dinner), with a choice of four or five dishes at each course.

Directions: The Manor Hotel is located in Meriden, signposted from the A45 Coventry to Birmingham road, approximately 6 miles to the west of Coventry.

### USEFUL INFORMATION

**SERVING TIMES:**
Lunch 12pm-2pm (Sun-Fri)
Dinner 7pm-9.45pm (every day)
**CLOSED:** Sat lunch
**SEATING CAPACITY:** 100
**C/C:** V, MC, S, D, AE, DC
**NO SMOKING** in the restaurant
**OFF-STREET PARKING:** yes

**NUMBER OF WINES:** 40
**HOUSE WINE:** £10.95
**RESERVATIONS:** advisable
**OUTDOOR EATING:** no
**CHILDREN:** welcome
**ACCOMMODATION:** 74 rooms
(D,B&B from £55 p.p. per night)

# THE RAVEN HOTEL

### Tel: (01952) 727251

Barrow Street, Much Wenlock, Shropshire, TF13 6EN

## A Selection from the A La Carte Menu

*Smoked Chicken and Cured Meat Salad  £4.60*
*A tossed salad of chicken, parma ham & pastrami,*
*with walnuts & a honey dressing*
*Tian of Avocado and Crab  £4.25*
*Avocado, apple & watercress bound with mayonnaise & cromer crabmeat,*
*layered between discs of tomato*
*Assiette of Seafood  £5.20*
*Fresh salmon with greenlip mussels, monkfish & tiger prawns,*
*surrounded by a crisp citrus salad & sauce vierge*
*~ ~ ~*
*Fresh Sea Trout with Smoked Salmon and Dill Ravioli  £12.25*
*Pan-fried sea trout set on a celeriac purée with a smoked salmon & dill ravioli*
*& a lemon grass scented sauce*
*Roast Saddle of Rabbit with Etuvée of Asparagus and Leeks  £13.00*
*Wild saddle of rabbit served with herb risotto, rosemary jus*
*& etuvée of asparagus & leeks*
*Chestnut, Spinach and Leek Crumble  £10.50*
*Roast chestnuts, baby spinach & leeks served on a base of creamed potato,*
*topped with a horseradish crumble & surrounded by a vegetable butter sauce*
*Magret of Duck on Braised Savoy Cabbage  £12.75*
*Pan-fried duck breast with a black peppercorn & honey coating,*
*braised Savoy cabbage & port sauce*
*Feuilleté of Pigeon with Wild Mushrooms  £11.90*
*Roast wood pigeon served in a feuilleté of puff pastry*
*with a wild mushroom, thyme & bacon sauce*
*Medallions of Beef "Penny Brookes"  £16.80*
*Pan-fried medallions of beef fillet presented on a bed of braised lentils du puy,*
*surrounded by a Madeira, truffle & pied de mouton sauce,*
*garnished with a garlic confit*
*~ ~ ~*
*Pan-fried Brioche  £4.25*
*Our own brioche pan-fried in caramel & served with caramelised hazelnuts*
*& rum & raisin ice cream*
*Warm Tart of Prunes & Armagnac  £4.25*
*An individual tart of prunes & armagnac with crème anglaise*
*A Light Mousse of Coffee & Pistachio  £4.25*
*A light mousse flavoured with coffee & pistachio resting on a tuile biscuit*
*& served with a coffee bean sauce*

The Raven Hotel is a privately owned 17th Century country town hotel with a fascinating connection to the modern day Olympic Games and a collection of prints and memorabilia relating to this history are on display. Originally a fine coaching inn, combined in later years with what are believed to be ancient alms-houses and a medieval hall, the hotel boasts character and charm of past times with beamed ceilings and open fires.

The à la carte dinner menu featured opposite is supported by the luncheon menu with dishes such as Salmon, Prawn and Avocado Salad (£6.90), Ham, Chicken and Mushroom Hotpot (£6.50), Mushrooms and Walnut Crêpe (£5.65), Char-grilled Brochette of Chicken (£7.75), Seafood Tagliatelle (£6.90) or Pheasant Salmis (£8.00).

Directions: The Raven Hotel is situated at the corner of Barrow Street and St. Mary's Road in the centre of Much Wenlock, approximately 5 miles to the south-west of Telford.

## USEFUL INFORMATION

**SERVING TIMES:**
Lunch 12pm-2pm (every day)
Dinner 7pm-9.30pm (every day)
**SEATING CAPACITY:** 40
**C/C:** V, MC, S, D, AE, DC
**NO SMOKING** in the restaurant
**OFF-STREET PARKING:** yes

**NUMBER OF WINES:** 65
**HOUSE WINE:** £10.00
**OUTDOOR EATING:** yes
**RESERVATIONS:** advisable
**ACCOMMODATION:** 15 rooms
(B&B single fr £48, double fr £85)

# THE CROWN AT MUNSLOW
### Tel: (01584) 841205
Munslow, Shropshire, SY7 9ET

## *DINNER MENU*

### STARTERS

**Mushrooms Bovary** in garlic butter, topped with grilled soft cheese  **£3.50**
**Soupe de Poisson** served with rouille, croutons & a clove of garlic  **£4.50**
**King Prawn & Prawn Gratin** in cream & mushroom sauce  **£5.25**
**Country Salad** with tomatoes, olives & red beans  **£2.75**
**Escargots** in shells with garlic butter & parsley  **£4.50**
**Tomato Salad** in olive oil & tarragon vinegar  **£2.25**
**Moules Marinières** in white wine and herbs  **£3.95**

### MAIN COURSES

**Fillet Oyster** grilled and stuffed with mushrooms & smoked oysters  **£13.95**
**Lamb Picardie** ground lamb, onion & tomatoes, topped with garlic mushrooms
& soft cheese  **£7.50**
**Beef Maison** strips of rump pan-fried with mushrooms in garlic butter  **£8.50**
**Beef Marie** strips of rump with mushrooms in a cream sauce  **£9.50**
**Pork Dijon** stripped pork in a Dijon mustard sauce  **£8.50**
**Vegetable Gratin** in a continental cream & onion sauce  **£6.75**
**Chicken Tarragon** in a white wine & cream sauce  **£8.50**
**Poulet Calvi** flambéed in brandy with tomato, olives, bacon & garlic  **£9.25**
**Plaice Mediterranean** stuffed with prawns in a lobster & cream sauce  **£9.25**
**Trout Grenobloise** grilled with herb butter, lemon & capers  **£8.50**
**Moules Marinières** main course in white wine and herbs  **£7.50**
**Salmon Normandy** with mushrooms in a cream sauce  **£8.95**

### HOME-MADE THAI SPECIALITIES

**Tom Yum Soup** hot & sour prawn soup  **£4.50**
**Thai-style Tiger Prawns** in garlic, ginger & coriander  **£9.95**
**Red Chilli Chicken** hot & spicy  **£6.95**
**Thai Green Curry** with coconut milk & Thai spices  **£6.95**

The Crown at Munslow is a traditional country pub in the heart of beautiful Corvedale. Its austere Georgian façade disguises an original Tudor interior with all the oak beams, nooks, crannies and ghost stories you would expect. Already a Hundred House and court, an inn was installed in the ground floor during the late 17th Century.

Meals are prepared to order, so there may be a slight delay during busy periods. Choices include standard bar food (served at lunchtimes), fresh fish, vegetarian dishes, Thai dishes, children's options and a French-influenced menu (an example of which is shown opposite) available every evening. Watch out for the owner's micro-brewery, with at least two of Vic's home-brewed bitters normally on offer at the bar!

Directions: The Crown is situated in the centre of the village of Munslow, which lies about 8 miles north of Ludlow on the B4368 Much Wenlock to Craven Arms road.

## USEFUL INFORMATION

**SERVING TIMES:**
Lunch 12pm-2pm (every day)
Dinner 7pm-9.30pm (every day)
**SEATING CAPACITY:** 40 in the dining room, 30 in the bar area
**C/C:** V, MC, S, D, AE

**NUMBER OF WINES:** 33
**HOUSE WINE:** £7.95
**RESERVATIONS:** advisable
**OUTDOOR EATING:** yes
**CHILDREN:** welcome
**OFF-STREET PARKING:** yes

# CHURCHE'S MANSION
## Tel: (01270) 625933
Hospital Street, Nantwich, Cheshire, CW5 5RY

*Starters*

*A warm salad of home smoked & grilled salmon, seared scallops, baby
leeks & asparagus bound in an 8 year old balsamic vinegar dressing
with crème fraîche & crisp angel hair*

*Tartlet of halibut brandade, spinach & soft hen's egg coated with a
lemon mousseline sauce & topped with keta caviar*

*Tian of avocado, red pepper & goats cheese with crostinis of beetroot,
served with curly endive & pickled walnuts*

*A winter game broth with chestnut dumplings, root vegetables,
haricot beans & fresh herbs*

*A confited terrine of guinea fowl & Cumbrian ham with pearls of
melon, spiced pear & figs*

*A Jerusalem artichoke, globe artichoke, rocket & dandelion salad
flavoured with truffle oil, served with shavings of Pecorino cheese*

*Pot roasted quail filled with liver stuffing on a red wine risotto with
crisp pancetta with Madeira & shallot sauces*

*Main Courses*

*Honey roasted breast of Lunsdale duck with onion marmalade, crisp
pastry of the leg & a port sauce flavoured with cassis*

*Fillet of Welsh lamb rolled with fresh herbs & mushroom duxelle,
wrapped & baked in puff pastry served on a truffle Madeira sauce*

*Seared fillet of Aberdeen Angus beef with an oxtail crepinette on braised
du pey lentils, winter vegetables purée, topped with a potato &
horseradish galette*

*Poached breast of corn fed chicken with buttered tarragon fettucini, a morel
mushroom sauce & fresh asparagus*

*Seared sea bass with fresh black olive crust, basil purée & a capsicum coulis*

*A pithivier of assorted mushrooms & nuts bound in a spinach &
hummus brandade on cherry tomato & herb sauces*

Served with a selection of seasonal vegetables & potatoes or a selection of lightly
dressed salad leaves

Churche's Mansion was built in 1577 by Thomas Cleese for Richard and Margery Churche as a symbol of their wealth. A fine example of a Merchant's house and an outstanding piece of decorated half-timbered architecture, it is now an elegant and popular restaurant.

At dinner there is an excellent table d'hôte menu (£26.75 for 3 courses and a sorbet) which changes every month. An additional fish course, chosen from the starters, may be taken for an additional £5.95.

The luncheon menu is also a monthly table d'hôte (£13.95 or £17.25 for 2 or 3 courses respectively), supplemented by a dish of the day.

Directions:  Nantwich is about 7 miles west of Junction 16 of the M6. Follow the A500 towards Nantwich over all roundabouts. At T-Junction turn right, and the car park is on the left immediately before the next roundabout.

## USEFUL INFORMATION

**SERVING TIMES:**
Lunch 12pm-2.30pm (Tues-Sun)
Dinner 7pm-9.30pm (Tues-Sat)
**CLOSED:** Sunday evening and all
day Monday, and 2 weeks in January
**SEATING CAPACITY:** 55
**C/C:** V, MC, S, D, DC

**NUMBER OF WINES:** 120
**HOUSE WINE:** £10.50
**RESERVATIONS:** compulsory
**CHILDREN** welcome at lunch
**OUTDOOR EATING:** yes
**OFF-STREET PARKING:** yes
**NO SMOKING** in the restaurant

# ROOKERY HALL

## Tel: (01270) 610016

Worleston, Nantwich, Cheshire, CW5 6DQ

**DINNER MENU £37.50**

Cream of Curried Parsnip and Apple Soup

Pithivier of Goats Cheese nested on a bed of Leeks and Tomatoes
with Shallot and Truffle Dressing

Carpaccio of Monkfish with Onion Marmalade and Orange

Escalope of Foie Gras on Saffron Brioche with a Raisin,
Apple and Muscat Butter

A salad of Smoked Pigeon and Figs on a Walnut Relish

**MAIN COURSES**

Fillet of Beef topped with Horseradish Mousseline and Celeriac
on a Port Sauce

Local Pheasant Supreme with Chestnuts, Smoked Bacon
and Garlic Confit

Steamed Fillets of Lemon Sole on Spinach Pasta
and Red Pepper Essence

Supreme of Chicken on Saffron Risotto and Wholegrain Mustard Sauce

Roast Rack of Lamb with Wild Mushrooms, Herb Dumplings
and Creamed Leeks

A Casket of Puff Pastry and Forest Mushrooms
on a bed of Tarragon Creamed Leeks

'Tart Tatin' of Shallot, Thyme and Leek on a Cider Grape Sauce

**CHEESE COURSE**

**DESSERTS**

Cafetière Coffee and Petits Fours

Rookery Hall was built in 1816 and enjoys a tranquil setting in its own 200 acre grounds. A recent change of ownership has not affected the high standards of cuisine and service that one has come to expect of this elegant hotel and restaurant. The personal greeting as you alight from your car is only an indication of the luxurious attention to come!

The extensive dinner menu, a sample of which appears opposite, changes regularly to incorporate seasonal specialities. Delicious home-made desserts may include Rich Sticky Toffee Pudding with Cornish Clotted Cream, or an Iced Banana Parfait between layers of Crisp Meringue on a Fresh Colombian Coffee Sauce. The table d'hôte luncheon menu (3 courses £17.50) offers a good choice of dishes, which change daily.

Directions: Follow the road signs towards Worleston, and Rookery Hall is signposted off the B5074 about 2 miles north of Nantwich.

## USEFUL INFORMATION

**SERVING TIMES:**
Lunch 12.30pm-2.30pm (Mon-Sat)
    12.30pm-3pm (Sunday)
Dinner 7pm-10pm (every day)
**SEATING CAPACITY:** 35
**C/C:** V, MC, S, D, AE, DC
**OUTDOOR EATING:** yes

**NUMBER OF WINES:** 148
**HOUSE WINE:** £12
**RESERVATIONS:** advisable
**NO SMOKING** in the restaurant
**OFF-STREET PARKING:** yes
**ACCOMMODATION:** 45 rooms
(single £110, double £150)

# THE OLD THREE PIGEONS

**Tel: (01743) 741279**

Nesscliffe, Shropshire, FY4 1DB

## TODAY'S FISH BOARD SPECIALS

### APPETISERS

Platter of Oak Smoked Scottish Salmon  £5.50
Sauté of Tiger Prawns with Garlic  £4.50
Salad of Welsh Smoked Trout  £4.50
Ripe Avocado with Mixed Shellfish  £4.50
Oak Smoked Haddock, Cream & Spinach  £4.50
fi Dozen Fresh Bluenose Oysters  £5.50

### MAIN COURSES

Fillet of Whitby Cod  £6.95
Fillet of Scottish Haddock  £7.50
Fillet of Irish Plaice  £6.95
Wing of Irish Skate  £6.95
Whole Pink Trout  £9.50
Fillet of Cornish Hake  £9.50
Greenland Halibut Steak  £12.50
Whole Welsh Sea Bass  £12.50
Whole Cornish Lemon Sole  £10.95
Fillet of Sea Trout  £9.50

*Sauces: Beurre Blanc, Provençale, Cream & Mushroom £1.50 extra*

### A SMALL SELECTION OF OTHER DISHES AVAILABLE

Crisp Roast Duck with Sweet Parsnip Mash  £13.95
Breast of Garlic Chicken with a Sweet Pepper Sauce  £9.95
Prime Sirloin Steak grilled with Pork & Stilton  £12.95
Creamed Mushroom Risotto with Grilled Zucchini  £7.50
Greek-style Marinated Vegetables on a Herb Squeak  £7.50
Baked Avocado with Mozzarella & Field Mushrooms  £7.50

The Old Three Pigeons is difficult to miss. This former coaching inn, the oldest part of which was built in 1405, is situated on the A5 opposite Nesscliffe Hill, reputedly where Humphrey Kynaston (the Robin Hood of Shropshire) plied his trade. But it is the collection of used military hardware on the front lawn that really catches your eye as you drive past.

When I paid a visit, the flavour of the moment was a Russian tank. Plans were afoot to add an old Dennis fire engine from the Windsor Fire Services - the only tender not to make it to the great fire at Windsor Castle, apparently because they couldn't find the key!

The menus here are all written up on the blackboards and change regularly. The proprietors own a trawler and pride themselves on offering one of the largest selections of fresh fish in the Midlands (but carnivores will not be disappointed as there is also a huge choice of grills from £7.30 to £13.95).

Directions: The Old Three Pigeons is situated on the main A5 road, midway between Shrewsbury and Oswestry.

### USEFUL INFORMATION

**SERVING TIMES:**
Lunch 12pm-2.30pm (every day, summer)
        12pm-2.30pm (Tues-Sun, winter)
Dinner 6pm-10pm (every day, summer)
        7pm-10pm (Tues-Sat, winter)
**CLOSED FOR FOOD:** all day Monday and Sunday evening in the winter
**OUTDOOR EATING:** yes

**NUMBER OF WINES:** 30
**HOUSE WINE:** £4.50
**RESERVATIONS:** advisable
**CHILDREN:** welcome
**C/C:** V, MC, S, D
**SEATING CAPACITY:** 60 in one restaurant, 30 in the other
**OFF-STREET PARKING:** yes

# MISCHA'S RESTAURANT
### Tel: (01952) 820636
128 High Street, Newport, Shropshire, TF10 7BH

### Appetisers

**Home-made Soup of the Day served with freshly baked bread**
**£3.50**
**Scottish Haddock with grilled Welsh Rarebit**
**served with Plum Tomatoes**
**£3.50**
**Sliced Smoked Duck Breast and Quails Eggs nestled on**
**Italian lettuce leaves with a Raspberry Vinaigrette**
**£4.00**
**Chicken Liver Mousse with Bloody Mary Sauce and Melba Toast**
**£3.90**
**Poached Pear stuffed with Cream Cheese and Pineapple**
**served on a bed of Sweet Peppers and Avocado**
**£3.80**

### Entrées

**Tenderloin of Pork with Orange and Basil Sauce**
**£11.75**
**Roast Loin of Lamb with a herb scented crust,**
**Candid Shallots and a light Lamb Jus**
**£14.50**
**Chicken, Apricot and Cardamon Parcels**
**served with a light Korma Sauce**
**£10.95**
**Stuffed Breast of Pigeon wrapped in Cabbage,**
**served with a Game Sauce**
**£10.50**
**Beef Olives with Black Pudding served with Onion Gravy**
**£12.00**
**Fillet of Salmon with a Saffron Fondue served with seasoned Mussels**
**£11.95**
**Fillet of Trout with Garlic, Spinach and Prawns cooked with White**
**Wine, Lemon Juice, Butter and Flaked Almonds**
**£10.50**
**Mischa's House Fillet stuffed with Avocado, wrapped in Back Bacon**
**and complemented with a Red Wine and Mushroom Sauce**
**£15.50**

*All served with a selection of freshly prepared Market Vegetables or salad*

It has only taken five years for the proprietors, Georgina and Mischa, to establish their restaurant as one of the most popular in the area, and it is easy to see why. The building itself is the Old School House, with a rather grand Georgian frontage and an elegantly decorated interior, and the atmosphere catches just the right mix of a relaxed brasserie and a more refined restaurant.

However it is Mischa's excellent cooking that ensures you will not leave here disappointed. A monthly à la carte (as shown opposite) is supplemented by daily specials and wonderful home-made desserts such as Hazelnut & Praline Meringue, or Almond & Amaretto Cheesecake with Caramelised Banana (£3 each). There is also a blackboard featuring lighter, brasserie style dishes which are especially popular at lunchtime, but also available in the evening. These change daily.

A traditional roast lunch is offered every Sunday (3 courses £11.50).

Directions: Easily found in the centre of Newport, which lies 5 miles north of Telford on the A41.

### USEFUL INFORMATION

**SERVING TIMES:**
Lunch 12pm-3pm (Tues-Sun)
Dinner 7pm-10pm (Tues-Sat)
**CLOSED:** Sunday evening and all day Monday
**SEATING CAPACITY:** 50
**C/C:** V, MC, S, D, AE, DC
**NO SMOKING** area available

**NUMBER OF WINES:** 34
**HOUSE WINE:** £8.25
**CHILDREN:** welcome
**RESERVATIONS:** advisable
**OUTDOOR EATING:** yes
**OFF-STREET PARKING:** yes
**ACCOMMODATION:** 3 rooms
(B&B single £40, double £55)

# NUNSMERE HALL

### Tel: (01606) 889100

Tarporley Road, Oakmere, nr Northwich, Cheshire, CW8 2ES

**A selection from the evening A La Carte**

### *Starters*

*A Fine Tart of Finnan Haddock*
*with poached egg, smoked salmon and caviar £8.50*

*Terrine of Local Rabbit*
*with foie gras and pencil leeks £11.00*

*Tortelini of Salmon and Sea Scallop*
*with roast bell pepper and basil essence £11.00*

*A Soup of Split Peas*
*and flaked ham knuckles £7.50*

*Winter Salad Tartare*
*with red mullet and fried vegetables £8.50*

*Wood Pigeon and Globe Artichoke Galette*
*with shallot and juniper choucroute £8.00*

### *Main Courses*

*Steamed Brill with Thai Spice,*
*wilted greens and lobster tempura £19.50*

*Grilled Seabass*
*with dauphinoise of fennel and tomato confit £20.00*

*Pot Roast Guinea Fowl*
*with marjoram, crushed parsnips and woodland mushrooms £18.00*

*Scotch Beef Fillet*
*with vegetable fondants and rich oxtail gravy £21.00*

*"Osso Bucco" Braised Veal*
*with langoustine tails, garden herbs and light pan juices £21.00*

*Gressingham Duck with Preserved Leg Pastry*
*and port sauce £19.50*

Nunsmere Hall was built around 1900 as a private home for Sir Aubrey Brocklebank, chairman of the famous Brocklebank Shipping Line. Enjoying a spectacular and unique setting in the middle of a 60 acre lake, it is now an elegant hotel which effuses an atmosphere of understated luxury.

The gourmet cuisine served in The Garden Restaurant has a modern French style with oriental influences. The excellent lunchtime table d'hôte menu (2/3 courses for £16.95 and £19.50 respectively) changes daily, and there is a terrace menu for those after a less substantial meal.

In the evening an extensive à la carte is offered (see opposite), together with a separate vegetarian menu featuring dishes such as Crispy Vegetable Salad (£7) and Tortellini of Goats Cheese (£16). Desserts are all £7.50 and may include Baked Clafoutis, Sugar Frosted Vanilla Risotto, or Roast Butterscotch Pear. Every Sunday there is a special table d'hôte menu.

Directions: Nunsmere Hall is about five miles south-west of Northwich, and is signposted off the stretch of A49 between the A54 and A556 crossroads.

### USEFUL INFORMATION

**SERVING TIMES:**
Lunch 12pm-2pm (every day)
Dinner 7pm-10pm (every day)
**SEATING CAPACITY:** 50
**C/C:** V, MC, S, D, AE, DC
**OUTDOOR EATING:** yes
**RESERVATIONS:** advisable

**NUMBER OF WINES:** 140
**HOUSE WINE:** £13.25
**NO SMOKING** in the restaurant
**OFF-STREET PARKING:** yes
**ACCOMMODATION:** 32 rooms
(single fr £105, double fr £140)

# THE HUNDRED HOUSE HOTEL
### Tel: (01952) 730353
Bridgnorth Road, Norton, nr Shifnal, Telford, Shropshire, TF11 9EE

## STARTERS

| | |
|---|---|
| **Cawl** - Welsh broth garnished with lamb & leeks | £4.50 |
| **Spiced Pumpkin Soup** with rum, raisin & warm almonds | £4.50 |
| **Coriander Cured Salmon** with lime, peanuts & beansprouts | £5.95 |
| **Duo of Bruschetta** - Italian garlic toast topped with sweet peppers, anchovies & marinated Mediterranean vegetables | £5.25 |
| **Marbled Terrine of Venison, Wild Boar & Local Game Birds** with plassey chutney and warm rolls | £4.75 |
| **Lightly Curried Tomatoes, Lemon Smoked Haddock** topped with tzatziki and deep fried leeks | £4.95 |

## MAINS

| | |
|---|---|
| **Cumin Roast Rack of Shropshire Spring Lamb** with chick pea and aubergine salad with spicy ginger & chilli salsa | £14.95 |
| **Breast of Hereford Duck** with green peppercorn sauce, rosti potato and spinach | £14.95 |
| **Charlotte of Roast Carrot & Coriander Mousse** wrapped in courgette, served with tomato coulis and baked shallots | £9.50 |
| **Thai Chicken Curry** with pickled cucumber, chilli, coriander and rice | £10.50 |
| **Breast of Chicken** stuffed with port & orange mousse on a port cream sauce with stuffed prunes | £13.95 |
| **10oz Sirloin Steak** garnished with sautéed mushrooms, tomato and mixed leaves | £12.95 |
| **Casserole of Venison** with soft polenta, beetroot jam and deep fried parsnips | £11.50 |
| **Pork Chop** marinated with lemon & sage, served with caponata | £9.95 |
| **Braised Shank of Lamb** with caper & mint sauce | £12.50 |
| **Whole Dover Sole** with anchovy butter, lemon and parsley | £16.50 |
| **Warm Salad of Spinach**, polenta, roast tomatoes, goats cheese | £9.50 |

## DESSERTS

| | |
|---|---|
| **Banana & Walnut Pudding** with butterscotch sauce & vanilla ice cream | £4.50 |
| **Pears Poached in Red Wine** served with cinnamon & raisin ice cream | £4.50 |
| **Coffee & Walnut Cheesecake** served with fresh cream & chocolate sauce | £3.50 |
| **Apple Pie** with custard | £3.50 |
| **Profiteroles** with hot chocolate sauce | £3.50 |

The Hundred House is a family-run hotel with an emphasis on good food and personal service. The main building is of Georgian origins and the interior has old quarry-tiled floors, exposed brickwork, beamed ceilings and oak-panelling. The hotel has been added to and modernised at various times, particularly during the 19th Century to cope with the expanded trade arising from the Industrial Revolution which started at nearby Ironbridge.

The à la carte menu featured opposite is served in the Dining Room, supplemented by 8 or 9 specials that change daily. The hotel also boasts a Brasserie and a separate bar menu, where you can enjoy the same high standard of cooking but in a slightly less formal atmosphere.

The traditional Sunday lunch is extremely popular, with two and three courses priced at £10.95 and £13.95 respectively.

Directions: The Hundred House Hotel is located in the centre of the village of Norton on the A442 Telford-Bridgnorth road, approximately 5 miles to the south of Telford.

### USEFUL INFORMATION

**SERVING TIMES:**
Lunch 11.30am-2.30pm (every day)
Dinner 6pm-10pm (Mon-Sat)
　　　7pm-9pm (Sunday)
**SEATING CAPACITY:** 50 in the dining room, 30 in the brasserie
**C/C:** V, MC, S, D, AE
**OFF-STREET PARKING:** yes

**NUMBER OF WINES:** 50
**HOUSE WINE:** £9.60
**RESERVATIONS:** advisable, but compulsory at weekends
**OUTDOOR EATING:** yes
**CHILDREN:** welcome
**ACCOMMODATION:** 10 rooms
(B&B single £65, double from £79)

# THE HINDS HEAD
## Tel: (01630) 653014
Main Road, Norton in Hales, nr Market Drayton, TF9 4AT

### A selection from the A La Carte

#### STARTERS

**Home-made Soup of the Day £1.90**
Served with a wholemeal roll and croutons
**Chicken Indienne £3.95**
Tender chicken bound in a creamy curried mayonnaise, accompanied by rice,
poppadoms and mango chutney
**Crispy Coated Brie £4.25**
Wedges of cheese coated in a mix of nuts and breadcrumbs, deep fried and served with a port
wine sauce
**Garlic Mushrooms £3.95**
Button mushrooms in a creamy sauce of garlic, white wine and cream,
served with French bread
**Traditional Prawn Cocktail £3.95**
Served with brown bread and butter
**Spinach Pancake £3.75**
Leaf spinach wrapped in a light pancake and topped with rich cheese sauce
**Barbecued Spare Ribs £3.85**
Coated in a sweet and sour sauce served with garlic bread and side salad

#### MAIN COURSES

**Traditional Steak and Kidney Pie £5.25**
Topped with a shortcrust pastry
**Lamb Shrewsbury £8.65**
Lamb cooked in a rich sauce of onions, mushrooms and redcurrants, with a hint of rosemary
**Home-made Lasagne £5.45**
Accompanied by garlic bread and salad
**Home-baked Roast Ham £5.85**
Accompanied by new potatoes and salad
**Fillet of Salmon £7.95**
Gently poached and served with a light creamy lemon and dill sauce
**"Posh" Fishcakes £6.95**
Our own recipe, fresh fillet of salmon and smooth potato, seasoned, breadcrumbed and deep
fried, then served on a lemon sauce
**Deep Fried Cod £4.95**
Served with mushy peas
**Chargrilled Chicken £5.65**
Chicken breast cooked on the barbecue, with a salad and a dish of our barbecue sauce

The Hinds Head, rather helpfully described by its owner John Griffiths as simply "very old", is a delightfully warm and inviting 18th Century coaching inn, with exposed beams and open fires.

The à la carte menu is extensive (only a small selection is shown opposite) and includes charcoal grills (from £9.65) and a choice of vegetarian dishes such as Home-made Nut Roast (£5.85) and Spinach Pancakes (£4.95). In addition to traditional pub meals like jacket potatoes (from £3.25) and sandwiches (from £2.25), there are also 'Light Bites' such as the Hinds Head Club Sandwich (£4.45) and Barbecued Sardines (£4.95).

The menu changes twice a year to incorporate the most popular specials that have appeared on the daily blackboard menu. This always offers a choice of at least 3 additional starters and 6 main courses, which may include tempting dishes such as Tarragon and Tomato Chicken (£7.65) or Lemon Sole Roulade (£7.95).

Directions:  The Hinds Head is easily found in the pretty village of Norton in Hales, which is signposted off the A529, A51, and B5415 a few miles north of Market Drayton.

## USEFUL INFORMATION

**SERVING TIMES:**
Lunch 12pm-2pm (Tues-Sun)
Dinner 6.30pm-9.30pm (Tues-Sat)
**CLOSED:** Sunday evening and all
day Monday for food
**SEATING CAPACITY:** 90
**C/C:** not accepted

**NUMBER OF WINES:** 14
**HOUSE WINE:** £7.95
**RESERVATIONS:** advisable
**CHILDREN** welcome at lunch
**OUTDOOR EATING:** yes
**OFF-STREET PARKING:** yes

# SEBASTIAN'S

**Tel: (01691) 655444**

45 Willow Street, Oswestry, Shropshire, SY11 1AQ

## A SELECTION FROM THE A LA CARTE MENU

### LES ENTREES

Bisque de Fruits de Mer  £4.50
*A seafood soup flavoured with tomatoes, prawns & mussels*
Champignons au Roquefort  £4.25
*Mushrooms sautéed in garlic, cream & roquefort cheese*
Assiette de Saumon Fumé  £7.95
*Slices of smoked Scottish salmon, timbale of potato & red onion salad*
Carpaccio de Boeuf Fumé  £7.50
*Slices of lightly smoked beef fillet, topped with roast aubergines, slices
of parmesan cheese, garnished with tossed french leaves*

### PLATS POUR LES VEGETARIENS

Mille Feuilles aux Champignons des Bois  £14.50
*A layered herb pancake filled with wild mushrooms & leeks,
served on a chive & cream sauce*
Brochette de Légumes  £11.95
*A brochette of mixed vegetables in breadcrumbs,
served on an olive oil, tomato & coriander sauce*

### LES VIANDES

Filet d'Agneau au Croûte des Herbs  £17.50
*Fillet of lamb with a garlic & herb crust,
served with a tomato sauce, garnished with stuffed courgettes*
Magret de Canard au Miel et Poivre  £16.50
*Breast of duck caramelized with honey & black peppercorns, served on
a blackcurrant sauce, garnished with sarladaise potatoes & shallots*
Filet de Boeuf Wellington  £18.95
*Fillet of beef with a duxelle of mushrooms
& a slice of foie gras, wrapped in puff pastry*

### LES POISSONS

Escalope de Saumon à la Ciboulette  £12.95
*Thin slices of salmon served on a chive & cream sauce*
Nage de Poisson au Coriandre et Carotte  £18.95
*Poached Dover sole, salmon, Dublin Bay prawns,
served on a coriander & carrot sauce*

Sebastian's started life in the mid-eighties as a bistro and has gradually matured into an excellent French restaurant, adorned with regional posters and with piped French music creating a relaxed and informal atmosphere. The 16th Century half-timbered building still appears to be growing, with the recent addition of three ensuite bedrooms (priced very competitively) to complement the dining area.

The extensive à la carte menu (a selection from which is featured opposite) is supplemented by a fixed price menu (priced at £16.95 for three courses) which changes each month. There is generally a choice of three dishes at each course, plus a small appetiser of the day.

For those of you in more of a hurry, the small luncheon à la carte menu offers dishes such as Fish Soup (£3.50), Savoury Crêpes (£3.75), Deep-fried Calamari with a Garlic Dip (£2.95), French Open Sandwiches (from £3.75) or Fillet Steak and Chips (£12.95). Alternatively, the monthly table d'hôte can be served, as long as you give prior notice.

Directions: On the one-way system from the town centre, follow the sign for Selatyn. Sebastian's is 150yds from Oswestry town centre on the left hand side.

## USEFUL INFORMATION

**SERVING TIMES:**
Lunch 12pm-2pm (Wed-Fri)
Dinner 6.30pm-10pm (Tues-Sat)
**CLOSED:** Tues & Sat lunch, and all day Sun & Mon
**SEATING CAPACITY:** 40
**C/C:** V, MC, S, D, AE
**OUTDOOR EATING:** yes

**NUMBER OF WINES:** 75
**HOUSE WINE:** £9.50
**RESERVATIONS:** advisable
**OFF-STREET PARKING:** yes, but for residents only
**ACCOMMODATION:** 3 rooms (single £30, double £38 room only)

# THE WALLS

### Tel: (01691) 670970

Welsh Walls, Oswestry, Shropshire, SY11 1AW

## DINING ROOM MENU

Lentil & Tomato Soup  £3.50
Duck Liver & Smoked Bacon Salad  £4.75
Rosette of Smoked Salmon with Prawns  £6.00
Fan of Melon with Raspberry Sorbet & Strawberries  £4.50
Duck & Parma Ham Salad with Orange & Pinenuts  £4.95

\* \* \* \* \*

Crispy Roast Duck with Orange & Mint Glaze  £17.00
Fillets of Salmon & Sole with White Wine Cream Sauce  £16.50
Roast Rack of Lamb with Caramelised Onions & Madeira  £16.00
Breast of Pheasant with a Port & Grape Sauce  £15.50
Fillet of Beef with Bacon, Mushrooms & Tarragon  £18.00
Garganelli with Field Mushrooms, Cumin & Shropshire Blue  £10.00

Vegetables and Potatoes

\* \* \* \* \*

Chocolate & Tia Maria Mousse  £4.00
Almond Meringue & Coffee Cream  £4.00
Orange & Treacle Tart  £4.00
Crème Brûlée  £4.00

\* \* \* \* \*

CHEESE BOARD  £5.00

\* \* \* \* \*

COFFEE AND CHOCOLATES  £2.00

If you have never visited The Walls, a former school converted into an "eating house and dining rooms", nothing can prepare you for the imminent assault on your senses. From the outside you could easily walk past, wondering why the children aren't causing mayhem in the playground. Then you step inside. Hundreds of rival restaurateurs must be tearing what little is left of their hair out in pure envy - because this place is absolutely stunning!

Indeed the owners, Geoff and Kate, recently won a "prestigious" award, beating none other than Le Manoir aux Quatr' Saisons into second place (admittedly it was in the Restaurant Loo of the Year category, but they all count!). Let's just say that the fact that they don't have a no-smoking policy is not an issue - the ceilings are so high and the tables in the dining room are so far apart that you probably wouldn't notice anyway.

In addition to the Dining Room menu opposite that changes daily, the Wine Bar area offers a wide variety of dishes such as Giant Mussels with Garlic Butter (£3.75), Pasta Carbonara (£5.50), Salmon and Thai Green Curry (£8.50), Seafood Salad (£8.50) and Fillet Steak in a Red Wine Sauce (£14.00).

Directions: The Walls can be found on the north side of Cae Glas Park.

## USEFUL INFORMATION

**SERVING TIMES:**
Lunch 12pm-3pm (every day)
Dinner 7pm-10.30pm (Mon-Sat)
**CLOSED:** Sunday evening
**SEATING CAPACITY:** 200
**C/C:** V, MC, AE
**OFF-STREET PARKING:** yes

**NUMBER OF WINES:** 100
**HOUSE WINE:** £8.00
**RESERVATIONS:** advisable, but
compulsory at weekends
**CHILDREN:** welcome (there are
baby-changing facilities)
**OUTDOOR EATING:** yes

# WILLIAM HARDING'S HOUSE

### Tel: (01785) 712955

Mill Street, Penkridge, Staffordshire, ST19 5AY

### *DINNER MENU*

*Seared Breast of Pigeon on a Sherry and Liver Sauce*

*Classical Soup of Tomato with Seasonal Vegetables Laced with Calvados Cream*

*Fanned Slivers of Smoked Breast of Duck with a Soft Gooseberry Mousse*

*A Melée of Summer Fruits with a Blackcurrant Coulis*

*Young Lamb's Sweetbreads on a Port and Shallot Sauce with Marinated Figs*

\* \* \*

*A Crisp Breast of Gressingham Duck Sliced onto a Peppercorn Sauce*

*Fillet of Chicken with Langoustines on a Piquant Lime Sauce with Thyme*

*Baked Strudel of Salmon and Halibut on a Sauce Variation*

*Roast Filleted Partridge on a Redcurrant Sauce*

*Medallion of Grilled Marinated Swordfish on Potato and Red Onion Salad*

*Fresh Seasonal Vegetables to Accompany*

\* \* \*

*Coffee and Vine Fruit Soufflé*
*Rich Mincemeat Jalousie*
*Dark Chocolate and Orange Parfait*
*Raspberry Roulade*
*or*
*A Selection of British Rural Cheeses*
*Tornegus - Pencarreg - Smoked Cumberland*
*Swaledale - with Fruits and Celery*

*Coffee or Tea with Chocolates*

*Our Set Price for Dinner is Nineteen Pounds Fifty Pence*

William Harding's House, a grade II listed building dating back to the late 16th Century, is tucked away in a quiet corner of Penkridge. Divided into two small rooms, each with oak beamed ceilings and their own open fireplaces, the atmosphere is delightfully intimate.

Using only original stocks and fresh, local produce wherever possible, Eric and Fiona Bickley prepare and serve wonderful home-made food. The table d'hôte menu, shown opposite, changes with the seasons and is very good value. The "Supper Club" menu (£15.50 for 4 courses and an aperitif) is offered on the first Thursday of every month. This is very popular so book early.

For those looking for something a little bit different to the traditional Sunday roast, then I strongly recommend the self-indulgent Victorian Breakfast (£22 including Champagne cocktails on arrival) which begins at 11.30am on the third Sunday of every month from October to March.

Directions:  Penkridge is about 6 miles south of Stafford. Leaving the M6 at junction 13, follow the signs to Penkridge. On entering the village, take the first left. After about 100 yards bear left again, and the restaurant is a short distance further along on the right.

### USEFUL INFORMATION

**SERVING TIMES:**
Lunch 1pm-2pm (first & last Sunday)
Dinner 7.30pm-9.30pm (Tues-Sat)
**CLOSED:** lunchtime, all day Monday
and Sunday evening
**SEATING CAPACITY:** 24
**C/C:** V, MC, S, D

**NUMBER OF WINES:** 45
**HOUSE WINE:** £8.75
**RESERVATIONS:** compulsory
**OFF-STREET PARKING:** no
**DRESS CODE:** jacket and tie are
requested
**OUTDOOR EATING:** no

# THE SMOKER

**Tel: (01565) 722338**

Plumley, nr Knutsford, Cheshire, WA16 0TY

## STARTERS

**Home-made Soup of the Day**
Freshly prepared by our chef £2.00

**Blini Pancake**
Pancake filled with smoked salmon, baked
in cream with black pepper £4.95

**Black Pudding**
Best Lancashire Black Pudding with a
mustard and white wine sauce £3.85

**Venison Sausage**
Venison Sausage on a pâté topped crouton
with bacon & cumberland sauce £3.95

**Chicken Liver Pâté**
Home-made and served with toast £3.85

**Chilled Melon** £3.25

**Smoked Salmon**
Served with a dill vinaigrette £4.95

**Prawn Cocktail**
Greenland prawns on a bed of lettuce £4.75

**Home-made Savoury Pancake**
Served with a filling of ham, mushrooms
and shallots £3.95

**Strawberries, Melon & Cucumber**
Melon balls with strawberries and cucumber
finished with black pepper £3.75

**Smoked Ham with Apricot Chutney**
Slices of lightly smoked ham served with
sweet apricot chutney £3.95

**Stuffed Mushrooms**
Mushrooms stuffed with our own pâté, deep
fried in breadcrumbs £3.75

**Goujons of Lemon Sole**
Deep fried & served with tartare sauce £3.65

**Seafood Pancake**
Savoury pancake with plaice, cod, salmon
and prawns in a white wine sauce £4.25

**Américaine Salad**
Slices of tomatoes & potatoes, julienne of
celery, onions & hard boiled eggs £2.95

**Niçoise Salad**
Beans, tomato quarters, potatoes, olives,
anchovies & capers £2.95

## MAIN COURSES

**16oz T-Bone Steak**
With mushrooms & onion rings £10.60

**Steak de Tabley**
Fillet Steak with stilton, topped with a port
wine sauce £10.95

**8oz Gammon Steak**
Served with egg or pineapple £6.95

**Beef Stroganoff**
Strips of steak in a rich creamy sauce £6.95

**Steak and Kidney Pie**
Prime steak and kidneys in a rich gravy with
pastry lid £6.85

**Minted Lamb Henry**
A trimmed, marinated shoulder of lamb on
the bone £6.95

**Asparagus Chicken**
Supreme of chicken in a white wine sauce
topped with ham & fresh asparagus £6.75

**Cumberland Sausage**
Made by our local specialist Butcher £5.95

**Fish and Chips**
Fresh cod in a home-made beer batter,
served with mushy peas £6.35

**Breaded Scampi**
Deep fried & served with tartare sauce £6.35

**Home-made Seafood Bake**
Plaice, cod, salmon, prawns, halibut in a
creamy sauce topped with cheese £6.55

**Tagliatelle**
Served with wild mushrooms, chicken and
ham in a cream sauce £6.35

**Vegetarian Tagliatelle**
Mushrooms and seasonal vegetables in a
cream sauce £6.35

**Vegetarian Pancake**
A savoury pancake with vegetables £5.95

**Vegetable Stir Fry** £5.95

*All Main Courses are served with a*
*choice of Chips, New Potatoes, Rice*
*or Salad*

Believed to have been built in the days of Elizabeth I, The Smoker is named after a horse owned by the first Lord de Tabley in the late 18th Century. Of the nineteen times the horse raced, he won twelve times, was second three times, third twice and unplaced twice. I know which two times I would have backed him!

The food here is excellent. An extensive à la carte menu, which changes twice a year, is complemented by a blackboard featuring six daily specials. There is also a good selection of sandwiches (from £2.30) and a Children's Menu. Every Sunday a set lunch is offered (3 courses £11.95), which includes a good choice of traditional roast dishes and tempting alternatives. It is very popular so be sure to make a reservation.

Directions:   Easily found on the side of the A556 between Northwich and Knutsford.

## USEFUL INFORMATION

**SERVING TIMES:**
Lunch 12pm-2.30pm (Mon-Sat)
Dinner 6pm-10pm (Mon-Sat)
Food served all day Sunday
**SEATING CAPACITY:** 80 in the restaurant, 70 in the bar
**C/C:** V, MC, S, D, AE, DC
**NO SMOKING** area available

**NUMBER OF WINES:** 52
**HOUSE WINE:** £8.55
**RESERVATIONS:** advisable at weekends
**CHILDREN** welcome
**OFF-STREET PARKING:** yes
**OUTDOOR EATING:** yes

# THE WHITE HOUSE RESTAURANT
### Tel: (01625) 829376
The Village, Prestbury, Cheshire, SK10 4DG

## *TO START WITH*

*FRESHLY MADE SOUP of the MOMENT £3.50*
*SCOTTISH MUSSELS with a LIME and BASIL FUME £4.50*
*CRISPY DUCK CONFIT with CHINESE SPICES, CUCUMBER*
*and GLASS NOODLES £6.50*
*WILD MUSHROM FRITTATA with an ONION, TOMATO*
*and ARUGULA RELISH £4.50*
*SKEWERED TIGER PRAWNS with PESTO DIPPING SAUCE £6.50*
*ROAST WOOD PIGEON with RED WINE, LENTILS and BACON £6.95*
*FILO PASTRY CROUSTADE of FETA CHEESE, LEEK and TOMATO*
*on BALSAMIC ONIONS £5.95*
*SEARED SCALLOPS on a PUREE of SWEET and SOUR PINEAPPLE*
*and VEGETABLE MATCHSTICKS £7.95*
*SAUTE DUCK LIVERS on SHALLOT TATIN and MELTING GOATS CHEESE £5.50*
*WARM CHARGRILLED VEGETABLE PRESSE on a DUO of SAUCES,*
*VIERGE and TOMATO £5.25*
*A SALSA of SMOKED SALMON, CUCUMBER and RADISH with*
*CREME FRAICHE BLINIS £7.95*

*PENNE with FLAKED HAM HOCKS, LEEK and MUSHROOM,*
*PARMESAN SHAVINGS Half £5.95  Full £10.50*
*WILD MUSHROOM RISOTTO CAKE filled with TALEGGIO CHEESE £5.75/9.50*
*FETTUCINE with ROAST VEGETABLE MEDLEY and TAPENADE SAUCE £5.25/9.00*

## *AND TO CONTINUE*

*WHOLE DOVER SOLE GRILLED with PARSLEY BUTTER £13.95*
*CHARGRILLED CORNISH SEA BASS with a TOMATO and FENNEL*
*FONDUE, CRISPY COURGETTES £12.50*
*TEMPURA FRIED MONKFISH on RICE NOODLES & CORIANDER DRIZZLE £11.50*
*HALF CRISPY DUCKLING with RED PLUMS and THREE-GRAIN PILAF £12.50*
*FILLET of BEEF FORESTIERE on ROSTI POTATO & RED WINE SAUCE £12.95*
*POT ROASTED CHESHIRE LAMB SHANK with GARLIC and HERBS*
*on BAKED TORTINO £11.50*
*GUINEA FOWL SAUSAGE with GINGERED PARSNIP & MADEIRA SAUCE £9.95*
*RIB EYE STEAK with a BALSAMIC VINEGAR, SHALLOT, ROSEMARY SAUCE £11.25*
*GRILLED MARINATED CHICKEN BREAST with YOGHURT & ASIAN SPICES £10.50*
*DUTCH CALVES LIVER and SMOKED BACON RASHERS*
*with CARAMELISED APPLE £11.50*
*"BLUE PLATE" SPECIAL - RESTYLED OLD FAVOURITES £M.P*

*MIXED or GREEN SALAD £3.50   SELECTION of MARKET VEGETABLES £3.00*
*DAUPHINOISE £1.75   TIMBALE of MEDITERRANEAN VEGETABLES £2.00*
*GARLIC MASH POTATOES £1.75   CHIPS £1.75*

The White House, dating back to the 17th Century, enjoys a central location in the pretty village of Prestbury. It is stylishly decorated and, whilst the emphasis is very much on refinement and elegance, the atmosphere is nonetheless friendly and relaxed. The contemporary English cuisine is interesting and often innovative, with influences from all over the world - often a direct result of the chef proprietor's latest holiday!

The à la carte shown opposite changes three times a year, and there is a limited version available at lunch. Good value table d'hôte menus are also offered at lunch (3 courses £12.95) and dinner (3 courses £16.95), and these change fortnightly. Desserts are all home-made and may include Bread Pudding Soufflé with Bourbon Whiskey Ice Cream, or Chocolate Galaxy, a Starburst of Warm Valhrona Chocolate Puddings, Mousses and Sorbets.

Directions: Easily found in the centre of the village of Prestbury, which is about 2 miles north of Macclesfield.

## USEFUL INFORMATION

**SERVING TIMES:**
Lunch 12pm-2pm (Tues-Sun)
Dinner 7pm-10pm (Mon-Sat)
**CLOSED:** Sunday night, Monday lunch
**SEATING CAPACITY:** 80
**C/C:** V, MC, S, D, AE, DC
**OUTDOOR EATING:** yes

**NUMBER OF WINES:** 100
**HOUSE WINE:** £11.50
**RESERVATIONS:** advisable
**OFF-STREET PARKING:** yes
**NO SMOKING** pipes or cigars
**ACCOMMODATION:** 9 rooms
(single from £40, double from £65)

# GASCON'S
## Tel: (01952) 461625
8 Market Place, Shifnal, Shropshire, TF11 9AZ

## DINNER MENU

Home-made Vegetable Soup £2.95
Warm Blackpudding & Avocado Salad with a Madeira Vinaigrette £4.95
Pan-fried Foie Gras & Caramelised Apples
served with a Balsamic Vinegar Butter Sauce £6.95
Crab & Vegetable Tartlet on a Light Stilton Sauce £4.95
Fresh Mussels with a White Wine & Cream Sauce £3.95
Home-made Tagliatelle flavoured with Coriander
served with a Light Curry Sauce & Red Kidney Beans £3.95
Goose & Port Pâté with toasted Bread & a Red Fruit Sauce £6.25
Home-made Lobster Ravioles with a Chicken Consommé
and Vegetable Brunoise £6.95

Breast of Duck with a Celery & Lemon Compôte
served with a Red Wine Jam Butter Sauce £10.95
Pan-fried Salmon on Spinach Leaves with a Sorrel Sauce £7.95
Red Snapper on a Bed of Aubergine, Tomato & Black Olives
with a Saffron Sauce £9.95
Fresh Brill with Mushroom Juice, Broad Beans & Chives £10.50
Swordfish with a Light Coarse Grain Mustard Sauce
& Feuilleté of Wild Mushrooms £11.50
Boneless Roasted Quail with Creamed Savoy Cabbage
& an Oregano Sauce £10.95
Lamb Noisettes with a Potato, Onion & Black Olive Gâteau
served with a Rosemary Jus £11.95
Whole, Corn-fed Coquelet flavoured with Dijon Mustard
& served with a Chicken Coulis £9.95

Fine Tarte Chaude aux Pommes, Sauce Anglaise
et Glace Vanille au Parfum de Cannelle £2.50
Crème Brûlée £2.95
Baileys Cheesecake served with a Crème Anglaise
Brandy & Meringue Parfait with a Red Wine & Strawberry Sauce £2.95
Chocolate Mousse flavoured with Rum with Crème Anglaise £2.95
Winter Fruit Salad with Vanilla Ice Cream £2.95
Lime Bavaroise served with a Raspberry Coulis
& Caramelised Lime Zests £2.95

Gascon's is a 16th Century town-house restaurant with a half-timbered black-and-white exterior. Chef Patron Patrick Gascon and his wife Sally continue to build on their reputation with a predominantly French-orientated menu that changes every two months and specialises in fish.

The à la carte featured opposite is supplemented by daily specials such as King Prawns with Garlic (£5.95) or Fresh Squid with Mango (£3.95). They always try to have fresh lobster on the menu and Patrick will even prepare dishes on request if you give him enough warning.

Special themed evenings, such as Bastille night, are a frequent attraction. Please telephone the restaurant to find out about forthcoming events.

Directions: Gascon's is easily found in the Market Place in the centre of town.

## USEFUL INFORMATION

**SERVING TIMES:**
Dinner 7pm-10.30pm (Tues-Sat)
**CLOSED:** every lunchtime and all day Sundays and Mondays
**SEATING CAPACITY:** 36
**C/C:** none accepted

**NUMBER OF WINES:** 25
**HOUSE WINE:** £5.95
**RESERVATIONS:** very advisable
**OUTDOOR EATING:** no
**CHILDREN:** welcome
**OFF-STREET PARKING:** no

# ALBRIGHT HUSSEY
### Tel: (01939) 290523
Ellesmere Road, Shrewsbury, Shropshire, SY4 3AF

### A LA CARTE MENU

## STARTERS

FRESHLY MADE SOUP OF THE DAY     £3.20
*Using seasonal ingredients*

DUET OF MELON WITH SEASONAL BERRIES     £3.80
*Laced with a light cinnamon syrup topped with home-made sorbet*

WILD MUSHROOMS & TARRAGON RAVIOLI     £4.50
*Laced with a saffron cream sauce*

GRILLED JUMBO MUSSELS     £4.80
*With cream cheese & garlic, glazed in white wine & chive sabayon*

FLAKED DUCK MEAT     £5.80
*Served with oranges sandwiched in a crisp potato galette on a
dressed green salad*

## MAIN COURSES

GATEAU OF AUBERGINE, COURGETTES,     £8.00
OYSTER MUSHROOMS, SWEET RED PEPPERS
*With a cherry tomato & shallot compôte*

SUPREME OF CHICKEN BREAST     £12.00
*Filled with a wild mushroom mousse, basil, served in a port wine*

FILLET OF PORK     £12.80
*Rolled with fresh asparagus served with a pink peppercorn sauce*

ROAST FILLET OF MONKFISH     £14.50
*Wrapped in smoked bacon, served in a mustard & tarragon sauce*

PAN FRIED VENISON STEAK     £15.60
*Served on a bed of fried cabbage with caraway seeds with a red
wine & juniper sauce*

BEST END OF LAMB CUTLET     £13.25
*Marinated in garlic & rosemary, served with a timbale of creamed
spinach & spearmint glaze*

**FRESH VEGETABLES OF THE DAY**     £2.50

**SELECTION OF HOME-MADE SWEETS from**     £3.85

**SELECTION OF ENGLISH CHEESES**     £4.20

The Albright Hussey is a listed Grade II moated country house hotel. The present manor house was built in two parts: the timber-framed half in 1524 with the brick and stone wing added by 1560. In 1634 the house was acquired by the Corbet family, when Robert Corbet married the Hussey heiress. During the English Civil War a few years later in 1642, the house was converted into a garrison for the Royalist troops of Charles I.

Nowadays the Albright Hussey is renowned for its superb food, fine wines and impeccable service. An à la carte menu is available for both lunch and dinner (an example is featured on the facing page). Alternatively you can choose from a set price lunch (£12.50 for four courses) or a table d'hôte dinner menu (£19.50 for four courses).

Directions: Albright Hussey is situated 2½ miles north of Shrewsbury town centre on the A528 Ellesmere road. The hotel is on your right as you drive north.

### USEFUL INFORMATION

**SERVING TIMES:**
Lunch 12pm-2.15pm (every day)
Dinner 7pm-10.15pm (every day)
**SEATING CAPACITY:** 90
**C/C:** V, MC, S, D, AE, DC
**NO SMOKING** in the restaurant
**OFF-STREET PARKING:** yes
**OUTDOOR EATING:** yes

**NUMBER OF WINES:** 140
**HOUSE WINE:** £9.75
**RESERVATIONS:** advisable
**CHILDREN:** welcome (over 3yrs)
**DRESS CODE:** jacket and tie
**ACCOMMODATION:** 14 rooms
(B&B single fr £65, double fr £85)

# THE ARMOURY
### Tel: (01743) 340525
Victoria Quay, Welsh Bridge, Shrewsbury, SY1 1HH

Soup with crusty bread  £2.45
Lentil and sundried tomato pâté with granary toast  £4.75
Pan-fried kidneys in grain mustard sauce  £3.50
Tiger prawns wrapped in filo pastry with plum dipping sauce  £4.95
Chicken liver, brandy and herb pâté with granary toast  £4.75
Smoked cheese, grape and apple salad  £4.95
Smoked salmon with coriander dressing and brown bread  £5.25
Field mushrooms in herb and garlic butter  £3.95
Chilli squid with mangetout and cherry tomatoes  £4.25

\* \* \* \* \* \* \* \* \* \*

Pan-fried chicken livers on salad leaves with ciabatta bread  £6.25
Char-grilled Mediterranean vegetables with cous cous  £6.95
Cajun chicken salad in warm pitta bread with minted yoghurt dressing  £5.75
Salmon and smoked haddock fishcakes
with sliced tomato, spring onion and lemon mayonnaise  £5.25
Lasagne with crisp mixed salad  £6.25
Thai chicken in coconut milk, lemon grass, ginger, green chilli and lime
sauce with Thai fragrant rice and stir fried vegetables  £8.25
Baked potato with mushroom and smoked bacon sauce  £4.95
Warm smoked mackerel with salad and hot ciabatta bread  £7.95
Farfelle pasta with broccoli and red onions in a blue cheese sauce  £7.25
Lamb and cashew nut curry with onion bhaji, nan bread and rice  £8.95
*Side orders: mixed salad, fries, potatoes, mixed vegetables, garlic bread - all £1.75*

Armoury Pie (beef, bacon, red wine and mushrooms)  £7.25
Braised half shoulder of lamb with pommery mustard
and tarragon sauce  £9.25
Char-grilled monkfish with red pepper essence  £11.25
Chicken, red wine and cranberry casserole  £8.95
10oz Rump steak cooked to your liking with garlic butter  £11.25
Grilled duck breast with a spiced blackcurrant jus  £11.25
Pork fillets with apple, sage and onion sauce  £10.75
*The above seven dishes are served with potatoes and vegetables*

\* \* \* \* \* \* \* \* \* \*

Pear and almond tart  £3.45
Fruit crumble and custard  £3.45
Chocolate truffle torte  £3.45
Steamed syrup sponge and custard  £3.45
Crème brûlée  £3.45
Bread and butter pudding with apricot sauce  £3.45

The Armoury is a modern pub/restaurant in a converted warehouse down by the River Severn. The floor area is huge (over 3,000 square feet) with old tables and chairs, antique prints on the walls, a real log fire at one end and, at the other, shelves stacked high with books.

In order to ensure that your food is served the same day, they have installed an amazing labour-saving device to get your order to the kitchens: a vacuum tube system meanders its way across the ceiling and provides hours of fun for those of us who haven't forgotten what it's like to be six years old.

Although you have to order your meal at the bar, the dishes are served to your table by friendly, efficient staff. The menu featured opposite changes every three months and is supplemented by 2 or 3 daily specials on the blackboard. One fascinating feature is the enormous array of spirits on the shelves behind the bar, over 300 at the last count. Pride of place within this collection goes to the twenty or so bourbons that are always in stock.

Directions: The Armoury is found down by the River Severn by Welsh Bridge.

### USEFUL INFORMATION

**SERVING TIMES:**
Lunch 12pm-2.30pm (Mon-Fri)
Dinner 6pm-9.30pm (Mon-Fri)
12pm-9.30pm (all day, Sat & Sun)
**SEATING CAPACITY:** 140
**C/C:** V, MC, S, D, AE
**OFF-STREET PARKING:** no

**NUMBER OF WINES:** 30
**HOUSE WINE:** £7.95
**OUTDOOR EATING:** no
**CHILDREN:** tolerated at lunch
**RESERVATIONS:** advisable, but
essential at weekends

# PRINCE RUPERT HOTEL
### Tel: (01743) 499955
Butcher Row, Shrewsbury, Shropshire, SY1 1UQ

---

### <u>Dinner Menu</u>

### £17.00

*Fan of Cantelope Melon set on a Strawberry & Mango Coulis
garnished with seasonal Fruit & Passion Fruit Sorbet
A warm salad of Queen Scallops, Avocado, Duck Livers & Fine Beans
drizzled with a Raspberry Vinaigrette
Smoked Salmon Cornets filled with Prawns & Sherried Marie Rose
set on a Lemon & Chive Cream
Venison, Pork & Wild Mushroom Terrine flavoured with Brandy & Juniper Berries
served with French Leaves & Cumberland Sauce
Cream of Celery & Roquefort Soup*

*Lemon-poached Darne of Seabass with Vegetable Tagliatelle
and a Saffron & Watercress Butter Sauce
Half a Roast Gressingham Duck accompanied by a Red Onion & Apple Confit
served with a Black Cherry Port Wine Sauce
Flash-fried Strips of Fillet Steak with Mushrooms, Tarragon, Paprika & Brandy
bound with Double Cream & served with Turmeric Rice
Sautéed Breast of Chicken stuffed with a Prawn & Chive Mousse
enveloped in a Coconut, Apricot & White Wine Sauce
Roast Rack of Lamb with a Dijon & Herb Crumb
garnished with Turned Vegetables
and served with a Redcurrant, Garlic & Rosemary Sauce*

*A selection of fresh seasonal vegetables and potatoes*

*A slice of Marquise de Chocolat
set on a pool of Caramel Sauce
Fresh Exotic Fruit Salad
laced with Kirsch & served with Double Cream
Light Fromage Frais Parfait
swirled with a duo of Rich Fruit Purées
Strawberry Shortcake layer
accompanied by Clotted Cream Quenelles*

*Freshly brewed Cafetière Coffee with home-made Chocolate Liqueur Truffles*

Situated in the heart of medieval Shrewsbury, The Prince Rupert is firmly established as the town's finest hotel. The former home of Prince Rupert, the grandson of King James I, it combines old-world charm with modern facilities and is an oasis of tranquillity in the centre of town, surrounded by cobblestoned streets and Tudor architecture.

The Cavalier Restaurant offers fine dining for lunch and dinner, with a choice of both à la carte and table d'hôte menus. An example of the evening table d'hôte, with three courses plus coffee costing £17.00, is shown opposite. The set price luncheon menu is priced at £11.00 per person.

Directions: The Prince Rupert Hotel is easily found in the town centre, opposite the Church of Saint Alkmond's Square.

### USEFUL INFORMATION

**SERVING TIMES:**
Lunch 12pm-2.15pm (every day)
Dinner 7pm-9.45pm (Sun-Thurs)
       7pm-10.15pm (Fri & Sat)
**SEATING CAPACITY:** 90
**C/C:** V, MC, S, D, AE, DC
**OFF-STREET PARKING:** no

**NUMBER OF WINES:** 40
**HOUSE WINE:** £9.75
**RESERVATIONS:** advisable
**CHILDREN:** welcome
**OUTDOOR EATING:** no
**ACCOMMODATION:** 65 rooms
(B&B from £70 per room)

# THE MOAT HOUSE
### Tel: (01785) 712217
Acton Trussell, nr Stafford, Staffordshire, ST17 0RJ

### *A selection from the A La Carte Menu*

*Chicken Parfait ~ Chicken Livers, Fresh Herbs, Brandy, Madeira, Onions and Garlic blended together and studded with Prunes, wrapped in Smoked Bacon and served with a toasted Brioche*

*Mousseline of Fish ~ Salmon and Sole Mousse gently poached in White Wine and set on a bed of Julienne of Vegetables napped with a Lime & Chive Sauce*

*Fan of Poached Pear served on slices of Fresh Mango, decorated with Black Grapes and topped with a scoop of Blackcurrant Sorbet*

*Home-made Soup of the Day served with Fried Snippets of Bread*

*Medley of Seafood ~ Mussels, Prawns, Scallops and Salmon steamed in Vermouth and napped with a sauce of Tomatoes, White Wine and Cream*

### *MAIN COURSES*

*Pan Fried Fillet of Scotch Halibut garnished with Turned Cucumber, Prawns and Capers in a Nut Brown Lemon Butter £24.75*

*Supreme of Pheasant filled with a Chestnut, Black Cherry and Orange Stuffing coated with a sauce of Dry Sherry and Cream £22.85*

*Loin of Venison stuffed with a Cranberry Forcemeat, roasted in the oven and served with a Venison Jus £24.75*

*Charcoal Grilled Aberdeen Angus T-Bone Steak £22.85*

*Oven Roasted Whole Partridge wrapped in Bacon served with Bread Sauce and Gravy £24.75*

*Pancake Purse filled with a Ratatouille of Vegetables accompanied with a Tower of Aubergine interleaved with a Spinach Mousse set on a Fresh Tomato and Basil Sauce £20.25*

*Mousse of Scotch Salmon wrapped in Spinach coated with a White Wine and Chive Sauce £23.25*

**The Price of the Main Course is inclusive of Starter, Dessert and Coffee**

The Moat House is a grade II listed building dating back to the 14th Century. With large ponds on two sides, and the Staffordshire and Worcestershire Canal on another, the setting is both dramatic and elegant, and the roar of the M6 motorway traffic really does pale into insignificance.

Owned and run by the Lewis family since 1988, the restaurant has gained an enviable reputation for its cuisine. The à la carte menu changes every month and an example is shown opposite. The desserts are all home-made and may include Steamed Sponge served with a Hot Orange Curd Sauce, or perhaps Chocolate Truffle Cake. A good value weekly table d'hôte menu is also available at lunch (£12.95) and dinner (£14.95). In the bar there is a daily blackboard menu featuring both light meals and more substantial dishes.

Directions:  A few miles south of Stafford on the A449 take the turning to Acton Trussell. Follow the road through the village and The Moat House is found on the right.

## USEFUL INFORMATION

**SERVING TIMES:**
Lunch 12pm-2pm (Mon-Sat)
        12pm-3pm (Sunday)
Dinner 6pm-9.30pm (Mon-Sat)
**CLOSED:** Sunday night
**SEATING CAPACITY:** 80
**C/C:** V, MC, S, D, AE, DC

**NUMBER OF WINES:** 120
**HOUSE WINE:** £9.50
**RESERVATIONS:** advisable
**OUTDOOR EATING:** yes
**NO SMOKING** in the restaurant
**OFF-STREET PARKING:** yes
**CHILDREN:** welcome

# THE WOOLPACK INN

### Tel: (01889) 270238

The Green, Weston, nr Stafford, Staffordshire, ST18 0JH

## APPETISERS

**Soup of the Day £1.60**
Served with a roll & butter
**Breaded Mushrooms £2.50**
With a blue cheese or garlic dip
**Prawn Cocktail £2.95**
Served with brown bread & butter
**Hot Smoked Peppered Mackerel £2.50**
Served with brown bread & horseradish

## MAIN COURSES

**Fried Whole Boneless Plaice £4.75**
Deep fried in golden breadcrumbs
**Whole Tailed Scampi £5.50**
Deep fried with tartare sauce
**Fresh Salmon Fillet £6.25**
Served with dill sauce
**Three Country Chicken £5.95**
Three pieces of chicken marinated in an
Indian, Mexican & Chinese style
**Broccoli & Cream Cheese Bake £4.95**
Florets of broccoli in a cream cheese topped
with potatoes & cheese
**Leek & Potato Dish £4.95**
With a cheese topping
**Balti of the Day £5.25**
Served with rice & naan bread
**8oz Sirloin Steak £8.75**
Served with mushrooms & onion rings
**Steak & Mushroom Pie £4.50**
Chef's own special with a puff pastry top
**Large Pork Chop & Apple Sauce £4.95**
Served with roast potatoes

*All our main meals (except curry & balti dishes) are served with a
choice of chips, sauté slices, new potatoes & vegetables of the day.*

**A selection of desserts from £2.00**

The Woolpack is a traditional 17th Century inn, enjoying a tranquil setting on a small village green a few miles outside Stafford. Part of the dining room was originally stables, and the ghost, or "grey lady" as she is known, reputedly still wanders here.

The menu offers a broad range of good food, all prepared and cooked fresh to order, and includes basic pub grub for those after a light lunch, such as Jacket Potatoes (fr £1.40) and Sandwiches (fr £1.50),. The Chef's specials, which are shown on a board and change daily, may include Beef Wellington served on a rich Port Sauce (£10.95), or Giant King Prawn Balti (£7.95).

Sunday lunch is very popular, as are the regular theme evenings like Gourmet Balti Night at £12.95 per person.

Directions: Three miles north-east of Stafford on the A518, turn right just before the A51 and The Woolpack Inn is about 150 yards on the left.

### USEFUL INFORMATION

**SERVING TIMES:**
Lunch 12pm-2pm (every day)
Dinner 6.30pm-9.30pm (Mon-Sat)
**CLOSED:** for food Sunday evening
**SEATING CAPACITY:** 55
**C/C:** not accepted
**OFF-STREET PARKING:** yes

**NUMBER OF WINES:** 20
**HOUSE WINE:** £4.50
**RESERVATIONS:** advisable at weekends
**NO SMOKING** area available
**OUTDOOR EATING:** yes
**CHILDREN:** welcome

# GRANVILLES
### Tel: (01785) 816658
Granville Square, Stone, Staffordshire, ST15 8AB

*SOUP & FRENCH BREAD £2.45*
*CAPONATA with FOCCACIA £3.95*
*sweet & sour aubergine salad with Italian olive bread*
*PORK RILLETTES with CRANBERRY RELISH £4.25*
*TART OF CARAMELISED SHALLOTS, STILTON & ROSEMARY £3.95*
*CAMEMBERT & POPPY SEED MUFFIN with TOMATO CHUTNEY £3.95*
*POTTED FETA, SUNDRIED TOMATOES & CAPERS £3.45*

*CHILLI & SWEET PEPPER KING PRAWNS £5.25 / £8.75*
*THREE-RICE RISOTTO of MIXED MUSHROOMS with SHAVED*
*PARMESAN £3.95 / £7.95*
*THAI FISH CAKES with SWEET & SOUR DIPPING SAUCE £3.95 / £7.95*
*SPINACH SALAD with BACON, EGG & CROUTONS £3.95 / £7.95*
*OPEN RAVIOLI of SCAMPI & LEMON BALM £4.25 / £8.45*
*with lemon sabayon*
*TAGLIATELLE with SMOKED CHICKEN & MUSHROOMS £4.25 / £8.45*

*GRILLED SALMON FILLET with SALSA VERDE £8.45*
*PEPPERED SIRLOIN STRIPS £9.95*
*on a bed of egg noodles dressed with chilli oil*
*DUCK LEG CONFIT & COUSCOUS £8.95*
*with Mediterranean vegetables & orange sauce*
*PAPRIKA-CRUSTED COD on SHREDDED LEEKS £8.95*
*with lemon dressing*
*CARAMELISED CHICKEN BREAST £8.95*
*on coriander scented white & wild rice*
*STEAK & KIDNEY PUDDING £8.95*
*with mushy peas & chips*
*MILLEFEUILLE of PARMESAN TUILLE £8.75*
*layered with asparagus, artichoke & goats cheese with tomato coulis*
*FILLET STEAK & FRIES £12.95*
*with Stilton Sauce / Sautéed Onions & Mushrooms or Naked*

Granvilles is found in a lovely listed building at the top end of Stone, and over the years it has developed an unsurprising popularity. The atmosphere is relaxed and friendly, with vibrant bistro colours complementing the wooden furniture, sanded floors and exposed beams. There is a jazz piano most nights, and live bands at weekends, with big names like Acker Bilk, George Melly and Alan Price regularly performing. But even when the restaurant is really buzzing, there are always a few quieter corners reserved for those after a more intimate evening.

The brasserie style food served here is very good. The menu (shown opposite) changes seasonally, and is supplemented by blackboard daily specials, with an emphasis on fresh fish dishes. Desserts are all home-made and may include Chocolate Brûlée or Sticky Toffee Pudding (£2.95 each).

At the time of going to press the kitchens had just been extended with a view to serving food all day and also opening on Sundays, so please bear in mind that some of the details below may well change!

Directions: From the A34 about 7 miles north of Stafford, turn right towards Stone town centre. Join the one-way system and after about 200 yards turn left opposite the entrance to the high street, and Granvilles is on your left.

### USEFUL INFORMATION

**SERVING TIMES:**
Lunch 12pm-2pm (Mon-Sat)
Dinner 7pm-10pm (Mon-Sat)
**CLOSED:** Sunday
**SEATING CAPACITY:** 70
C/C: V, MC, S, D, AE, DC

**NUMBER OF WINES:** 40
**HOUSE WINE:** £9.45
**OFF-STREET PARKING:** no
**RESERVATIONS:** advisable
**OUTDOOR EATING:** yes

# ALVESTON MANOR

### Tel: (01789) 204581

Clopton Bridge, Stratford-upon-Avon, Warwickshire, CV37 7HP

*A selection from the*
*A LA CARTE*

### STARTERS

**A Warm Timbale of Asparagus and wild Mushrooms**
*perfumed with Truffle and Shallot Vinaigrette £5.95*
**Scoops of Seasonal Melon on an Advocaat Lime Sauce**
*with Strawberries and Crispy Citrus Zest £4.95*
**Court Bouillon of Seafood with Aromatic Vegetables**
*infused with Saffron and Pernod £6.95*
**Whisky Cured Scottish Salmon**
*served with a Light Spa Dressing £8.95*

### ENTREES

**Spinach Rolled Monkfish and Red Snapper**
*with Ribbons of Carrot and Courgette on a Ketia Caviar Cream £16.95*
**Pink Roasted Duck Breast with Confit of Leg**
*served on a Classical Orange Sauce enhanced with Juniper £17.95*
**Cannon of Cornish Lamb, Ravioli of Crab and Ginger**
*brought together with a Spicy Eastern Sauce £16.95*

### GRILLS

**Whole Dover Sole**
*grilled plain or with Lemon and White Wine Butter Sauce £21.95*
**Fillet Steak £18.95, Sirloin Steak £18.95, Rib Eye Steak £19.95**
*each served with a choice of Herb Butter, Pepper, or Chasseur Sauce,*
*and garnished with grilled tomato, mushrooms and fresh watercress*

### DESSERTS

**Chocolate Teardrop filled with a Lychee Bavois**
*served with a Ball of Fresh Raspberry Ice*
**Majolaine set on a Cream of Crème de Cacao**
*layered with dark Chocolate, Hazelnut Praline, Light Meringue and Sponge*
**Bread and Butter Pudding**
*made with Croissants and Brioche and served with a Brandy infused Sauce*
*All prepared in-house for £4.95 each*

Alveston Manor is a 16th Century hotel, which stands in seven acres of grounds and landscaped gardens, a short walk from the centre of Stratford-upon-Avon. The original stage directions of Shakespeare's "A Midsummer Night's Dream" indicate that the play was probably premiered here.

The beautiful restaurant serves award-winning cuisine. In addition to the extensive à la carte menu, there are three course table d'hôte menus available at lunch and dinner, priced at £14.95 and £23.95 respectively.

Directions: Alveston Manor is easily found on the outskirts of Stratford-upon-Avon, just off the large roundabout where the A422 meets the A3400.

## USEFUL INFORMATION

**SERVING TIMES:**
Lunch 12.30pm-2pm (every day)
Dinner 6pm-9.30pm (Mon-Sat)
        7pm-9.30pm (Sunday)
**SEATING CAPACITY:** 60
**C/C:** V, MC, S, D, AE, DC
**OFF-STREET PARKING:** yes

**NUMBER OF WINES:** 20
**HOUSE WINE:** £16.00
**OUTDOOR EATING:** no
**RESERVATIONS:** advisable
**NO SMOKING** in the restaurant
**ACCOMMODATION:** 106 rooms
(single £95, double £110)

# ETTINGTON PARK

**Tel: (01789) 450123**

Alderminster, Warwickshire, CV37 8BU

---

*CHEF'S DINNER MENU OF THE DAY*

*Asparagus, Beetroot and Parmesan Salad, Balsamic Dressing*

*Fresh Home-made Soup of the Day*

*Seared Monkfish Fillet, Smoked Salmon, Pesto Cream*

\*\*\*\*\*

*Pork fillet, Rosti Potato, Glazed Apricots, Marsala Sauce*

*Lemon Sole Fillets, Salmon Mousse, Creamed Potato, Chive Butter*

*Char-grilled Breast of Chicken, Roasted Potato and Mediterranean
Vegetables, Tomato Olive Oil*

\*\*\*\*\*

*Seasonal Fruits and Berries Coated and Glazed with a
Champagne Sabayon*

*Dark Chocolate Torte, Glazed Poached Pear, Drambuie Sauce*

*Selection of English Cheese with Banana Bread and Biscuits*

\*\*\*\*\*

*Freshly Brewed Coffee or Choice of Teas and Chocolates
(£2.50 supplement)*

*£29.50 per person*

Ettington Park, a Grade I listed Victorian Gothic mansion, is set in 40 acres of gardens and parkland on the banks of the River Stour.

The Oak Room with its 19th Century family crests and rococo ceiling provides an elegant setting. Original paintings, antiques and magnificent stained glass windows create a marvellous atmosphere in which to dine. There is a set luncheon menu (two courses priced at £10.00, three courses £14.00), whilst in the evening one may choose from a daily table d'hôte menu, or the full à la carte.

Directions: heading south from Stratford-upon-Avon on the A3400 towards Alderminster, the hotel is signposted on the left after about five miles.

## USEFUL INFORMATION

**SERVING TIMES:**
Lunch 12.30pm-2pm (every day)
Dinner 7.30pm-9.30pm (every day)
**SEATING CAPACITY:** 40
**C/C:** V, MC, S, D, AE, DC
**NO SMOKING** in the restaurant
**DRESS CODE:** jacket and tie

**NUMBER OF WINES:** 125
**HOUSE WINE:** £15
**RESERVATIONS:** advisable
**CHILDREN:** welcome
**OFF-STREET PARKING:** yes
**OUTDOOR EATING:** yes
**ACCOMMODATION:** 48 rooms
(single £115, double £152)

# THE BELFRY

## Tel: (01675) 470301

Wishaw, North Warwickshire, B76 9PR

## *THE FRENCH RESTAURANT*

### *Chef's Special Dinner Menu*
### *£28.50*

Terrine of Foie Gras and Artichoke with Brioche
and Lime and Apple Compôte
Deep Fried Cod with Mushy Peas and Tomato Sauce
Honeyed Duck Breast Salad with Sultana and Chestnut Chutney
Lamb and Mint Sausage with Braised Cabbage and Rosemary Sauce

~~~~~~~~

Passion Fruit and Apricot Water Ice
Carrot and Coriander Cappuccino Soup

~~~~~~~~

Canneloni of Chicken, Sweetcorn and Bavarian Ham
with Basil Mash and Smoked Sauce
Petit Fillet of Beef with Welsh Rarebit, Field Mushrooms and Cocotte Potato
Roasted Loin of Local Venison
with Humous, Fine Beans and Roasted Beetroot Sauce
Fillets of Red Mullet and Sea Bass with Potato, Leek and Ratatouille Gâteau
Open Lasagne of Stir Fried Vegetables with Satay Sauce
*Each main course is presented with integral vegetable accompaniments*
*to enhance and complement the dish*

~~~~~~~~

Hot Malibu Soufflé with Coconut Ice Cream
Glazed Lemon Tart with Lime Anglaise Sauce
and Home-made Griottine Cherry Ice-Cream
Chocolate and Peppermint Mousse served with Duo of Sauces
Apple Tart Tatin with Vanilla Sauce and Dairy Ice-Cream
Cheese and Biscuits with Grapes and Celery

~~~~~~~~

Situated in 500 acres of Warwickshire countryside, nestling in the tiny hamlet of Wishaw, The Belfry Resort boasts three championship golf courses and has been the venue of three Ryder Cups (with a fourth returning in 2001).

Enjoying panoramic views of the famous Brabazon Course, The French Restaurant offers a fine dining experience. Head Chef Eric Bruce and his dedicated team maintain the highest standards of quality and presentation, creating superb four-course dinner menus (which change weekly) supported by an à la carte of traditional favourites.

The lunchtime menu, generally with a choice of five dishes at each course, is reasonably priced at £16.50 for three courses including coffee and there is also an excellent two-course set business lunch at £10.95.

Directions: Leaving the M42 at Junction 9, The Belfry is one mile along the main A446 road towards Lichfield.

## USEFUL INFORMATION

**SERVING TIMES:**
Lunch 12.30pm-2pm (Sun-Fri)
Dinner 7.30pm-10pm (Mon-Sat)
**CLOSED:** Sat lunch & Sun evening
**SEATING CAPACITY:** 80
**C/C:** V, MC, S, D, AE, DC
**OFF-STREET PARKING:** yes
**DRESS CODE:** gentlemen prefer
to wear a collar and tie, or jacket,
for dinner

**NUMBER OF WINES:** 90
**HOUSE WINE:** £13.50
**RESERVATIONS:** advisable
**OUTDOOR EATING:** lunch only
**ACCOMMODATION:** 327 rooms
(from £44.50 per person per night
for dinner in the Garden Room and
B&B - supplement for upgrade to
The French Restaurant opposite)

# NEW HALL

### Tel: (0121) 378 2442

Walmley Road, Sutton Coldfield, West Midlands, B76 1QX

**3 Courses £34.00**   DINNER MENU   **2 Courses £28.50**

*Creamy Butternut Squash Soup*
with toasted goats cheese croûtons
*Terrine of Venison En Croûte*
with apple and celeriac salad and mustard dressing
*Grilled Tuna*
on a bed of carrots flavoured with ginger, saffron and coriander
*Potted Duck Confit with Foie Gras*
in port jelly
*Spinach Gnocchi with Roast Tomato Sauce*
topped with melting Swiss cheese

*Crispy Fried Seabass*
on angel hair pasta and a light vanilla and basil sauce
*Char Grilled John Dory*
on marinated red peppers, confit fennel, sautéed potatoes and chilli salsa
*Chilli, Lime and Coriander Marinated Chicken Breast*
char grilled, with vegetable spaghetti, ginger crisps and soy butter sauce
*Braised Lamb Chump Chop*
with roasted winter vegetables, crispy potatoes and rosemary jus
*Roast Partridge (supp £2.50)*
with wild mushroom polenta, parsnip crisps and a rich red wine sauce
*Pan Fried Beef Fillet and Mushroom Duxelle (supp £5.00)*
with roast tomato, rosti potato and béarnaise sauce
*Spinach, Mushroom and Tomato Lasagne*
with basil cream

*Chocolate Soufflé*
with white chocolate sorbet
*Olive Oil and Sauterne Cake*
with citrus syrup, poached fruits and marmalade ice cream
*Warm Spiced Pear and Prune Pithivier*
with cardamom anglaise
*Banana Torte with Biscotti*
and chocolate sauce

Reputedly the oldest moated manor house in England, New Hall is now a country house hotel of unrivalled style and presence. Set in twenty-six acres of private gardens and surrounded by a lily-filled moat, it is steeped in history and full of romantic charm.

The dining room, with its beautiful oak panelling and stained glass windows, has its origins in Anglo-Saxon times. The moulded stone fireplace is late 17th Century and the 16th Century Flemish glass has old Dutch wording. The innovative set price dinner menu, an example of which is shown on the facing page, is changed on a seasonal basis.

Directions: From Birmingham, take the A38 Aston Expressway to the Sutton Coldfield turn off. Then follow the A38 signed Lichfield until bearing left into the B4148 signed Walmley/Falcon Lodge. Continue for approximately 1 mile and at a large roundabout take the 2nd exit signed Walmley. Continue on the B4148 through Walmley village and after a further mile turn left into New Hall.

### USEFUL INFORMATION

**SERVING TIMES:**
Lunch 12.30pm-2pm (Sun-Fri)
Dinner 7pm-10pm (Mon-Sat)
       7pm-9.30pm (Sunday)
**CLOSED:** Saturday lunch
**SEATING CAPACITY:** 60
**C/C:** V, MC, S, D, AE, DC

**NUMBER OF WINES:** 300
**HOUSE WINE:** £13.25
**RESERVATIONS:** advisable
**OFF-STREET PARKING:** yes
**NO SMOKING** in the restaurant
**ACCOMMODATION:** 60 rooms
(some rooms at £63 pp pn B&B)

# FITZHERBERT ARMS

**Tel: (01782) 796542**

Swynnerton, nr Stone, Staffordshire, ST15 0RA

## STARTERS

**Tiger Prawns £4.95**
*Fan-tailed, Shell-on, Pan fried in Garlic & Sesame Oil on a Bed of Mixed Leaves*
**Spare Ribs £3.25**
*Japanese Style Pork Ribs with a Teriyaki Dipping Sauce*
**Deep Fried Camembert £3.25**
*Served with Fruits of the Forest Sauce & Crisp Salad Garnish*

## FISH 'n' FAVOURITES

**Fish 'n' Chips £4.95**
*A generous portion of Battercrisp Fish served with
Chips, Peas & a Slice of Bread & Butter*
**Rob Roy Trout £7.95**
*Two boneless Pink Trout Fillets rolled together in Oatmeal and Baked in Butter
served with Chips or New Potatoes in their Skins & Vegetables*
**Beef & Real Ale Pie £5.60**
*Served with Chips or New Potatoes in their Skins & Vegetables*
**Cod & Prawn Pie £5.85**
*Served with Chips or New Potatoes in their Skins & Vegetables*
**Pasta Bake £5.45**
*Choice of Tuna or Chicken, Cheesy Pasta Bake served with a Crisp and
Crunchy Salad & a White or Brown Crusty Roll*
**Fruity Duck £9.10**
*Boneless Breast of Duck with an Orange Sauce with Fruits of the Forest*
**Chicken, Apricot & Asparagus £6.95**
*Boneless Breast of Chicken with an Apricot Glaze garnished with Asparagus*
**Currant Lamb £7.95**
*Juicy Lamb Steak with Redcurrant Sauce*

## SIMMER & SHIVER SALADS

**Warm Chicken Salad £6.95**
*Pan Fried strips of Chicken Breast in a Sesame, Ginger, Garlic & Soy Sauce*
**A Simmering Vegetarian Salad £5.95**
*Baby & New Vgetables Pan Fried in a Sesame, Ginger, Garlic & Soy Sauce*

Locals are united in the belief that Longfellow's words *'Under the spreading chestnut tree, the village smithy stands'*, found their inspiration here in Swynnerton, and more specifically in the chestnut tree opposite the Fitzherbert Arms.

This friendly pub restaurant, a converted farmhouse dating back to the 18th Century, now offers a wide selection of good food in a relaxed atmosphere. The main à la carte menu, a sample of which is shown opposite, is updated every six months to include the most popular specials which have appeared on the blackboard. The Light Bite menu carries both old favourites such as Cheddar Ploughmans (£3.65), as well as something a little different, like a Stilton and Spinach Pancake (£3.60).

The excellent steaks, from the 5oz Rump (£5.15) to the 1lb Rump (£10.30), are very popular, and if you have not eaten for a few days then I suggest the enormous Fitzherbert Farmyard Platter (£10.40).

Directions: The Fitzherbert Arms is found in the village of Swynnerton, which is signposted off the A51 and the A519, about four miles west from Stone.

### USEFUL INFORMATION

**SERVING TIMES:**
Lunch 12pm-2.15pm (every day)
Dinner 7pm-9.30pm (Sun-Thurs)
Dinner 7pm-10pm (Fri-Sat)
**CLOSED:** Boxing Day evening
**SEATING CAPACITY:** 65
**C/C:** V, MC, S, D, AE

**NUMBER OF WINES:** 25
**HOUSE WINE:** £6.90
**RESERVATIONS:** advisable
**NO SMOKING** area available
**OFF-STREET PARKING:** yes
**OUTDOOR EATING:** no

# THE RISING SUN

## Tel: (01829) 732423

High Street, Tarporley, Cheshire, CW6 0DX

### STARTERS

**Prawn Cocktail £3.65**
**Scampi Mornay £3.75**
**Smoked Fish Platter £3.95**
**Assorted Dim Sums £4.15**
**Stuffed Mushrooms £2.95**
**Melon au Porto £3.25**
**Spinach Pancake £3.15**
**Tagliatelle Carbonara £3.00**

### FISH

**Rainbow Trout** grilled with butter and sliced almonds **£7.50**
**Whole Dover Sole** grilled in butter and topped with prawns **£10.95**
**Sole Bonne Femme** poached in a white wine, cream and mushroom sauce **£7.50**
**Salmon Asparagus** salmon steak in a hot asparagus and cream sauce **£7.25**

### POULTRY

**Chicken Prawn Lobster** breaded chicken filled with prawn and lobster sauce **£6.25**
**Sweet and Sour Chicken** deep fried strips of chicken breast in a home-made sweet and sour sauce **£6.95**
**Chicken Fumé** chicken breast cooked in a cream, cheese and smoked ham sauce **£7.25**
**Chicken Piri Piri** a whole poussin, boned out, coated with a traditional Portuguese spice blend & grilled **£6.65**
**Half Honey Roast Duckling** served with a choice of orange, black cherry or honey and lemon sauces **£8.50**

### MEATS

**Veal Jardin** a casserole of diced veal with mixed vegetables in a white wine sauce **£7.25**
**Venison Casserole** diced venison cooked in a rich red wine sauce with mushrooms and carrots **£7.25**
**Kidney Sauté** kidneys, mushrooms & sausage in a rich sherry sauce **£7.25**
**10oz Fillet Steak** served with fried onions and mushrooms **£10.25**
**Sirloin Chasseur** cooked to your liking in a rich chasseur sauce **£9.75**
**Medallions of Beef Bordelaise** slices of fillet steak served with a bordelaise sauce and baby mushrooms **£10.75**
**Beef Stroganoff** prime strips of fillet steak in a rich cream, brandy and mushroom sauce **£7.95**

### SIZZLING STYLE DISHES

**Cajun Chicken** American spiced chicken with mixed peppers **£7.25**
**Cantonese Prawns** jumbo prawns with mixed vegetables in an aromatic Cantonese sauce **£7.25**
**Teriyaki Beef** strips of beef and vegetables in a sweet, savoury Teriyaki sauce **£7.25**

### VEGETARIAN

**Vegetable Stroganoff £6.95**
**Vegetable Moussaka £6.95**
**Broccoli and Cheese Pancake £6.95**
**Vegetable Medallions £6.95**

*All main courses are served with a selection of vegetables and potatoes*

The Rising Sun is a traditional 17th Century inn which enjoys a quiet location in the picturesque village of Tarporley. Inside you are welcomed by an atmosphere of olde worlde charm, with original open fires, low doorways and exposed beams everywhere.

The food here is very popular, not least because the choice of dishes is so extensive, with the evening restaurant menu (a sample of which appears opposite) boasting about thirty starters! The bar menu is a little cheaper but with an equally amazing selection of main dishes and specials. At lunch the same menu operates throughout all the dining areas, and includes basic pub grub such as jacket potatoes and sandwiches, as well as more imaginative choices like Chicken in Stilton (£6.05) and Seafood Provençale (6.25). Every Sunday there is a traditional roast (3 courses £9.25).

Directions:   Tarporley is situated just off the A51 between Chester and Nantwich. The Rising Sun is easily found in the village high street.

## USEFUL INFORMATION

**SERVING TIMES:**
Lunch 12pm-2pm (Mon-Sat)
Dinner 5.30pm-9.30pm (Mon Sat)
Food served all day Sunday
**SEATING CAPACITY:** 38 in the dining room, 40 in the bar
**C/C:** V, MC, S, D

**NUMBER OF WINES:** 40
**HOUSE WINE:** £8.75
**RESERVATIONS:** advisable at weekends in the dining room only
**OFF-STREET PARKING:** yes
**CHILDREN:** welcome at lunch
**OUTDOOR EATING:** yes

# THE SWAN HOTEL

### Tel: (01829) 733838

50 High Street, Tarporley, Cheshire, CW6 0AG

## BOHARS BRASSERIE MENU

### STARTERS AT THE SWAN

| | |
|---|---|
| A WARM SALAD OF SAUTE POTATOES, APPLES, SMOKED CHICKEN AND CASHEW NUTS with a blackberry dressing | £5.25 |
| A SPINACH AND FLAKED COD PANCAKE with smoked salmon glazed with a rich cheese sauce | £4.95 |
| WAFERS OF RIPE MELON WITH EXOTIC FRUITS and raspberry coulis | £4.50 |
| DEEP FRIED CRAB, GINGER AND POTATO FRITTERS with oriental oyster sauce | £4.75 |
| GRILLED FIELD MUSHROOMS with garlic and herb butter and goats cheese on a tomato butter sauce | £5.50 |
| DEEP OCEAN FISH TERRINE with spring leaves and lemon dressing | £6.25 |
| PORK AND SAGE RILLETTE bramley apple sauce, gherkins & croutons | £5.25 |
| SAUTE CHICKEN LIVERS with an orange and thyme sauce, served with mixed spring leaves and potato ribbons | £5.25 |
| AN OPEN RAVIOLI OF LOBSTER, KING PRAWNS, SCALLOPS AND SALMON | £8.25 |
| WARM WAFERS OF SMOKED BLACK FOREST HAM with toasted mozzarella cheese on a tomato salad with olives and pesto | £5.25 |

### MAIN COURSES

| | |
|---|---|
| GRILLED MONKFISH BROCHETTE with peppers and bacon served on a bed of Thai spiced cous cous | £11.45 |
| ROAST PORK FILLET wrapped in Parma ham and carved around a timbale of herb and cheese spetzle | £11.95 |
| COLLOPS OF VENISON served with a ginger and rhubarb sauce with red cabbage confit | £12.25 |
| ROASTED COD FILLET on a coriander and carrot sauce speckled with peppers | £10.95 |
| CONFIT OF LAMB studded with garlic and herbs and layered with parsnip purée on a red wine jus | £12.45 |
| ESCALOPE OF TURKEY with rondells of black pudding and crispy rashers of pancetta | £11.25 |
| CHAR GRILLED FRESH TUNA on a warm yellow pepper coulis with a tomato garlic roast | £11.95 |
| FRIED LAMBS LIVER with smoked bacon rashers, garlic mash and caramelised onion sauce | £10.95 |
| SUPREME OF SALMON baked with a pesto crust on a spring onion butter sauce | £11.25 |
| MEDALLIONS OF BEEF with roast shallots and peppercorn sauce | £12.95 |
| ROAST DUCKLING with chorizo sausage, sauerkraut and orange sauce | £12.25 |

The Swan is a charming period hotel dating back to the 16th Century and it enjoys a central location in the picturesque village of Tarporley. Chris Sharp, the General Manager of The Swan, likes to compare the atmosphere here with that of a good local, and the exposed beams, open fires, olde worlde furnishings and friendly staff certainly support that impression.

The food served here, however, is far better than that of your average pub, with imaginative dishes carefully prepared and presented. In addition to the à la carte menu (a selection from it appears opposite) there is a daily table d'hôte featuring 2 or 3 courses at £9.95 and £13.50 respectively. Vegetarian dishes and a good range of home-made desserts are always available.

Directions: Tarporley is found just off the A51 between Chester and Nantwich. The Swan is in the middle of the high street.

## USEFUL INFORMATION

**SERVING TIMES:**
Lunch 12pm-2pm (every day)
Dinner 6pm-10pm (every day)
**SEATING CAPACITY:** 70
**C/C:** V, MC, S, D, AE
**CHILDREN:** welcome
**OUTDOOR EATING:** no

**NUMBER OF WINES:** 45
**HOUSE WINE:** £8.25
**RESERVATIONS:** advisable
**OFF-STREET PARKING:** yes
**ACCOMMODATION:** 17 rooms
(single £48.50, double £62.50)

# MADELEY COURT

### Tel: (01952) 680068

Castlefields Way, Telford, Shropshire, TF7 5DW

## EXPRESSIONS BRASSERIE

### Opening Expressions

Oven baked Goats Cheese Croûte, roast Garlic, Tomato and Curly £4.50
A smoked Ham Salad with home-made Mustard Pickle £4.50
Marinated Sardines in a pungent Rosemary and Tomato Salsa £4.75
Grilled Herb and Garlic Polenta with creamed Mushrooms £4.75
Dill marinated Salmon with a Lemon and Pepper Oil,
Pink Grapefruit and a ripped Salad £5.95
Deep fried Basil Risotto on a jumble of Tomato, Red Onion and Pancetta £3.95
Chinese Chicken Noodle Salad with a Peanut and Chilli Dressing £4.95
Spinach, Chick Peas and Courgette Pâté
with Garlic Toast and Provolone Cheese £3.95

### Catchy Expressions

Oven roast Cod with a Potato Crust,
stir-fried Leek and a Grain Mustard Dressing £12.50
Deep fried Salmon Pavette, Horseradish and Caper Mayonnaise £12.95
Mixed Seafood with Sausage, mashed Celeriac and Parsnip,
Saffron and Parsley Butter Sauce £13.50

### Simple Expressions

Roast Rack of Pork, baked Onion Pudding and deep fried Sage Leaves £12.95
Braised Shank of Lamb with Minted Winter Vegetables £13.75
Grilled Sirloin of Beef, hand cut Fries and an Onion and Mushroom Relish £14.95

### Expressive Expressions

Local Venison stuffed with Almond, Lemon and Thyme,
served with Creamed Beetroot Casserole £14.00
Wok fried Sirloin of Beef seasoned with Ginger
Lime Leaf, Garlic and Seasame tossed Noodles £14.50
Pan-fried Potato Terrine with a warm Mixed Bean and Fennel Salad £11.75
A warm Tomato and Pecorino Cheese Tartlet
served with a Gratin of creamed Macaroni £11.75
Crispy Roast Duck with Chilli, Sweet and Sour and Wilted Pak Choi £14.75
Poached Breast of Chicken with a sauce of Smoked Salmon,
Coriander and Green Onion £12.95

The heart of the 16th Century Madeley Court Manor House was the Great Hall, now the setting for The Priory Restaurant, which offers gourmet à la carte dining on Friday and Saturday evenings, and Sunday luncheons.

Situated in the undercrofts of this Elizabethan country house hotel is the recently refurbished Expressions Brasserie. In addition to the à la carte menu featured opposite, which changes seasonally, a three-course set price menu is available at £14.95. There is an added incentive to turn up early, as parties of up to 4 people who place their order between 6.30pm and 7.30pm from Monday to Saturday receive a 20% discount off their total bill.

Directions: 3 miles south of Telford, signposted from Castlefields Way (B4373)

## USEFUL INFORMATION

(EB) refers to Expressions Brasserie    (PR) refers to the The Priory Restaurant

**SERVING TIMES:**
Lunch (EB) 12pm-3.00pm (Mon-Sat)
    (EB) 12pm-2.30pm (Sunday)
    (PR) 12pm-2.30pm (Sundays only)
Dinner (EB) 6.30pm-10.15pm (every day)
    (PR) 7pm-10pm (Fri & Sat only)
**SEATING CAPACITY:** 70 in the
brasserie, 50 in the restaurant
**C/C:** V, MC, S, D, AE, DC
**OFF-STREET PARKING:** yes
**OUTDOOR EATING:** yes

**NUMBER OF WINES:** 85
**HOUSE WINE:** £10.50
**NO SMOKING** in the restaurants
**DRESS CODE:** (PR) jacket & tie
**RESERVATIONS:** essential for
restaurant, advisable in brasserie
**CHILDREN:** welcome
**ACCOMMODATION:** 47 rooms
(leisure breaks fr £55pp per night,
for D,B&B, 3rd night £35pp)

# FINDONS

**Tel: (01926) 411755**

7 Old Square, Warwick, CV34 4RA

## TWO COURSE MENU  £19.95

\* \* \* \* \*

CREAM OF BEETROOT SOUP

BAKED GOATS CHEESE WITH A MUSHROOM CRUST,
RED ONION RELISH AND A SALAD OF HERBS

FRESH MUSSELS
WITH WHITE WINE, SHALLOTS AND CREAM

HALF A DOZEN ROCK OYSTERS ON ICE

FLAKED SMOKED HADDOCK
WITH SAVOY CABBAGE AND AN ENGLISH MUSTARD SAUCE

KING PRAWN WITH SAUCE STAR ANISE
AND A BEETROOT SALAD

\* \* \* \* \*

FILLET OF BEEF
WITH A GREEN TAPENADE AND TRUFFLE JUS

PAN FRIED SCALLOPS
WITH SWEET CHICORY AND LEMON SAUCE

CHUMP OF LAMB
WITH GREEN LENTILS AND GARLIC WITH A MINT AND BASIL FUMET

BREAST OF BARBARY DUCK
WITH GREEN PEPPER SAUCE AND ORANGE STUFFING

BUTTON MUSHROOM PEPPER FARCI
WITH A PARMESAN HERB CRUST AND TOMATO OIL

MEDALLIONS OF VENISON
WITH A MOUSSE OF PEAS AND A PORT SAUCE

FILLET OF SEABASS
WITH A CHERVIL AND RED WINE SAUCE

Findons is a town-house restaurant with a cheerful and unstuffy "English country house" ambience of charming pictures, old books, original beams and flagstone flooring. It occupies the ground floor of a handsome Georgian building, looking across Old Square to the historic landmark of St. Mary's Church (an episode of the TV series *Dangerfield* was filmed here recently). Relaxing and comfortable surroundings, friendly and efficient service and, above all, the best of modern British cooking are the hallmarks of this first-class establishment in the heart of Warwick.

The set menu, presided over by proprietor Michael Findon, changes seasonally and is complemented by a two-course variation on the same theme, tremendous value at £10.95 (except on Saturday nights). A *plat du jour* is available at lunch, costing £6.95 per person. The accompanying dessert menu features home-made favourites such as Lemon Crème Brûlée (£4.95), Bread & Butter Pudding (£4.50), Chocolate Mousse (£4.95) or Terrine of Fruits with a Passion Fruit & Mint Coulis (£4.50).

Directions: Findons is situated in Old Square opposite St. Mary's Church.

## USEFUL INFORMATION

**SERVING TIMES:**
Lunch 12pm-2pm (Mon-Fri)
    12.30pm-2.30pm (Sunday)
Dinner 7pm-10pm (Mon-Sat)
**CLOSED:** Sat lunch & Sun night
**SEATING CAPACITY:** 40
**C/C:** V, MC, S, D, AE, DC

**NUMBER OF WINES:** 60
**HOUSE WINE:** £8.95
**RESERVATIONS:** advisable
**OUTDOOR EATING:** yes
**OFF-STREET PARKING:** yes,
there is a public car park at the back
of the restaurant

# THE OLD BEAMS RESTAURANT
### Tel: (01538) 308254
Waterhouses, Staffordshire, ST10 3HW

**DINNER MENU**
Full Meal  £39.50
Two Course Meal with Appetiser  £29.00 (weekdays only)

Appetiser of the day

-------

Fillets of red mullet
in a saffron nage garnished with spring vegetables
Terrine of ham hock and foie gras
with a madeira vinaigrette
Ravioli of wild mushrooms
served on a truffle scented risotto with a sauternes beurre blanc
Duet of crab mousse and home smoked salmon
with a spicy thai dressing

-------

Sorbet

-------

Fillet of home salted marinated cod
on a bed of wild rice with a mild curry sauce
Braised pigs trotter
boned & filled with a light chicken & truffle mousse served with a madeira sauce
Confit of duck
roasted with honey and lemon on a light tarragon jus
Pan fried fillet steak
topped with creamed wild mushrooms on a black olive sauce
Roast breast of wood pigeon
served on a cep jus with seasonal vegetables

-------

Iced parfait of white chocolate and fudge
served on a raspberry coulis
Gratin of lemon and cinnamon
served upon slices of caramelised pear

-------

Cheese and biscuits from the trolley (£7.50 if taken as an extra course)

-------

Copious coffee and home-made petits fours

Nigel and Ann Wallis' dream was to strive to create a top provincial restaurant known for the warmth of its reception and the quality of food and service to its customers. Their success in achieving this goal bears testimony to their dedication and culinary expertise.

The restaurant mirrors the building's history with oak beams, open fires and an abundance of fresh flowers, which is complemented by the palm court atmosphere of the Conservatory with its grand piano and lush foliage.

Each change of menu reflects the character of the season, from the lightness of salad days and the soft fruits of spring and summer, to the strength and richness of soups and exciting game in the winter. The table d'hôte menu on the facing page is an example of the choice available at dinner and the set price lunch costs £21.00 for the full meal, or £15.95 for just two courses with appetiser.

Directions: The Old Beams Restaurant with Rooms is situated in the village of Waterhouses, which lies approximately 7 miles to the north-west of Ashbourne on the main A523 Leek-Ashbourne road.

## USEFUL INFORMATION

**SERVING TIMES:**
Lunch 12pm-1.30pm (Wed-Fri & Sun)
Dinner 7pm-9.30pm (Tues-Sat)
**CLOSED:** Sunday night, Saturday & Tuesday lunch, all day Monday
**SEATING CAPACITY:** 40
**C/C:** V, MC, S, D, AE, DC
**NO SMOKING** in the restaurant

**NUMBER OF WINES:** 160
**HOUSE WINE:** £15.75
**RESERVATIONS:** advisable, but compulsory at weekends
**OFF-STREET PARKING:** yes
**OUTDOOR EATING:** no
**ACCOMMODATION:** 5 rooms
(B&B single £65, double £75)

# THE OLD SCHOOL HOUSE
### Tel: (01543) 480009
Weeford, nr Lichfield, Staffordshire, WS14 0PW

## A selection from the A La Carte

**CREVETTES ROSES EN CROUTE**                                £7.50
*King Prawns wrapped in Filo Pastry and served with a light*
*Curried Fruit Sauce*
**MELON GLACE AU JAMBON DE SERRANO**                         £5.95
*Slices of Melon with Serrano Ham*
**SAUMON D'ECOSSE FUME**                                     £6.75
*Scottish Smoked Salmon with Brown Bread*
**NOUILLES A L'AIGLEFIN FUME MORNAY**                        £4.75
*Green Noodles with Smoked Haddock with a Cheese Sauce*
*glazed with Parmesan Cheese*
**BISQUE DE CRABE AU COGNAC**                                £4.25
*Chef's home-made Crab Soup laced with Brandy*

## Les Entrées

**CARRE D'AGNEAU A LA PORTO ET GROSEILLES ROUGES**   £15.75
*Roast Best End of Lamb with a Port Wine, Herb & Redcurrant Sauce*
**BROCHETTE DE FRUIT DE MER THERMIDOR**                      £15.25
*A Mixed Fish Kebab with a Cheese Sauce seasoned with Mustard*
**MEDALLION DE SAUMON VERONIQUE**                            £14.75
*Fresh Scottish Salmon with a White Wine and Grape Sauce*
**FILET DE BOEUF ROI DU FROMAGE**                            £16.95
*Pan-fried Fillet Steak topped with Stilton Cheese and served*
*with a Madeira Sauce*
**MAGRET DE CANARD AUX CASSIS**                              £14.75
*Breast of French Barbary Duck, cooked pink and served with*
*a Blackcurrant Sauce*

## Entremets £3.75

**MERINGUES A LA MACEDOINE DE FRUITS**
*Meringue filled with various fruits, served with whipped Cream*
**CREME BRULEE**
*The classic Cream and Egg base with a Caramel top layer to break through*
**FRAMBOISES CHAUDES GLACE VANILLE**
*Hot Raspberries served with Vanilla Ice Cream*
**ASSIETTE DE SORBETS AUX FRUITS**
*A selection of high quality Sorbets*

The Old School House was built around the turn of the century as the village school, which it remained until the late 1960s. Retaining many original features, it opened as an elegant and sophisticated country restaurant in 1984, and quickly established itself as one of the finest in the area.

The main menu is an extensive à la carte (a small selection is featured opposite) which changes seasonally and is complemented by daily specials. At lunch there is also a good value table d'hôte (3 courses £10.25), and in the evening a set menu (3 courses £12.95) is offered, together with a table d'hôte (3 courses £16.25), which has a very good choice of dishes.

Directions: The Old School House is opposite the church in the village of Weeford, which lies about 3 miles south of Lichfield and is signposted from the A38 and A5.

## USEFUL INFORMATION

**SERVING TIMES:**
Lunch 12pm-2pm (every day)
Dinner 7pm-9.30pm (Mon-Sat)
**CLOSED:** Sunday evening
**SEATING CAPACITY:** 120
**C/C:** V, MC, S, D, AE, DC
**NO SMOKING** area available

**NUMBER OF WINES:** 94
**HOUSE WINE:** £8.95
**OFF-STREET PARKING:** yes
**RESERVATIONS:** compulsory
**OUTDOOR EATING:** yes
**CHILDREN:** welcome

# THE BOOT AND SLIPPER
## Tel: (01270) 528238
Long Lane, Wettenhall, Winsford, Cheshire, CW7 4DN

### A selection from the A La Carte

**Caribbean Melon £3.90**
*A fan of melon drenched in malibu and served with an exotic
fruit purée and mango sorbet*
**Deep Fried Camembert £3.95**
*Served with a port and redcurrant sauce and a crisp salad garnish*
**Spinach and Mushroom Pancake £3.50**
*A wafer thin pancake filled with mushrooms and spinach coated
in a cream cheese sauce and grilled*
**Moules Marinières £4.95**
*Fresh mussels gently cooked in a white wine, parsley, onions, a hint
of garlic and cream, served with slices of French bread*

### Main Courses

**Mauritian Chicken £8.95**
*A pan fried fillet of chicken studded with black peppercorns and served
with a mild curry sauce and garnished with coriander*
**Fillet of Lamb Farci £10.95**
*A fillet of lamb served pink, layered with a home-made pâté and crowned
with a pastry lattice, served with a blackcurrant flavoured jus*
**Fillet Grand Duke £12.50**
*A pan fried fillet steak just cooked, filled with stilton and wrapped in
bacon, served with a red wine gravy*
**Rack of Lamb £9.50**
*Served with a redcurrant and mint gravy and garnished with a
bouquet of watercress and cranberries*
**Half Crispy Roast Duckling £9.50**
*Served with a tangy orange sauce or a plum flavoured with brandy*
**Dover Sole Baguette £16.95**
*A whole dover sole filled with a mousseline of prawns, parsley and
zest of lemon, glazed with butter and grilled*
**Peppered Salmon £8.95**
*A poached fillet of salmon coated in a green peppercorn sauce*
**Grilled Royal Mullet £9.95**
*A whole red mullet marinated in lime juice and lightly grilled, served
with a lime and cream sauce*

*All main course dishes are served with a selection of vegetables & potatoes*
**Head Chef: Ivor Tatlow**

The Boot and Slipper is a popular 16th Century inn found down a winding lane in the middle of Cheshire countryside. A converted farmhouse, it has been tastefully extended to include a restaurant and upstairs accommodation.

The à la carte menu offered in the restaurant is quite extensive, and only a small selection from it is shown opposite. Vegetarian dishes such as home-made Lasagne Verdi (£7.50) and Vegetable Stroganoff (£7.50) are available, and there is a good choice of desserts which may include Sticky Toffee Pudding (£2.45), White Chocolate Gateau (£2.70) or Passion Cake (£2.40). A bar menu featuring more traditional pub grub is also offered.

Directions: Wettenhall is a small village found about 6 miles north of Nantwich, and is signposted from both the A51 and B5074.

### USEFUL INFORMATION

**SERVING TIMES:**
Lunch 12pm-2pm (every day)
Dinner 6pm-9.30pm (every day)
**SEATING CAPACITY:** 50 in the restaurant, 25 in the bar
**C/C:** V, MC, S, D
**OUTDOOR EATING:** yes

**NUMBER OF WINES:** 30
**HOUSE WINE:** £7.50
**RESERVATIONS:** advisable at weekends
**OFF-STREET PARKING:** yes
**ACCOMMODATION:** 4 rooms (single £30, double £45)

# RED COW

**Tel: (01746) 783665**

Ackleton, nr Wolverhampton, Shropshire, WV6 7JH

## A SELECTION OF BLACKBOARD SPECIALS

Grilled Rainbow Trout £6.75

Turkey & Leek Pie £5.95

Half a Roast Duck, served crispy £9.75

Horns of Ham, filled with leeks, carrots and mushrooms £6.75

Half Pheasant Casserole £7.50

Stilton Chicken £7.25

Cod, Prawn and Broccoli Mornay £6.95

Lamb Rogan Josh £6.95

Smoked Haddock Linguine £6.95

Three Game Pie £6.95

Grilled Fillet Steak in Brandy and Cream Sauce £10.95

Grilled Gammon with Peaches £7.25

Grilled Whole Lemon Sole £9.00

Duck, Leek and Blackpudding Pie £5.95

* * * * *

Apple Pie £2.50    Crème Brûlée £2.75

Tiramisu £2.50    Banoffee Pie £2.50    Lemon Bavarois £2.50

The Red Cow is a 200-year-old Georgian country pub that looks out over Badger Dingle. You can walk down to this local beauty spot via the country lane nearby. The inn is situated between Dudley and Telford in a small village just off the road known locally as *The Rabbit Run*.

There is no separate restaurant, but there is waitress service in the bar area and the meals served here are of a high standard. In addition to the blackboard specials, there is an extensive snack menu which contains dishes such as Spanish chicken (£6.25), home-made lasagne verde (£3.95), chicken tikka masala with rice (£6.95), home-made pie of the day (£5.95), spinach, leek and garlic mushroom bake (£6.50), smoked haddock with tagliatelle in mornay sauce (£6.95), deep-fried scampi with salad and fries (£6.95), 20oz T-bone steak with all the trimmings (£11.50), various ploughmans (£4.95) and salmon and asparagus mornay (£6.95).

Directions: Ackleton is located about 5 miles to the north-east of Bridgnorth and 7 miles to the south-east of Telford. The village is signposted from the B4176 Dudley-Telford road. The Red Cow is easily found in the village approximately 800 yards from this turning.

### USEFUL INFORMATION

**SERVING TIMES:**
Lunch 12pm-2pm (Tues-Sun)
Dinner 6pm-9.30pm (Mon-Sat)
**CLOSED FOR FOOD:** Sunday night and Monday lunch
**SEATING CAPACITY:** 60

**NUMBER OF WINES:** 22
**HOUSE WINE:** £8.75 (litre)
**C/C:** none accepted
**OUTDOOR EATING:** no
**RESERVATIONS:** advisable
**OFF-STREET PARKING:** yes

# THE OLD PARSONAGE
### Tel: (01785) 284446
High Offley, Woodseaves, Staffordshire, ST20 0NE

### First Courses

*Sweet red onions gently caramelised with balsamic vinegar, poured into a garlic-flavoured pastry case and accompanied by a saffron vinaigrette*

*Scottish salmon, poached and mixed with fresh whiting, formed into a small fishcake and served with wilted leaves and a coriander sauce*

*A warm salad of local pigeon breast with wild rice and blueberries*

*Fresh spiced sausage made from pork, chicken and Parma ham, served with roasted tomato salsa*

### Second Courses

*The Chef's Caesar salad garnished with shavings of fresh pecorino*
*or*
*Chef's soup of the day*

### Main Courses

*Pan-fried breast and boned leg of guinea fowl with a Madeira and tarragon sauce, set on a bed of creamed leeks*

*Roast fillet of pork set on a ratatouille of sweet red and yellow peppers, wild mushrooms and a hint of chilli pepper*

*Lightly grilled fillets of fresh turbot and brill served on a bed of sautéed celery with a grain mustard sauce*

*Seared roe deer steak accompanied by garlic mashed potato and a game sauce*

*Breast of chicken gently sautéed and served with a sauce of English goats cheese and fresh rosemary*

*Layers of aubergine, tomato and courgette, topped with mozzarella cheese and served with a tomato salsa*

All main courses are served with an accompaniment of fresh market vegetables and potatoes, or a mixed salad

The Old Parsonage is a delightful restaurant in a converted coach-house, which enjoys a tranquil location and lovely views over Staffordshire countryside.

The evening table d'hôte menu (£23.50 for 4 courses and coffee), a sample of which appears opposite, offers a good selection of dishes. Delicious puddings may include Clementine filled with Honey and Almond Nougatine served with a Clementine Sauce, or Sticky Gingerbread Toffee Pudding with a Ginger Wine and Brandy Sauce.

At lunch there is also a table d'hôte menu (£15.50 for 3 courses and coffee), and the Sunday lunch (£13.50) is always very popular.

Directions: On the A519 between Eccleshall and Newport, take the turning to High Offley from Woodseaves. After about a mile and a half, take a left fork and The Old Parsonage is 100 yards on the right.

## USEFUL INFORMATION

**SERVING TIMES:**
Lunch 12pm-2pm (every day)
Dinner 7.30pm-9pm (every day)
**SEATING CAPACITY:** 45
**C/C:** V, MC, S, D, AE, DC
**NO SMOKING** area available
**OFF-STREET PARKING:** yes

**NUMBER OF WINES:** 60
**HOUSE WINE:** £11.95
**RESERVATIONS:** compulsory
**CHILDREN** welcome
**OUTDOOR EATING:** yes
**ACCOMMODATION:** 4 rooms
(B&B single £45, double £55)

# THE FALCON INN

### Tel: (01630) 647230

London Road, Woore, Nr Crewe, Shropshire, CW3 9SF

### A Selection from the Menu

#### STARTERS

Soup of the Day £1.95
Mussels in Garlic Butter £3.95
Smoked Salmon and Spinach Pancake £4.95
Chinese Spare Ribs in Barbecue Sauce £4.50
Mediterranean Prawns in Garlic Butter £4.95
Platter of Chinese Hors d'Oeuvres £10.95

#### MAIN COURSES

Tournedos Rossini, with Pâté en Croûte and Madeira Sauce £12.45
Folded Sirloin Steak filled with Smoked Salmon in a Mushroom,
Cream and Whisky Sauce £12.45
Chicken Breasts in Cream, White Wine and Asparagus Sauce £8.45
Crown of Melon filled with Chicken, Spring Onions and Ginger £8.95
Medallions of Pork with a Cream and Sherry Sauce £8.95
Steak and Kidney Pie £6.65
Kidney au Porto, Lambs Kidneys in Port Wine, in Dijon
Mustard Sauce, served on a bed of rice £8.45
Smoked Guinea Fowl with Tomato, Cream and Red Wine Sauce £10.95
Fillet of Beef Stroganoff £11.95
Mushroom Tagliatelli £7.95
Stir Fried Vegetables with Hoy Sin, Szechuan or Plum Sauce £7.95
Cheese and Broccoli Pancake £7.95

*All main course dishes are served with a choice of baby roast, chipped, new or
jacket potatoes and a full selection of fresh vegetables or a salad if preferred*

#### DESSERTS

Profiteroles £2.50
Apple Pie £2.50
Coffee and Hazelnut Meringue £2.75
Chocolate and Brandy Pavlova £2.75
Raspberry Crowdie £2.75
Jam Roly Poly Pudding £2.25

Despite a rather plain roadside location, this 17th Century country inn is well worth a visit. Not only do you receive a warm welcome in 'The Gallery', a bar so named due to the wealth of pictures all over the walls, but you also cannot help but be impressed by the choice and quality of the food on offer.

There is one main menu with an enormous selection of dishes, supplemented by a weekly specials board with over twenty fish dishes, fresh from Manchester Fish Market. This may feature Swordfish Coated in a Wholegrain Mustard with a Sweet Chilli Salsa (£10.25), a Sizzling Melange of Stir Fried Fish (£10.25), or perhaps Tuna Fish on a bed of Couscous with Garlic and Herb Butter (£10.95). There are also special starters, special menu cards, and special lunchtime cards where everything is £4.95. In fact, for lovers of fresh seafood, 'special' just about sums it up!

Directions: Easily found on the side of the A51 in the centre of Woore, which is about nine miles south of Nantwich.

## USEFUL INFORMATION

**SERVING TIMES:**
Lunch 11.30pm-2.30pm (Mon-Sat)
12pm-2.30pm (Sunday)
Dinner 6.30pm-9.30pm (Mon-Sat)
7pm-9pm (Sunday)
**SEATING CAPACITY:** 90
**C/C:** V, MC, S, D, AE

**NUMBER OF WINES:** 25
**HOUSE WINE:** £9.00
**RESERVATIONS:** advisable in the week, and compulsory at weekends
**OUTDOOR EATING:** yes
**OFF-STREET PARKING:** yes

# THE BULL'S HEAD
### Tel: (01564) 792511
Stratford Road, Wootton Wawen, Warwickshire, B95 6BD

## STARTERS

Home-made Soup with Crusty Bread £2.95
Coarse Country Terrine with Cumberland Sauce £4.95
Smoked Salmon on Warm Buckwheat Blinis with Dill Crème Fraîche £4.50
Smoked Haddock Chowder with Crusty Bread £4.95
Caesar Salad with Fresh Anchovies £3.95
Field Mushrooms with Crispy Pancetta £4.95
Roast Pepper and Goat's Cheese Tart £4.70
Seafood Linguine with Garlic Bread £4.25
Choux Pastry filled with Creamed Spinach topped with a Poached Egg £4.95
Warm Chicken Liver and Frizzled Chorizo Salad £3.95

## MAIN COURSES

Seared Breast of Duck with Honey and Chinese Five Spice £10.75
Oven Roasted Red and Yellow Peppers
filled with Mushroom and Parmesan Risotto £7.00
Chargrilled Chicken Breast with Fresh Basil Pesto on Toasted Ciabatta £7.95
Slow-cooked Lamb Shank with Rosemary and Garlic £9.50
Pork and Leek Sausages with Bubble & Squeak and Red Onion Gravy £6.95
Chargrilled Spiced Lamb Kebabs with Yoghurt, Mint and Coriander Dressing,
served with Steamed Cous Cous £7.25
Crisp Roast Loin of Pork on Dijon Mash with Madeira Gravy £8.25
Pan-fried Calves Liver and Smokey Bacon £10.50
Chargrilled 8oz Sirloin Steak £10.95
Fresh Seafood Platter (min 2 persons) £17.50 each

Side orders: mixed leaf salad £1.60, creamy mash £1.10, vegetables £1.25

## PUDDINGS

Banana and Toffee Pancakes with Clotted Cream £3.25
Sticky Ginger Cake with Stem Ginger Syrup and Clotted Cream £3.25
Berry Pavlova with Clotted Cream £3.25
Chocolate and Grand Marnier Mousse £3.50
Pecan Pie £3.25
Farmhouse Cheeses with Crusty Bread and Bath Olives £4.95

The Bull's Head is a "chocolate-box country pub", most people's idea of the quintessential English country inn. The mellow, black-and-white timbered building dates from the 16th Century. Inside, the flagstone floors, exposed beams, gleaming brass and loose rugs provide the perfect backdrop for an extensive menu of freshly prepared food.

Seafood and fresh fish, straight from the markets, are the speciality here, with eight dishes changed daily on the blackboard. These might include Supreme of Salmon with Sweet Peppers & White Wine (£9.25), Red Snapper Fillet with Leeks & Smoked Bacon (£9.75), Peppered Monkfish in a Citrus Butter Sauce (£9.95), Grilled Lemon Sole with Parsley & Lemon Butter (£9.95) or Oven-baked Rainbow Trout with Oyster Mushroom & Peanut Sauce (£9.25).

There really is nothing better than sitting at a marble table under their pergola on a dusky Summer's evening with the chef's outstanding Seafood Platter and a bottle of chilled Sancerre.

Directions: The Bull's Head nestles alongside the main A3400 Birmingham to Stratford-upon-Avon road, approximately 1 mile south of Henley-in-Arden.

## USEFUL INFORMATION

**SERVING TIMES:**
Lunch 12pm-2.30pm (Mon-Sat)
12pm-3pm (Sunday)
Dinner 7pm-10pm (Mon-Sat)
7pm-9.30pm (Sunday)
**SEATING CAPACITY:** 50 in the restaurant, 50 in the bar area

**NUMBER OF WINES:** 93
**HOUSE WINE:** £9.50
**RESERVATIONS:** advisable
**OUTDOOR EATING:** yes
**OFF-STREET PARKING:** yes
**C/C:** V, MC, S, D

# BROWN'S RESTAURANT
### Tel: (01905) 26263
24 Quay Street, Worcester, Worcestershire, WR1 2JJ

## Dinner Menu
## £32.00

### Starters

Soup of the Day
Fresh Oak Smoked Scotch Salmon
Warm Salad of Chicken Livers, Croûtons & Bacon
Thai Style Fresh Salmon with Yoghurt & Cucumber
Tartlette of Mushroom, Poached Egg & Béarnaise Sauce
Fresh Squid Sautéed with Lemon & Butter

### Main Course

Roast Carré of Lamb with Mint & Pease Pudding
Charcoal Grilled Fillet of
Aberdeen Angus, Herb Butter or Red Wine Sauce
Roast Duck with Pomegranate, Limes & Ginger
Fresh Fish of the Day
Roast Boned Quail with Leeks & Bacon on Polenta
Mediterranean Vegetable Cassoulet

### Sweets & Cheese

Crème Frangipan
a Cream Caramel with Sultanas soaked in Brandy
Chocolate Royale
Dark Chocolate Mousse, Coffee Bean Sauce & Chocolate Meringue
Bread & Butter Pudding
Plum Ice Cream & Hot Plum Sauce
Framboisier
A Raspberry Charlotte with a Raspberry & Liqueur Sauce

Coffee or Infusions

Brown's is a modern, light, airy restaurant that was converted from a corn mill in 1980. The building has high ceilings and large picture windows that look out onto the River Severn. One of the hallmarks of this restaurant is the very friendly service which, combined with the high quality of the cooking, has helped to build Brown's an enviable reputation in the area.

The three course lunch costs £17.00 and is a slightly simpler version of the dinner menu that appears opposite. The menus change every three to four weeks.

Directions:  Brown's is located down by the River Severn on Quay Street near to the city centre.

## USEFUL INFORMATION

**SERVING TIMES:**
Lunch 12.30pm-1.45pm (Sun, Tues-Fri)
Dinner 7.30pm-9.45pm (every day)
**CLOSED:** Saturday lunch, Sunday evening and all day Monday
**SEATING CAPACITY:** 90
**C/C:** V, MC, S, D, AE
**DRESS CODE:** smart casual

**NUMBER OF WINES:** 100
**HOUSE WINE:** £11.50
**RESERVATIONS:** advisable
**OFF-STREET PARKING:** no, but use the adjacent public car park
**OUTDOOR EATING:** no
**NO SMOKING** area available (segregated but not separate)

# THE OLD VICARAGE HOTEL
### Tel: (01746) 716497
Worfield, nr Bridgnorth, Shropshire, WV15 5JZ

## *DINNER*

### *3 Courses £32.50   Additional Course £6.50*

**Spicy Parsnip & Apple Soup**
*with Griddled Cheese & Onion Bread*
**Terrine of Shropshire Turkey, Red Pepper & Smoked Bacon**
*with Marinated Vegetables*
**Boudin of Smoked Haddock**
*with Potato & Spring Onion Salad, Baby Spinach & Horseradish Cream Dressing*
**Grilled Loch Fyne Scallops**
*with Avocado & Red Onion Salsa and Red Wine Dressing*
**Homecured Bresaola**
*with Marinated Broccoli & Lemon Olive Oil*

\* \* \* \* \*

**Chargrilled Fillets of Cornish Red Mullet**
*with Polenta, Roasted Tomatoes and Basil Dressing*
**Seared Cannon of Shropshire Lamb**
*with Bubble & Squeak, Truffle & Madeira Jus*
**Glazed Breast of English Duck**
*with Spicy Risotto of Pearl Barley & Wholegrain Mustard Butter Sauce*
**Chargrilled Fillet of Local Beef**
*with Fondant Potatoes, Crispy Celeriac and Balsamic Lentils*
**Steamed Fillet of Cornish Seabass**
*with Saffron, Mussel & Chive Fricassée*

\* \* \* \* \*

**Selection of Traditional and New British Cheeses**

\* \* \* \* \*

**Iced Pistachio Praline Parfait**
*with Toasted Almond & Amaretto Ice Cream*
**Warm Spiced Carrot Cake**
*with Glazed Banana & Honey Ice Cream*
**Light Chilled Coffee Soufflé**
*with Blackcurrant Sauce and Rum & Raisin Ice Cream*
**White Chocolate Crème Brûlée**
*with Dark Chocolate Ice Cream*

The Old Vicarage is an Edwardian red-brick building that has been transformed by Christine and Peter Iles into a superb country house hotel.

The emphasis in the restaurant is very much on the fresh and natural. Shell and sea fish from the West Country, wild salmon from the Severn and Wye, Welsh lamb, local game, traditionally reared pork, beef and poultry, together with home-made bread, ice cream, sorbets, jams and preserves, all help to make dining here an unforgettable experience.

The vegetarian dishes are worthy of a special mention, such as Crostini of Griddled Aubergine, Tomato and Basil Fondue, Melted Mozzarella and Pesto. The dinner menu featured opposite changes daily and is supplemented by a three-course supper menu priced at £25.

Directions: The village of Worfield is approximately 3 miles to the north-east of Bridgnorth and is signposted from the A454 Bridgnorth-Wolverhampton road. Once you turn off the main road, simply follow the signposts to the hotel.

## USEFUL INFORMATION

**SERVING TIMES:**
Lunch 12pm-2pm (Sundays only)
Dinner 7pm-8.30pm (Mon-Sat)
    7pm (one sitting on Sundays)
**CLOSED:** lunchtimes (Mon-Sat)
**SEATING CAPACITY:** 45
**DRESS CODE:** no jeans
**C/C:** V, MC, AE
**OUTDOOR EATING:** no

**NUMBER OF WINES:** 200
**HOUSE WINE:** £13.00
**RESERVATIONS:** advisable, but compulsory at weekends
**NO SMOKING** in the restaurant
**OFF-STREET PARKING:** yes
**CHILDREN:** welcome (over 8 yrs)
**ACCOMMODATION:** 14 rooms
(B&B sgl fr £69.50, dbl fr £100)

# THE DUSTY MILLER

### Tel: (01270) 780537

Wrenbury, nr Nantwich, Cheshire, CW5 8HG

### Starters at the Mill

Home-made Soup (from our own stock) £2.50
Crostini of Field Mushrooms with Garlic and Herbs £3.95
A Warm Salad of Smoked Bacon, Avocado, Croutons and
Mustard Dressing £4.75
Chicken Liver and Cognac Parfait with warm bread £3.75
"Traditional" Prawn Cocktail £4.75
Welsh Rarebit melted onto Olive Bread Toasts with Tomato Relish £3.75
Deep-Fried Feta Cheese with Cranberry £4.75
Smoked Haddock and Prawn Staffordshire Oatcake
glazed with Cheddar £4.25
Ripe Honeydew Melon with Raspberry Sauce £2.75

### Main Courses

Sautéed Fillet of Beef Strogonoff served with Rice £7.95
Supreme of fresh Salmon, baked in filo pastry with Cheshire Cheese
and served with a Prawn Butter Sauce £10.25
Grilled Cumberland Sausage with Black Pudding, tomato and egg £5.95
Fresh Cod Fillet deep-fried in beer batter served with mushy peas £6.95
Pan-Fried Chicken Supreme wrapped in smoked bacon, stuffed with
mushrooms, sun-dried tomatoes & olives with a tomato & garlic sauce £10.25
Sirloin Steak served with onion rings, tomatoes and mushroms £8.95
Smoked Salmon tri-colour pasta with garlic bread
and parmesan shavings £5.95
Baked Lasagne made with roast vegetables £5.95
Beef Cobbler, beef braised in Old Tom topped with a cheese dumpling £5.95
Hot Beef and Mushroom Madras with Rice £5.95
Somerset Pheasant braised in Cider, finished with cream and Calvados £8.95

### A Selection of Puddings £3.25

### Stotties

Tuna and Sweetcorn £2.95
Cheshire or Mature Cheddar Cheese and Pickle £2.95
Smoked Salmon, Cucumber and Black Pepper £3.95
Hot Smoked Bacon and Black Pudding £3.95
Sirloin Steak and Onion £3.95

Formerly a working mill dating back to the 16th Century, The Dusty Miller is now a popular country pub restaurant, which enjoys a delightful setting on the Llangollen Branch of the Shropshire Union Canal at Bridge No. 20.

There is an extensive blackboard menu, as shown opposite, which greets you as you enter the main bar. It changes daily, but always caters for all tastes and appetites. The new chef proprietors Mark and Julie Sumner have made an excellent start. Using only fresh ingredients and local produce, the emphasis is on serving generous portions of very good home-made food at reasonable prices - the huge starters are almost meals in themselves, and their unique stotties so much more than ordinary sandwiches.

Directions:  Wrenbury stands between Nantwich and Whitchurch, signposted off the A530 and A49. The Dusty Miller is easily found at the west end of the village.

### USEFUL INFORMATION

**SERVING TIMES:**
Lunch 12pm-2pm (Mon-Sat)
        12pm-2.30pm (Sunday)
Dinner 7pm-9.30pm (Mon-Sat)
        7pm-9pm (Sunday)
**SEATING CAPACITY:** 80
**C/C:** V, MC, S, D

**NUMBER OF WINES:** 20
**HOUSE WINE:** £8.50
**RESERVATIONS:** advisable at weekends
**OFF-STREET PARKING:** yes
**OUTDOOR EATING:** yes
**CHILDREN:** welcome

# THE YOCKLETON ARMS
**Tel: (01743) 821254**
Yockleton, near Shrewsbury, Shropshire, SY5 9PG

## *Starters*

Curried Parsnip Soup  £2.50
Duck Liver, Pork & Port Wine Pâté  £3.25
Ham & Asparagus baked in a Cheese Sauce  £3.25
Garlic Mushrooms  £3.25
Melon & Parma Ham  £3.25
Roquefort & Bacon Salad  £3.25
Grilled Goats Cheese with Cranberry Jelly  £3.25
Grilled Black Pudding with Hot Apple Sauce  £3.25
Prawn & Salmon Terrine  £3.25
Garlic Bread  £1.50

## *Main Courses*

Grilled Salmon with Herb Butter  £7.95
Salmon poached in White Wine, Cucumber & Cream  £8.50
Grilled Red Bream with Sun Dried Tomatoes  £8.50
Sole Fillets filled with Prawn & Crabmeat, glazed with Cheese  £8.95
Gnocchi & Mushrooms, Tomato Sauce, topped with baked Pepper  £6.95
Curried Nut Loaf with Yoghurt & Mango Chutney  £6.95
Beef in Red Wine with Mushrooms  £8.50
Roast Local Duck with Walnut Stuffing & Mandarin Sauce  £8.50
Pan Fried Chicken Breast with Bacon, White Wine & Cream  £8.50
Lamb Kebab with a Redcurrant Glaze  £8.50
Sirloin Steak  £9.50
Rump Steak with Port & Stilton  £10.50
Fillet Steak  £11.50

## *Puddings*

Fruits in Cassis  £2.95     Amaretto Brûlée  £2.95
Chocolate Marquise with a Cherry Compôte  £2.95
Raspberry Pavlova  £2.95     Lemon Sorbet in Vodka  £2.95
Carrot Cake with a Cream Cheese topping  £2.95
Turkish Delight with Chocolate Chip Ice Cream  £2.95

The Yockleton Arms used to be a traditional country pub and still looks from the outside like a traditional country pub, but is in fact a restaurant.

The oldest part of the building dates from the 18th Century and the main dining area still retains much of the exposed brickwork and oak beams, with old prints and plates lining the walls. Comfortable sofas for pre-dinner drinks add to the cosy atmosphere.

The menu, which changes regularly, is written out on blackboards and contains dishes that reflect the good honest home cooking of chef/proprietor Ken Maynard and his partner Michael Melody.

The restaurant is open for dinner every day of the week, but Sunday is the only day when lunch is served. That menu offers 6 fish or vegetarian options in addition to the two traditional roast meats (priced at £6.95).

Directions: The Yockleton Arms is on the B4386 Shrewsbury to Montgomery road, midway between the two villages of Yockleton and Westbury.

## USEFUL INFORMATION

**SERVING TIMES:**
Lunch 12pm-1.30pm (Sundays only)
Dinner 7pm-9.30pm (Mon-Fri)
      6.30pm-9.30pm (Sat)
      7pm-9pm (Sun)
**CLOSED:** lunchtimes (Mon-Sat)
**SEATING CAPACITY:** 54
**C/C:** V, MC, S, D

**NUMBER OF WINES:** 17
**HOUSE WINE:** £8.50
**RESERVATIONS:** only taken for Sunday lunch or parties of 6+
**CHILDREN:** welcome
**OFF-STREET PARKING:** yes
**OUTDOOR EATING:** yes

# CORSE LAWN HOUSE

### Tel: (01452) 780771

Corse Lawn, Gloucestershire, GL19 4LZ

| Table d'hôte Luncheon | Table d'hôte Dinner |
|---|---|
| £14.95 for two courses | £24.95 |
| £16.95 for three courses | |

Table d'hôte Luncheon

Roast Aubergine Soup
Terrine of Vegetables
with Beurre Blanc
Confit of Duckling
with Port & Honey Sauce
Bavaroise of Smoked Trout
wrapped in Smoked Salmon

\*\*\*

Pan Fried Skate Wing
with Capers & Black Butter
Haunch of Venison with Port
Sauce & Wild Mushrooms
Crisp Spiced Poussin
with Spinach & Piquant Sauce

Selection of Vegetables
or Mixed Leaf Salad

\*\*\*

Orange Caramel Cream
Chocolate Pithiviers
Fresh Fruit in Champagne Jelly
& Peach Sauce
Cheese Trolley

\*\*\*

Coffee with Petits Fours £2.30

Table d'hôte Dinner

Oxtail Soup
Avocado Guacamole
Moules Marinières
Marinated Salmon
with Lime & Fennel

\*\*\*

Baked Stuffed Trout
with Tomato Vinaigrette
"Tournedos" of Braised Beef
with Burgundy & Red Cabbage
Poulet de Bresse
Pigeon Breasts
with Red Wine & Lentil Risotto

Selection of Vegetables
or Mixed Leaf Salad

\*\*\*

Bread & Butter Pudding
Banana Fritters
with Elderberry Ice Cream
Hot Butterscotch Pudding
Cheese Trolley

\*\*\*

Coffee with Petits Fours £2.30

Corse Lawn House Hotel is an elegant Queen Anne Grade II listed building, set back from the village green and fronted by an unusual ornamental pond.

Baba Hine and Tim Earley preside in the kitchen where their team prepare the dishes for both the main Dining Room and the more informal atmosphere of the Bistro. In addition to the set price menus featured opposite, the Dining Room offers more elaborate dishes on the à la carte menu such as Roast New Season Partridge (£19.95) or Lobster Thermidor (£25.00).

The Bistro provides a more moderately priced alternative, with dishes (all under £10.00) such as Atlantic Fish Soup with Garlic Croutons (£4.95), Baked Queen Scallops with Provençale Stuffing & Noodles (£9.95) or perhaps Chargrilled Chicken Breast with Coriander & Wild Rice (£8.95).

Directions: Corse Lawn is approximately 5 miles to the south west of Tewkesbury. Follow the A438 towards Ledbury and then look for the B4211 (signposted Corse Lawn). The hotel is set back from the village green.

## USEFUL INFORMATION

**SERVING TIMES:**
Lunch 12pm-2pm (every day)
Dinner 7pm-10pm (every day)
**SEATING CAPACITY:** 50 in the restaurant, 35 in the bistro
**OUTDOOR EATING:** yes
**NO SMOKING** in the restaurant, but it is permitted in the bistro

**NUMBER OF WINES:** 400
**HOUSE WINE:** £9.95
**RESERVATIONS:** advisable
**CHILDREN:** welcome
**C/C:** V, MC, S, D, AE, DC
**OFF-STREET PARKING:** yes
**ACCOMMODATION:** 19 rooms
(DB&B £135 p.n. for two people)